The River © 2017 by Mike Nicholson

All rights reserved. No part of this publication may be reproduced, distributed, or transmitted in any form or by any means, including photocopying, recording, or other electronic or mechanical methods, without the prior written permission of the publisher or author, except in the case of brief quotations embodied in critical reviews and certain other noncommercial uses permitted by copyright law. For permission requests, email the publisher or author at addresses below:

Contact the author:
michaelnicholson@rogers.com

Contact the publisher:
Unprecedented Press LLC - 495 Sleepy Hollow Ln, Holland, MI 49423
www.unprecedentedpress.com | info@unprecedentedpress.com
twitter: @UnprecdntdPress | instagram: unprecedentedpress

Unless otherwise indicated, all Scripture quotations are taken from the Holy Bible, New Living Translation, copyright ©1996, 2004, 2015 by Tyndale House Foundation. Used by permission of Tyndale House Publishers, Inc., Carol Stream, Illinois 60188. All rights reserved.

Scripture taken from the Holy Bible, Today's New International Version™ TNIV. ® Copyright© 2001, 2005 by International Bible Society®. All rights reserved worldwide.

ISBN-10:0-9987602-1-8
ISBN-13:978-0-9987602-1-6

Printed in the United States of America
Ingram Printing & Distribution, 2017

First Edition

Unprecedented
Press

"Then the angel showed me a river with the water of life, clear as crystal, flowing from the throne of God and of the Lamb. It flowed down the centre of the main street. On each side of the river grew a tree of life, bearing twelve crops of fruit, with a fresh crop each month. The leaves were used for medicine to heal the nations.

No longer will there be a curse upon anything. For the throne of God and of the Lamb will be there, and his servants will worship him."

(Revelation 22:1-3)

THE RIVER

A 30-day study on the role
of the Holy Spirit in the
church, the world and you

MIKE NICHOLSON

TABLE OF CONTENTS

Introduction   1

Part One: Springs of Water

Day 1. Drinking from the River and Enjoying God to the Full   7
Day 2. The River that Flows from His Heart   17
Day 3. The River of Life is Available Now   27
Day 4. Springs of Water: Ask and It Will be Given to You   37

Part Two: Jumping in the River

Day 5. Baptism in Water   49
Day 6. If You Only Knew, You Would Ask   59
Day 7. Living in the Light   69

Part Three: A River of Justice

Day 8. Why Aren't You Impressed?   81
Day 9. A Mighty Flood of Justice   93
Day 10. Trust in Your Money and Down You Go!   103
Day 11. Rivers of Light: Being the Light of the World   113

Part Four: A River of Help in Times of Need

Day 12. Trumpet Blast: Let the World Hear Us!   123
Day 13. Rivers of Difficulty   133

Day 14. Faithfulness 143
Day 15. The God Who Answers 153

Part Five: The River in Flood

Day 16. Water for the Thirsty, Strength for the Weak 163
Day 17. The Restoration of All Things 171
Day 18. All the Families on Earth 179
Day 19. A River of Favour: God is on Your Side 187
Day 20. The River in Flood 197

Part Six: Ezekiel's River

Day 21. Ezekiel's River 207
Day 22. Seeing the Stream: Living with Your Eyes Open 217
Day 23. Deep River: Deepening Your Experience of God 227
Day 24. Life Giving River: From Death to Life 237
Day 25. Food and Healing 245

Part Seven: As the Waters Cover the Sea!

Day 26. A Well-Watered Garden: He Came to Give Us Full Lives 257
Day 27. Strike the Water: Getting to Do God's Work 267
Day 28. To the Ends of the Earth 275
Day 29. God So Loved the World 285
Day 30. Glory! 293

Afterword 301
About the Author 302
Everyone Global Giving 303
Other Titles 304

DEDICATION

To Keri and Carol, Tony and Hazel, Bryn and Edna, river-dwellers all, for your covenant love, for your life-changing teaching from Word and life, and for faithful leadership. In hope that you will see in these pages some encouragement that all the good seed you sowed did lead to a harvest time.

ACKNOWLEDGEMENTS

With sincere thanks to my lovely wife Hazel whose wisdom, love, and revelation were essential factors in the bringing to birth of this book. I'm grateful also to my much-loved family for their constant encouragement. Also to my publishers, Josh and April Best at Unprecedented Press for their great skill and creative abilities. Finally to my brother elders and the saints at All Nations Church in Ottawa, especially those whose stories can be found in this book to the glory of King Jesus.

INTRODUCTION

"Then I heard a loud voice shouting across the heavens, 'It has come at last—salvation and power and the Kingdom of our God, and the authority of his Christ…For the accuser of our brothers and sisters has been thrown down to earth…And they have defeated him by the blood of the Lamb and by their testimony." (Rev 12:10, 11)

This book is essentially about the Holy Spirit, and my hope is that reading it will draw you closer to him. I've written it as a resource to take you through a month of meditation on the scriptures with a prayerful seeking after the Spirit of Jesus, one chapter a day for thirty days. The book relies heavily on the image of the Holy Spirit as God's river of delights, a river of life that flows out of heaven, through the Christ of the cross, and out of you and me into a thirsty, needy world. I ask you to join with me in calling on God to greatly increase the flow of that healing stream, offering ourselves as servants of Christ and bringing living water to all the families of the Earth.

Our world seems to be in danger of fracturing into ever smaller groups with a narrowing of our understanding regarding who is our neighbour, our brother, sister, and friend. As we call on God, I believe that the saints will remember that they are indeed their brothers' and sisters' keepers, as God's love for the whole world invades our hearts afresh. We can call on God to cause the river that flows out of us to become a torrent; that the Earth might be covered with an awareness of his glory; that heaven and earth will be joined in purpose and power as the river flows and brings life not just to my nation but also to all the nations under heaven.

As the Holy Spirit pursues his mission to glorify Jesus Christ throughout the world, he will tear down walls and build bridges between us. He will open our eyes to see that all men and women are God's creation, his much-loved children, destined to be part of one family and one body under Christ. Women and girls will no longer be treated unfairly, suffer abuse, or be taken captive by violent men, as the Spirit reveals them as daughters of the King. Men will no longer despise their brothers because they don't identify with their exact beliefs or share their history; they will love and accept them as true brothers in the family of our great Father God. The Holy Spirit is poured out on the Earth like a mighty river so that we might be reconciled to God by what Jesus has done and reconciled to each other by that same mighty victory on the cross. The precious and powerful blood of the Lamb will prove to be more than able to set us free from hatred, distrust, and separation from our global family; the heavens will rejoice at the reality of the unity and love between the daughters and sons of God.

If you are not yet a believer in Christ or come from a church family unfamiliar with the workings and operation of gifts of the Spirit in your meetings, I would ask for your understanding and patience as you read through these daily studies. I have prayed as I have been writing that the Lord will help you to open your heart and mind to what may seem at first to be a little strange. If you are used to the gifts of the Spirit, my prayer for you, and for us all, is that this generation of believers might fully understand that the Holy Spirit is not fully occupied in helping countless church meetings go well around the world. He will indeed help you interpret that message in an unknown heavenly language if that is what you need next. But we must lift up our heads to see that he is intently focussed on glorifying Christ by bringing the good news of his kingdom to all nations. The Holy Spirit is lifting up the cross of Christ for everyone to see and be saved; he is remembering the poor and promoting justice for all peoples everywhere; he is working to ensure that God's promise to Abraham will be fully kept, and that every family on Earth will be blessed.

I feel sure that if you will join with your brothers and sisters in reading a chapter each day, taking time to memorize God's words, pray, and give thanks, that the flow of God's river out of you will increase in power and effectiveness. Your concern for all nations, your active faith in seeing all families blessed, your love for the poor, and your pursuit of justice for all will increase. As the Holy Spirit flows through you he will destroy all fear of your sisters and brothers, and no one will seem like a stranger to you.

Open your hearts to the Holy Spirit. Memorize God's breathed-out word as you learn the scriptures. Make your nation great again by interrupting your life journey to help your injured brother or sister, whether in your own community or on the other side of the world. Don't allow your fears for your own safety to be the reason for passing by on the other side, leaving the innocent and hurting to suffer still more at the hands of their oppressors. Open your hearts, and let the Holy Spirit move you into action to show the love of Christ to all. Let the hungry eat at your table, and give that second shirt of yours to the child of God who has none. Do these things and the God of heaven will be pleased to use you to fill the Earth with the river of his glory!

Part One:
SPRINGS OF WATER

DAY 1

Drinking from the River and Enjoying God to the Full

"How precious is your unfailing love, O God! All humanity finds shelter in the shadow of your wings. You feed them from the abundance of your own house, letting them drink from your river of delights. For you are the fountain of life, the light by which we see."
(Psa 36:7-9)

God is good, as he is full of kindness, mercy, and love for people everywhere. He "cares for people and animals alike" (Psa 36:6), and the health of the world matters to him. He shelters and protects us; he feeds us and gives us drink that satisfies. He is a delightful, joyful God, and he "rejoice(s) over (us) with joyful songs" (Zeph 3:17).

God is a great god, and he is restoring all things, "as God promised long ago through his holy prophets" (Acts 3:21). He is restoring his church, equipping his people, stirring faith in his word and drawing this generation to himself. He is restoring our bodies by healing them. He is saving our souls by showing mercy to all who call on his name for forgiveness. He is making peace for us, reconciling us to his Father and drawing us close into the life of heaven. He is restoring health and peace to troubled minds. He has not forgotten the poor and the oppressed, and is against the tyranny of violent men. He is, to us all, the fountain of life, and the light by which we see. One of my most powerful moments of understanding God's way of working in the world came many years ago when I first realised that God is advancing, not retreating. He is restoring all things, not allowing them to crumble away to nothing. Many Christians around me at that time seemed to accept as an obvious truth that the church was shrinking, and that a small band of faithful believers would one day need to be rescued from an evil world. But here was the Lord himself declaring that he is a god of restoration and that heaven must keep Jesus until all things have been renewed. Walls that have fallen will be rebuilt. Spiritual gifts that have gone missing from the real experience of many Christians will be seen in action once more to the glory of God. If your life is a tough one, with the disappointments and challenges that are the burden of so many, then you should know that help and compassionate understanding is available. God loves you and is redirecting his "river of delights" to flow over you too!

"A river brings joy to the city of our God, the sacred home of the Most High. God dwells in that city; it cannot be destroyed. From the very break of day, God will protect it."
(Psa 46:4-5)

There is a river of life that brings joy to the city where God makes a home for himself. A river of crystal-clear, life-giving, thirst-quenching water, filled with gladness. For all of us, the invitation is clear: come and live in this joyful city with the God who "is our refuge and strength," who is "always ready to help in times of trouble" (Psa 46:6). I thank God that he is not coming to those of us who are overcome with sadness or depression only to tell us to "cheer up." He knows that that is just not how it is with us, and that his help has to be real, to be effective in our lives. He sends us more than empty advice; he sends us a river from heaven that brings joy to our souls. The world that we live in can seem to be a troubled one, with war, violence, and division on every side. But for those who live in the joyful, life-giving river of God, who dwell in his city, there can be no fear. "We will not fear when earthquakes come" (Psa 46:2) for we know that this river and this city cannot be destroyed. Jesus' power to transform us from the inside out is real, as he remembers each one of us in his mighty work of restoration. When I became a Christian at the age of eighteen, all I did was put my hand up in a meeting when the preacher asked, "Who wants to know God?" I didn't understand enough then to appreciate how complete a process this "new birth" would be, but the change in my life was unbelievably far-reaching. I started then a lifetime of drinking from God's river and of living an adventure with the Spirit that just keeps getting better.

The psalmist declares that "the nations are in chaos" (46:6) and everything around us seems to confirm that observation. We are often invited to respond with fear: to arm ourselves, to build walls, to look after "our own people." The psalmist sees everything very differently, as he compares the joyful river flowing through the unshakeable city with the crumbling kingdoms of this world. Why would we fear when "the Lord of Heaven's Armies is here among us" (46:7)? Who can be afraid when "the God of Israel is our fortress" (46:7)? We don't need to build walls to defend ourselves against our brothers and sisters. God has built an unbreakable wall around his city and invited us to live inside that joyful place with him. He is not a god of heaven only but of all the earth. He will help all his children who cry out to him, one united family of every colour, every nation, and every language, rich and poor alike. He is not distant; he is Immanuel, the God who lives with us: "His voice thunders, and the earth melts!" (46:6) rejoices the psalmist.

"Be still and know that I am God! I will be honoured by every nation. I will be honoured throughout the world." (Psa 46:10)

It is a glorious truth to realize that we are all called to live in God's river of delights and drink our fill. It comforts us all to understand that the place where God lives is our home too, and that it is a joyful, happy place because of the river of life that flows through its very centre. God is not a god of empty religion, of meetings and organizations only. He is a homebuilder, and he is full of life and joy. He is, and always will be, attentive to the cry of the hurting and inclined to answer by exerting his greatness and power in loving defense of the poor. The prisoner and the oppressed have a champion and a joyful city to take refuge in! If you will cry out to your loving Father to help you, he will fill you to overflowing with his river of delights.

We have often listened to his instruction to "be still, and know that I am God!" (Psa 46:10). We have calmed our minds and sought to bring our hearts and our spirits into a peaceful, restful place, to meditate on the truth that he is God. This has brought us into a place of faith, a delightful experience of comfort in his mighty presence. It is always better to find peace than to live in fear, and in the stillness, we remember many things about our awesome God. He reminds us about our frequent deliverances from trouble and encourages us to believe him for today. And yet the psalmist has quite a different idea, of course, not focused on our individual experience alone, but on the entire world. He wants us to be still and to know that the Lord is truly God of all the earth, of every people, and that he "will be honoured by every nation" (Psa 46:10). This is the foundation on which we will all see that God is, in fact, Lord of all. Every nation will honour him. Not a few, not just a selection, but every nation will honour the Lord whose city is joyful because of the river that flows through it. Don't give up on any nation, any people group, or on yourself! The church should reject as a lie any thought that we are just too helpless to divert the flood of violence, greed, and hatred that arises around us.

We have the answer, and it is not a sea of weapons but a river of eternal joy. "I will be honoured throughout the world," (Psa 46:10) declares the Lord, who knows the power of the Holy Spirit, the glorious, inexpressible joy of the river of life. Those of us who know and love the Lord are filled with the same certainty of faith that the whole earth will be touched by this joyful river of life. Because we have been saved by Jesus and filled to overflowing with his Holy Spirit, we know that:

"As all the waters fill the sea, the earth will be filled with an awareness of the glory of the Lord."(Hab 2:14)

The City of God, the river of delights, and the joy-giving river of life: these images are not an abstraction, not metaphors of an unreachable experience. They are all as real as Jesus Christ himself and closer to us than we imagine. We can reach out and drink from the life-giving river. We are surrounded by advice: diets, exercise equipment, and self-help manuals, and most of us struggle to be our best. But this is different; this is an offer from heaven, not to improve us or polish up our lives, but to drink from a different well. Jesus doesn't ask us to try harder, or even to try religion! He invited those who know that they are thirsty to drink from him.

"On the last day, the climax of the festival, Jesus stood and shouted to the crowds, 'Anyone who is thirsty may come to me! Anyone who believes in me may come and drink! For the scriptures declare 'Rivers of living water will flow from his heart.' (When he said 'living water' he was speaking of the Spirit, who would be given to everyone believing in him.)'" (John 7:37-39)

I wonder if you are ready to accept this offer, to admit your thirst and to tell the Lord "yes," that you will come to him and drink. Will you devote yourself to drinking deep from the river of delights, to throwing yourself with abandon into the river of the Holy Spirit that fills God's city with joy and gladness? Say yes, and not for yourself only. The generation that gives itself without reserve to drinking the waters of life will surely remember to bring that water to all who thirst. As the river of God fills you and drives you along, you will also find yourself filled with love and hope for the poor. As we look ahead to the whole earth being filled with an awareness of the Lord's glory, we can make a start on this tremendous promise by being filled with a keen awareness of his glory in our own lives. Being aware of the present glory of Jesus all around us will prevent us from thinking small, and we will feel compelled by that glory to let our own rivers flow out into other lives, knowing that this glorious river of life will never run dry.

The river of the Spirit of life in Christ Jesus "has freed (us) from the power of sin that leads to death" (Rom 8:2) and shall free many more of our brothers and sisters in every part of God's world. We are united in believing that God "will be honoured in every nation" as the river of God brings joy and freedom from slavery to sin "throughout the whole world" (Psa 46:10).

We can dare to believe that God is great, and that he is engaged in the restoration of all things. That he is filling his servants with the joyful river of life that is the Holy Spirit and powerfully equipping his servants. The river of life that begins its flow from beneath the throne of God and of the Lamb flows out to bring gladness to the whole earth. That same river is the one that flows out of you and me to bring life to all who thirst.

I have known times, as have many of you, when the Holy Spirit has come upon me with strength, and filled me with this river of joy that is so real. I remember one occasion, in a community outreach meeting in South Wales, when I rolled on the floor weakened and delighted by uncontrollable laughter. On that occasion, I believed that I understood the purpose of the experience, as it struck me as incredibly funny that I should have been so worried, for so long, about so little! My concerns faded away in the face of his greatness, and I surrendered myself to a river mightier than me.

Jesus kept his promise and has poured out the river of his Holy Spirit upon us all. That river will carry us out into the nations to announce his salvation, love and grace. Will you let go of the riverbank, and allow that river to move you to where you can serve the purposes of our great God?

"May the grace of our Lord Jesus Christ be with your spirit. Amen." (Gal 6:18)

MEDITATE & MEMORIZE:

Memorize this scripture and speak it out loud as often as you can, taking time to meditate on it and asking the Holy Spirit to open it up for you. Let faith come as you hear your own voice declaring the true word of God.

"Be still and know that I am God! I will be honoured by every nation. I will be honoured throughout the world." (Psalm 46:10)

PRAY & PROCLAIM:

Pray for a nation that you care about or are linked to in some way, or ask the Lord to put a particular nation on your heart. Pray for that nation and also for your own, that the glory of God might be seen clearly there. Proclaim over the people of both countries that the blessings of the Lord will overtake them, and that love and mercy might crush hatred and division to the glory of God.

GIVE THANKS & WORSHIP:

Worship Jesus as ruler and saviour to every nation, and give him thanks for the river of the Holy Spirit that he has caused to flow out of all believers.

TESTIMONY
Have you heard what God is doing in Ontario?

My life was changed by Jesus, and it was an experience that I will not forget. It happened in November 1983. At that time in my life, at 24, I was working in Marmora, Ontario and much of the work I did meant that I was alone. In previous years, I did similar work farther up north in Wawa, Ontario. Basically, I was very lonely, looking for friends and longing for a family.

After moving closer to civilization in Marmora, I spent weekends with my oldest sister, Linda, in Peterborough. Both of us were raised in the Lutheran church, which was very religious. I sensed that there was so much more to be discovered in the Christian life than attending church services. She invited me to attend a series of meetings by evangelist Don Brankel at the local Calvary Pentecostal Church. I attended every meeting from Friday to Sunday and absorbed great revelation of who Jesus really was and how he loved me so much. A call to the altar was given at the close of the preaching each night to make a change in our lives by receiving Jesus, but I held back because of my intense shyness.

At the end of the third meeting the evangelist heard from the Lord that he should extend the meeting to a fourth night, to Monday, and said he was doing so because there was someone in the meetings who still needed to receive Jesus. I knew at that moment that that person was me.

At the end of the fourth meeting, Don made a call to receive Jesus and invited us to respond by walking to the front. I did, and in the process, the Lord allowed most of my senses to experience his goodness, his forgiveness, and his awesome love.

At the front, I stood in the middle of a row of people who also wanted to receive the Lord into their lives. We prayed a prayer of repentance and then Don proceeded to pray for each person in the line. As he approached me, he started to laugh very loud, like deep belly laughing. I had no idea why, but I will never forget that moment! He had seen something in the Spirit and it was worthy of laughing! Then as he prayed over me and with my eyes closed, I saw a most bright intense white light and naturally opened my eyes, but there were no lights above me!

I continued to wait at the front and at another point my sense of smell was filled with a fragrance I had never experienced before. It was a beautiful experience of freshness, with a unique burning, yet not annoying but satisfying. At another point, I felt a brush of something beside my left side and actually touched my arm to check. Again, I opened my eyes but no one was there. I know that God was reassuring me of his presence with me. He has never left my side since!

The foremost experience that night was the lightness I felt in my chest, a lightness that I still feel in my heart today. I really had not experienced any heaviness before, but it was the most memorable feeling among all the other experiences that night. I knew in my mind that this lightness was a result of the removal of my sin and the end of my alienation from God. Something was definitely removed. Yet it was not a void; I knew my spirit was filled with his great love for me, and I then knew that Jesus was living in me. I can still hear myself telling my sister how light my chest felt. I was definitely forgiven and now a child of God.

Not long afterward, and after several instructive meetings about water baptism, I was baptized, burying my old self and rising in the power of God into a new life in Jesus. But there was more.

In one young adult meeting we were instructed to worship with all our hearts. It was a powerful time and Jesus was there. As I sang, my words changed to a language that I could not understand, and I became quite confused and scared. I didn't tell anyone about this experience, but I found out later that this other language or "tongues of angels and of men" was one sign of being filled with the Holy Spirit. I did not experience it again until several meetings later, when I started singing in an obscure language and then knew in the Holy Spirit that this was Jesus speaking through me. Wow, God is so good—a good, good Father!

Murray Kreuzer,
Marmora, Ontario

DAY 2

The River that Flows from His Heart

"Anyone who is thirsty may come to me! Anyone who believes in me may come and drink! For the scriptures declare, 'Rivers of living water will flow from his heart.'" (John 7:37-38)

Jesus came to bring hope and help to the thirsty. He came for the hungry, the sick, and the oppressed of this world. In the tradition of the judges, he came to deliver a defeated people from their enemies and to restore the lives of those living in darkness and captivity. Jesus came to save us from our sin and to baptise us all in his Holy Spirit. Every man and woman, every boy and girl, all who call out to him for help, was to be filled to overflowing with the river of his Holy Spirit. Simeon understood the magnitude of this promised deliverance, this defeat of death and filling with life. Taking the child Jesus in his arms he praised God, saying:

"I have seen your salvation which you have prepared for all people. He is a light to reveal God to the nations, and he is the glory of your people Israel!" (Luke 2:30-32)

The calling of the thirsty to come to Jesus and drink is an offer made to all people, everywhere. The only requirement is thirst. He always hears the poor, searches out the hungry, the hurting, and the lost. All can experience the love of a good, compassionate God, expressed in the outpouring of grace that we see in his Son. No matter how dark your life has been, no matter how deeply you have been buried by the cares of life, there is light and life for you as you accept Jesus' offer to drink deeply of his love for you. Isaiah understood just how brightly the light of Christ would shine into our dark world:

"In the land of Zebulun and of Naphtali, beside the sea, beyond the Jordan River, in Galilee where so many Gentiles live, the people who sat in darkness have seen a great light. And for those who lived in the land where death casts its shadow, a light has shined." (Mat 4:15-16)

In recent years there has been an increase in the darkness touching so many parts of our troubled world. There has been an exaltation of violence as terrible acts have been carried out by men filled with hate and devoid of mercy. Nowhere seems safe, and the temptation to isolate ourselves from the world as we try to build our walls against our brothers and sisters is very great. It is so easy to retreat from this terror and to forget that all the people of this world are made in the image of God, and that he loves us equally. It is into this world that Jesus walks, asking, "Is anyone thirsty?" We can be certain that if we cry out to our loving God and ask him for help that he will hear us and answer from heaven, "for he satisfies the thirsty and fills the hungry with good things" (Psalm 107:9).

But at what cost does he meet our need and satisfy our hunger and thirst? Jesus has indeed done enough to save us from our darkest sin, to release us from the deepest prison, but only at the cost of his own suffering and death. Peter declares that "Christ suffered for you," and that:

"He personally carried our sins in his body on the cross so that we can be dead to sin and live for what is right. By his wounds you are healed. Once you were like sheep who wandered away. But now you have turned to your Shepherd, the Guardian of your souls." (1 Pet 2:21, 24-25)

We are saved by his suffering, by his wounds, by his death and resurrection. He saved us from the thirst of the desert and gave us lives filled with the fast-flowing river of life. He guarantees that we will never thirst again, but at the cost of his own terrible suffering and death. Peter not only recognises this suffering of Christ as real, but accepts it as a pattern for our lives too, as we follow in Christ's steps. In the same way, Matthew witnesses Jesus healing all who are sick and troubled by demons, and alludes to the same "suffering servant" passage in Isaiah 53:

"He cast out the evil spirits with a simple command, and he healed all the sick. This fulfilled the word of the Lord through the prophet Isaiah, who said, 'He took our sicknesses and removed our diseases.'" (Mat 8:16-17)

Jesus set people free from captivity. He healed all who were sick, raised the dead, and brought good news to the poor and the oppressed. He showed selfless compassion to people who were struggling to live their lives without a shepherd. He gave drink to the thirsty and food to the hungry. All of this came at the cost of his own suffering and death. At the end, nailed to the cross, having breathed his last and given up his spirit, a soldier approached him. Having broken the legs of the two men crucified beside him in order to hasten their death the soldier saw that Jesus was already dead. So, "one of the soldiers…pierced his side with a spear, and immediately blood and water flowed out" (John 19:34). A river flowed out from the very heart of Jesus, so that a river of living water might flow from ours. Blood and water flowed from his pierced side to cleanse us and fill us with overflowing life.

Peter begins his first letter by rejoicing over the obedience of God's people who "have been cleansed by the blood of Jesus Christ" (1 Pet 1:2). He goes on to recognise that Jesus has rescued us all as we believe in his death on the cross and that a ransom has been paid to save us.

"And it was not paid with mere gold or silver…It was the precious blood of Christ, the sinless, spotless Lamb of God." (1 Pet 1:18)

Out of his side flows a river of his precious blood, paying a ransom for all who will believe in him and receive his help. Paul understood the value of this precious river.

"For God presented Jesus as the sacrifice for sin. People are made right with God when they believe that Jesus sacrificed his life, shedding his blood." (Rom 3:25)

My childhood was spent in a warm, religious atmosphere with Jesus hanging on the cross as an ever-present image. Pictures of Jesus with his heart exposed, encircled by the crown of thorns, his suffering made graphically evident, were in my family home and in my school setting. One Easter season, one of our classroom teachers spent over an hour describing in detail the process and experience of crucifixion, letting us know that it was humiliating and excruciating for Jesus, and it was all our fault. I found this emotionally arduous and unsettling, but failed to understand in any way the "why" of it all. To have been taken through such an exercise as a young teenager by someone who had no knowledge of the saving power of the cross was pain without purpose. The cross of Christ robbed of its certain hope of salvation and reconciliation with God is an empty, cruel place. It was only later, as a first-year university student, that the power of Christ's death to bring me into life was finally made clear. Paul understood that Jesus didn't suffer and lay down his life to make me religious. He did it to save me, to usher me into his Father's house, clean and forgiven. He took away my sins and removed my guilt. He took away my sickness and removed my disease. He took away my isolation and removed my loneliness. He took away my religion and led me to his cross.

"Those who are trying to force you to be circumcised want to look good to others. They don't want to be persecuted for teaching that the cross of Christ alone can save." (Gal 6:12)

"He personally carried our sins in his body on the cross so that we can be dead to sin and live for what is right. By his wounds we are healed." (1Pet 2:24)

In recent times, I have become more and more aware of the suffering of Christ on my behalf and on behalf of all peoples everywhere. The precious nature of the blood of Jesus has come to mean everything to me, and it seems to be true that the ministry of the Holy Spirit in our world will not allow a drop of that blood to be wasted, not a second of Jesus' suffering to be robbed of its effect. I have had to realise that much of my Christian life has been spent on small matters and trivial issues compared to the limitless value of Christ's precious blood. I have been blessed to spend many years in leadership roles in a number of churches and can only pray that some of it has been to the glory of God. But when I consider my efforts in the light of Jesus' suffering I am quickly brought to tears. The staggering reality of Christ's torture and death, and the Father's immeasurable love for the lost in allowing this sacrifice to happen as heaven looked on, must now serve to transform me and all his disciples into a truly surrendered kingdom of priests. To live in isolation from the needs of the world or to be constantly distracted by a thousand unimportant things is surely not an option for our generation. As we consider the river that flows from the heart of our crucified Lord, our response must be at a level that honours the immensity of his sacrificial covenant love. We have not been reconciled to religion, to doctrine or to Sunday meetings. We have been reconciled to our Father and are now citizens of heaven, called to share in the sufferings and mission of our King. If you feel that way too, then let us give ourselves without reservation to bringing the good news of Jesus' Kingdom to all. In the face of such sacrifice, such selfless love from heaven, where shall we go to live a life of faith and sacrifice? Where shall we stand to declare that our lives are surrendered to the work of Christ, rejoicing in our salvation and setting our hearts on pilgrimage so that all families on earth might be blessed? The writer to the Hebrews encourages us all to share in Christ's sacrificial ministry by standing with him in his place of suffering.

"So let us go out to him, outside the camp, and bear the disgrace he bore. For this world is not our permanent home; we are looking forward to a home yet to come."(Heb 13:13)

~~~~~~~

MEDITATE & MEMORIZE:
Memorize this scripture and speak it out loud as often as you can, taking time to meditate on it and asking the Holy Spirit to open it up for you. Let faith come as you hear your own voice declaring the true word of God.

"He personally carried our sins in his body on the cross so that we can be dead to sin and live for what is right. By his wounds we are healed." (1 Pet 2:24)

PRAY & PROCLAIM:
Pray that no part of his suffering, no drop of his precious blood, should be robbed of its reward in a mighty harvest of saved souls. Proclaim Christ crucified, buried and risen from the dead. Shout out that Jesus is alive!

GIVE THANKS & WORSHIP:
Express your deepest thanks to Jesus for suffering so that you could live a transformed new life. Worship him, acknowledging that he has done everything that was needed to heal you in your body, save your soul, bring lasting peace to your mind, and joy to your heart.

TESTIMONY
Have you heard what God is doing in North Africa?

My name is Aboubacar, and I was born in Africa in a devoted Muslim family. My father was one of the respected elders of the local mosque, and since my childhood, I used to follow him to go to pray in the mosque. However, growing up, I was really thirsty for God. I wanted to know Him and be assured of my salvation. So when I was a teenager, I used to ask myself many existential questions like where would I go after life on earth? Given the multitude of religions, all claiming to be the right way to heaven, which religion was the best and only way to God? These questions were trotting continually around my mind, especially as I had many doubts about Islam. Indeed, when I watched the Muslim community to which I belonged and in particular, my Muslim friends, I was scared. People who should be examples for me were so violent and aggressive and were not good examples to me. In addition to all this, I had a thirst for God that I was looking to quench but found no satisfaction in Islam.

In my desperation, one day I heard that a German preacher, Evangelist Reinhardt Bonnke, was coming in my town for an evangelistic crusade. Advertising posters of the crusade were posted throughout the city. Various radio and television advertisements were also regularly made. These ads presented God as full of love for humanity. Also, they emphasized the miracles of healing and restoration that will accompany the preaching of the word of God. These advertisements made me look forward to the day of the crusade to go to listen to the evangelist and to see with my own eyes the miracles that were going to happen.

The day of the crusade, I went to the venue where the meeting was to be held. The place was full of people: men and women of all ages came to listen to the preacher. In addition, several people with different kinds of diseases had come in the hope of finding healing. When the meeting began with songs of praise and worship, an unusual peace filled my heart, and I was filled with an unexplainable joy. I was convinced that God was there at the meeting, and that I was going to meet the God I had been looking for since my childhood. When Bonnke began his message, his preaching was about the prodigal son whom the Bible speaks about in Luke 15:11-20. What struck me in his message was that "the younger son got together all he had, set off for a distant country and there squandered his wealth in wild living. After he had spent everything, there was a severe famine in that whole country, and he began to be in need…When he came to his senses, he said, "How many of my father's hired servants have food to spare, and here I am starving to death! I will set out and go back to my father and say to him: Father, I have sinned against heaven and against you…But while he was still a long way off, his father saw him and was filled with compassion for him; he ran to his son, threw his arms around him and kissed him." Wow, what a love. I was so touched by this way God loves mankind.

What also struck me in the message of Bonnke is that he said that when the prodigal son left, his father looked for him, his father missed him so much, and his father wanted him be with him at home. He knew at home was his son's rest; there was his joy and well-being. Thus, the day the father saw his son coming home, he could not help running to meet him. Bonnke added that "if we take a step toward God, God actually takes a thousand to us." This dramatically changed the understanding I had of God. Islam taught me about a terrible God, always angry, awaiting the day of judgment to throw sinners into eternal fire. However, Reinhardt Bonnke portrayed a God full of love and compassion who does not wish the sinner to go to eternal damnation, but rather that he accepts Jesus as his personal Saviour and Lord and is saved.

I was greatly touched by these words, and I heard in my heart God calling me to him. It seemed like I was not a stranger to that voice. It seemed to me that I have heard this voice resound in me several times without knowing where it was coming from. I then found myself before the presentation of this God of love by Reinhardt Bonnke. It was like meeting someone you've always been on the phone with without having once seen him. The first time when you meet the person, from his first words you know this is the person you have always listened to on the phone. After the message, I was so convinced that I had met God. When the evangelist made the call to people who wanted to give their life to Jesus Christ, I was among those who raised their hands. He then prayed for us and I committed myself to follow Jesus all my life.

However, my conversion to Christianity would not be without difficulties. People from my neighbourhood went to tell my father that I had become a Christian. My father, furious as he was, came to me that day as I was studying, jumped on me and started to beat me up. He said he had heard I had become a Christian, and to know that if I am a Christian, I cannot stay in his house.

Seeing the high tension between my father and me, I decided to go to Côte d'Ivoire, a neighbouring country to spend the holidays. After three months,

I returned home. The day I arrived, I still had my hand luggage when I greeted members of the family. I wanted to drop my bags in my room when my father told me to drop them at the entrance, and he charged my younger brother to call all the family members. When the whole family gathered, my father asked me to choose between Christian life and Muslim life. He told me that if I persisted in my choice to be a Christian, he would simply ask me to take everything that belonged to me and to leave the family home. In front of the whole family, I told my father that I had become a Christian, and I was not turning back to Islam. My father then asked me to leave the family. That's when I took everything that belonged to me and left home.

After two years, my father changed his mind. God has been working in his heart. He sent friends to tell me that he would like that I come back home. When I returned, he gave me the freedom to go to church and to practice my Christian faith as I wanted.

Aboubacar,
North Africa

DAY 3

The River of Life is Available Now

"Then the angel showed me a river with the water of life, clear as crystal, flowing from the throne of God and of the Lamb. It flowed down the centre of the main street. On each side of the river grew a tree of life, bearing twelve crops of fruit, with a fresh crop each month. The leaves were used for medicine to heal the nations." (Rev 22:1-2)

"Then the angel showed me a river…" The church is once again remembering that we are a supernatural body of believers, born from above. Birthed from heaven, "born again, but not to a life that will quickly end. Your new life will last forever because it comes from the eternal, living word of God…And that word is the Good News that was preached to you" (1 Pet 1:23, 25). There is nothing ordinary about the people of God. We understand the glorious reality of a spiritual world whose life flows from heaven itself. We receive joyfully the evidence of God's extraordinary Kingdom as expressed in the life and work of his son Jesus Christ. So it is no great surprise to see John, our "brother and partner in suffering and in God's Kingdom" (Rev 1:9) guided into revelation by an angel. We must all throw off the last chains that bind us to the thought that we are on our own, subject to our own best efforts to be holy. We are not calling out across an abyss to a distant heaven, desperate for God to hear us and draw near. We have been, by the work of Christ, made a part of the heavenly community.

"You have come to Mount Zion, to the city of the living God, the heavenly Jerusalem, and to countless thousands of angels in a joyful gathering. You have come to the assembly of God's firstborn children, whose names are written in heaven.

You have come to God himself, who is judge over all things. You have come to the spirits of the righteous ones in heaven who have now been made perfect.

You have come to Jesus, the one who mediates the new covenant between God and people, and to the sprinkled blood, which speaks of forgiveness." (Heb 12:22-24)

Perhaps it seems more than enough for us to believe that we will spend eternity with Jesus in heaven when our lives are over, to know that we will never again be separated from God's fatherly love. But that is not all that Christ's magnificent victory on the cross achieved. We are also instantly delivered by his grace into a heavenly kingdom expressed on earth to every nation. We are not dwellers in the darkness with a dream of eventual heavenly light. We have come to Mount Zion, to a city, to countless angels, to a joyful assembly of our brothers and sisters. We have already come to God himself, to Jesus who speaks for us, and whose sprinkled blood speaks of love, forgiveness, mercy and acceptance. Let us all live as citizens of heaven, with the Holy Spirit to guide us everywhere we need to be, giving us all the words that we need to say. Ours is a joyful, noisy community, confident of God's love, walking by faith in his unending grace.

In considering my own experience of leaving behind dead religion to embrace a life of faith in Jesus, I have concluded that the difference has been that I am enjoying today a life that I thought was available only after I was dead. The thought that God is watching us from a distance now seems rather cold and uninvolved and a little creepy. This perceived gulf between earth and heaven leads hurting people on many occasions to wonder, "where was God when I needed him?" The reality that Jesus has brought me all the way back into the centre of his family, to live each day in heaven's company, to hear clearly the voice of my loving Father. This is exactly what I used to think the afterlife was all about! Religion made church an endurance test for me; faith in Jesus makes his church community heaven on earth.

The angel showed John a mighty river, flowing from the throne of God and of the Lamb. The water of life that flows out of our hearts as we receive Jesus' promised gift of the Holy Spirit originates from the throne of heaven. We live this transformed life as a river flowing. We are not mere observers, not conduits only, not extras in someone else's movie. We are rivers of life, bringing help, forgiveness and hope to all that we meet. Our lives will be spent echoing the words of God that we first heard for ourselves.

"Then I will sprinkle clean water on you, and you will be clean… And I will give you a new heart, and I will put a new spirit in you. I will take out your stony, stubborn heart and give you a tender, responsive heart. And I will put my Spirit in you… The ruined cities will be crowded with people once more and everyone will know that I am the Lord." (Ezek 36:25-27, 38)

I have a dear friend who has in her possession a stone that is in the shape of a heart. I have heard her on a number of occasions use this stone to preach the gospel from Ezekiel's declaration to those who need to find Jesus. Her words leave no doubt in any of her listeners that the impact of following Jesus involves total surrender to God and a complete transformation of life. When the river of life touches a person then their old, stony heart is ripped out, to be replaced by a tender heart that is able to hear and understand the words that come out of the Father's mouth and to be responsive to them. The old has gone and the new has come! The river of life that flows from the good news of Jesus come into our world has the power to kill the old life and give new birth to all who call on his name.

The flowing of this river of life, crystal clear and beautiful, touches many, not few. The outpouring of our new hearts results in blessing for all who see us and hear our words. This river is too influential to be merely a cure for individual thirst. The river of God's life-giving Holy Spirit flows from the throne, through our new hearts and out into the world, resulting in ruined cities becoming crowded with life once more. The waters of God's river are filled with transforming life, and its course takes it right down the centre of Main Street. As individual believers in Jesus Christ, we daily rejoice in our salvation. But oh, how marvelous it is to see cities rebuilt and communities restored across our world! We must never concede that the victory of Calvary has power to save individual believers but that the world is lost, too vast and complicated for us to stir our faith for the restoration of the nations; for on both sides of this life-giving river grows a tree of life. This is the very tree that was denied to us in our fallen, sinful nature. "What if they reach out, take fruit from the tree of life, and eat it?" says the Lord God. "Then they will live forever!" (Gen 3:22). Our loving father had no desire to see us trapped eternally with the consequences of our sin, no intent to abandon us to a hell of our own choice. And so "he placed a flaming sword that flashed back and forth to guard the way to the tree of life" (Gen 3:24).

How extraordinary, then, to see this heavenly fulfillment of that garden from which we were excluded restored and openly accessible to all who believe in

Jesus! If you know yourself to be a believer, a disciple of Jesus, then this is the city made for you to enjoy, a river of life flowing down Main Street, crystal clear and refreshing. The tree of life is opened once more to you because Christ has saved you and cleansed you from sin. Take fruit from the tree and eat it, knowing that there will be a fresh crop for you to enjoy each month.

You may wonder if this water of life, this fruit of the tree of life, is truly available to you. Listen to the heart of God, and the cry of his servant Moses: "Oh, that you would choose life so that you and your descendants might live!" (Deut 30:19). Your loving Father has always urged you to choose life, not death. Accept his offer of help and live the life that he has suffered so greatly to make available to you. To drink from his river and eat from his tree, to sit down at his banquet table and revel in his fellowship is exactly what God is drawing you into. Choose life! Scripture even gets you started on how to make this decision real: "You can make this choice by loving the Lord your God, obeying him, and committing yourself firmly to him. This is the key to your life" (Deut 30:20).

As you learn to reject a lonely life lived in the desert and accept a life lived with your faith-filled brothers and sisters in the river of the Holy Spirit, you will understand what Jesus came to give you.

"Those who come in through me will be saved. They will come and go freely and will find good pastures… My purpose is to give them a rich and satisfying life." (John 10:9-10)

Thank you Lord for saving me so fully! My religious upbringing as a child made me fully aware of my sin, and I knew how far I had fallen. Not until I was 18 years of age did anyone ever tell me that Jesus had answered the need and closed the gap between me and our Father, that he hadn't come to rub my nose in my obvious sinfulness, but that he had come to save me. I would have expected to find myself on probation at best, and I was astounded to find Jesus giving me a rich, satisfying life. What an exchange!

But what about the suffering, oppressed peoples of the world? You and your church are so completely blessed, filled so full that all are overflowing. But what will become of the persecuted? What of the hungry? Who will protect the women and girls carried off into captivity and abused and mistreated? Who will speak out for the victims of violence and end the terror of hate-filled men? Who can restore so many failed states, so many nations turned into graveyards of desolation?

"The leaves were used for medicine to heal the nations." (Rev 22:2)

I have to confess that I am a bit of a news and current events addict, believing that my life cannot be lived in isolation from the world around me. Having benefitted from God's great mercy and grace, I am unable to enjoy this newly created life of freedom while ignoring the more painful reality of others. God loves me, certainly. But it was his love of the whole world that moved him to send his own Son to die that multitudes in every nation might enjoy the same mercy and freedom. As I watch reports from so many troubled regions of our world, it convinces me that our loving Father doesn't want me to build a protective wall around my glorious new existence; he commands me to get up, go out, and tell others about Jesus!

It is too small a thing for Jesus to save me and you, only to leave everyone else to suffer their fate. The church must not live as if we have been taken out of the world into our own personal heaven, leaving behind the poor and the oppressed, without hope or help. God's love is greater than that, and Christ's death will reap a greater harvest than we have yet witnessed. What kind of spirit is it that would delight in personal rescue for the fortunate few while turning our backs on the weak and victimized of the world that Jesus came to save? Certainly not the Spirit of Christ, who will fill our hearts and minds with a love for the lost that will cause us to cry out in prayer that no one should be left behind. If our generation will rise up in love and faith, crying out to God to give us the nations, then he will give us success. No oppressed people will be forgotten; the widow and orphan will be defended, no matter where they live. Prayer will lead to faith, which will lead to financial giving and to action. We are not a weakened, self-centred faith community, looking only for our own comfort. There will be no rapture that will remove the saints from their God-given mission to go into every nation with the love, grace and salvation offered to the poor by King Jesus; no ending of our responsibility to love our enemies; no excuse to fly away or turn our backs on the troubles of strangers when so many need us to lay down our lives for God's flock. No rest will be asked or given to Christ's servants until every family is blessed. We are brothers and sisters to Jesus, and we will give ourselves to the work of God until the full harvest of the redeemed is brought in to his house.

We who drink from the river of life and eat the fruit of the tree of life must turn our eyes afresh and with overcoming faith to the nations. We will not build walls to seal them out or bar them from drinking from the river that brings life. We will remember that our brothers and sisters are family, every one made in the image of God. And we will take God at his word that the leaves of the tree are medicine to heal the nations. We understand that we who are believers in Jesus are Abraham's spiritual children, for "Abraham is the spiritual father of those who have faith" (Rom 4:11).

We acknowledge that "God told (Abraham), 'I have made you the father of many nations'" (Rom 4:17). As spiritual children by faith we will walk in the light of Abraham and refuse to give up on any nation, culture, or individual who calls to the Lord in their hunger or thirst for deliverance. Abraham "never wavered in believing God's promise. In fact, his faith grew stronger, and in this he brought glory to God. He was fully convinced that God is able to do whatever he promises" (Rom 4:20-21). We will be children who make Abraham proud because we will exhibit faith like his.

God has promised that a result of the existence of this river of life, the river of his Holy Spirit, is that a tree is growing whose leaves will bring healing to the nations. Generations of saints long dead were consumed with passion for the salvation of all nations. Men and women believed the Lord and gave their lives in relentless outreach to unreached peoples. This present generation will do no less, bringing the light of Christ to those dwelling in oppression, hunger, and poverty. Jesus is the vine, we are the branches, and we will produce leaves; we will grow life-giving, bible-believing, Holy Spirit empowered ministries that will bring the healing of the cross of Christ to the whole world. Where are the nations? They are to the north, and to the south, the east and the west. They stretch to the ends of the earth. They are right next door to where you live, in your own communities. They are within arm's reach and within the sound of your voices.

"The sovereign Lord will show his justice to the nations of the world. Everyone will praise him! His righteous will be like a garden in early spring, with plants springing up everywhere." (Isa 61:11)

~~~~~~~

MEDITATE & MEMORIZE:
Memorize this scripture and speak it out loud as often as you can, taking time to meditate on it and asking the Holy Spirit to open it up for you. Let faith come as you hear your own voice declaring the true word of God.

"The leaves were used for medicine to heal the nations." (Rev 22:2)

PRAY & PROCLAIM:

Pray for your neighbours, for the citizens of the entire world. Proclaim that the message of Jesus will heal the whole world, and fill it with an awareness of his glory. Jesus is the vine and we are the branches; branches that produce leaves that will bring his healing to all nations.

GIVE THANKS & WORSHIP:

Give thanks to the Lord that he has forgotten no one, and that he is King of all peoples; every language, every culture will know his blessing and life. Thank him that no one will be left behind, or denied his mercy if they seek him. Worship the God who is Lord of the heavens and the earth.

TESTIMONY
Have you heard what God is doing in every life that receives him?

One of my favourite jobs I was given while working for Teen Challenge, Brooklyn, was pioneering a coffee house outreach. I would walk through the Projects and invite people to join us. Some would describe the neighbourhood I worked in as extremely dangerous and very hopeless, but I only saw men, women, and children Jesus had died for, and I loved them dearly. At first people only came for coffee and food, but God gave us favour and soon we were praying with people, leading them to Jesus, baptizing them in water, and seeing them baptized in the Holy Spirit. They joined us to learn the Bible during the week and joined us for Sunday meetings. We prayed for many desperate lives.

Sally was one of the first to be saved, then Bernice, then their children. Bernice was addicted to alcohol. She was very difficult to work with and she didn't care for white people, but she kept coming. One night she bowed her heart to Jesus and her life was transformed. She was free from alcohol. She was free from hatred. She was free! Soon she was recruiting others to come, and she was organizing and running the clothing room and food distribution with us. Men were taken into Teen Challenge's year long drug rehabilitation program. Families' lives were changed. Thank you, Jesus!

Vicki Kreuzer
Ottawa
Owner of the stone heart!

DAY 4

Springs of Water: Ask and It Will Be Given to You

"Caleb asked her, 'What's the matter?' She said, 'Give me another gift. You have already given me land in the Negev; now please give me the springs of water, too.' So Caleb gave her the upper and lower springs." (Josh 15:18-19)

Caleb had promised his daughter in marriage to whomever captured the town of Debir, and Othniel succeeded. The town was now theirs, and Caleb's promise was kept, but the community had no water supply. So Caleb's daughter Acsah wisely asked for a second gift that would make the first gift (of a town) become a living, workable community. She asked for water. Her father gave her the rights to two springs that were closest to the town, but far enough away that they needed to be gifted separately. Now Acsah and her husband Othniel had a place to live that had its own water supply. As we contemplate the many promises and extravagant blessings found in Jesus, we must be wise and bold enough to ask him to give us the rivers of water that are needed to keep us in fullness of life.

"When the poor and needy search for water and there is none, and their tongues are parched with thirst, then I, the Lord, will answer them." (Isa 41:17)

Our Father in heaven loves us with endless compassion and deep understanding and knows that we depend on him for every breath, declaring "I, the God of Israel, will never abandon them" (Isa 41:17). Believers can be certain that our Christian lives are not destined to be lived in frustration or disappointment. Whatever God gives us will work; when he gives us land he will water it. We may feel that the task is too hard for the Lord, that our desert is too dry, our lives too barren. The enemy can so easily distract us with his endless lies: "It's not working because God is angry with you. You've sinned too much; your faith is so small!"

We can waste our time arguing with the devil's lies, or simply learn to laugh at them. We laugh at his lies because we know that "humanly speaking, it is impossible. But with God, everything is possible" (Mat 19:26). Living in the river of life is not a concession earned by our goodness, but a loving provision of a Lord who understands our absolute need of his grace. Having enough water tells us that God is good, and always does good things, not that we have earned his life-giving supply. No matter how messed up our lives are, a cry for help to the Lord will result in restoration of life.

"I will open up rivers for them on the high plateaus. I will give them fountains of water in the valleys. I will fill the desert with pools of water. Rivers fed by springs will flow across the parched ground." (Isa 41:18)

No one has grown to be so high or so important that God cannot get his water up to them. No one has sunk so low in life that God's fountains cannot get down to them. No one is so dried out that the waters of life in Christ Jesus cannot refresh them. No matter how parched your soul has become, no matter how little hope is left in your heart, your Father can cause "rivers fed by springs" to flow into every part of your life. He knows that this is impossible for us to achieve without his help.

"I am doing this so all who see this miracle will understand what it means – that it is the Lord who has done this, the Holy One of Israel who created it." (Isa 41:20)

When I gave my life to Jesus it was because I felt in crisis: lost, shy, lonely, and quite overwhelmed by the challenges of life. I've heard some say that the only people who find God are the weak and hopeless. Whether that is true for everyone or not, it was certainly true for me. I had been raised in a warm, loving family and educated in a religious setting. But when it came down to it, when I needed help that was more than theory, when I needed to be rescued, I discovered that I wasn't even sure that God existed. That may sound to you to be a terrible admission, but there it is. Eighteen years of religious education and I couldn't even stand on an understanding that God was real. I did the only thing that I could think to do. I knelt by my bed in the dark, told God that I wasn't sure if there was anyone there who could hear me, or that cared enough to listen, but if he was there then please help me now. And he did. Having had no one knock on my door for five months, two days after my prayer a young woman knocked and asked me if I would like to come to a Christian meeting. She looked so timid and so utterly shocked when I said yes, that I concluded she had not enjoyed very many friendly responses to her invitation! I went to the meetings, got saved without understanding anything that was preached, and started a transformed life with Jesus. When I was thirsty, God gave me water to drink. He would not turn his back on me, and he will never turn his back on you. He takes us out of the desert and turns us into springs of water.

God is a great God, and he is restoring all things. He has raised up an army, a people belonging to him, and given us extraordinary promises. He does not leave us without the water supply needed to take all the land promised to his people, and draws our attention to the glorious ministry of the Holy Spirit. In a loud, clear voice he calls out "Rivers of living water will flow from (the believer's) heart. (When he said 'living water' he was speaking of the Spirit, who would be given to everyone believing in him)" (John 7:38-39).

To "his chosen apostles" (Acts 1:2) he "talked…about the Kingdom of God" (1:3). He promised that they would tell everyone the good news about him everywhere, to their own neighbours, throughout the regions and to "the ends of the earth" (1:8). Before they could leave, they were commanded to wait until the Father sent the fire and water promised to give them success. "In just a few days you will be baptized with the Holy Spirit" (1:5).

"You will receive power when the Holy Spirit comes upon you." (Acts 1:8)

Our troubled world needs us to wait on God for the power needed to spread the good news of Jesus to our neighbours. We need the fire of the Spirit to guide our journey and to light up the lives of those living in darkness. We need the Holy Spirit so that those "rivers of living water" (John 7:38) will flow out of us high and low into the parched earth.

Waiting on the Lord for his Spirit is an important part of our life of faith. Waiting on God for everything needs to be a habit of our daily life, and the church must not allow this experience of waiting on the Lord to fade away in our "instant" world. Waiting on God will be rewarded. I have learnt to recognise over the years that where I wait, and who I surround myself with in my waiting times, are key elements of true waiting on the Lord. A friend of mine once waited for 25 years to be baptized in the Holy Spirit in a Pentecostal church based in a city that was the headquarters of a major Pentecostal denomination. Her wait had been way too long and had become a disappointment and confusion in her life. She was a wonderful woman of faith, strong, gifted, and loving to all around her, and yet her wait for such a simple thing seemed endless. One day, we were visited by a young woman who was working as a nurse on the mission field in Asia. When hearing the story of this wonderful Pentecostal lady who had waited for a quarter of a century to be baptized in the Spirit, her response was immediate and caring: "Oh, you poor thing, come with me right now!" She took my friend by the hand and led her next door. Just a few minutes later they returned, my friend radiant and filled to overflowing with the Holy Spirit and speaking in tongues! You can wait for 25 years for something that will only take 25 minutes when you find a person of faith and experience. Be sure that you have joined yourself to a faith-filled community, where the answers you seek can be found. Set your heart on pilgrimage, seeking fervently for a deeper life with God and his people, surrounded by travelling companions who feel the same way!

"In the beginning God created the heavens and the earth. The earth was formless and empty, and darkness covered the deep waters. And the Spirit of God was hovering over the surface of the waters." (Gen 1:1-2)

Are you hungry and thirsty for the workings of the Spirit in your life? Are you ready to fall on your knees right where you are and declare your thirst before the Lord? Have you finally come to an end of yourself, an end to trying hard and doing your best? Have you finally realized that to reach your neighbour, to evangelize your region, to teach about Jesus is well beyond your capacity? Then call on the Spirit with all your heart. Let him hear your voice and recognize your earnestness. Tell him how much you love all the peoples of the earth, and how much it means to you to see the nations become aware of the glory of the Lord.

The Spirit is hovering over you right now, waiting to shape you into the servant of God that your Father has destined you to be. Jesus promised, "I will not abandon you as orphans – I will come to you" (John 14:18). He has asked the Father to give us another advocate who will never leave us: "He is the Holy Spirit, who leads into all truth" (John 14:17). Receive the Holy Spirit with an open heart, and he will fill you to overflowing, so that rivers of life rush out of your heart. Just tell him how hungry and thirsty for more you are; speak it out loud with conviction and sincerity, and he will rush into your life to answer your cry.

God is in the business of transforming us: born again, with a new heart, filled with his Spirit, sent preaching and healing into the city. That is God's plan and provision for all his children.

"Let God transform you into a new person by changing the way you think." (Rom 12:2)

The Holy Spirit is hovering over your lives, asking you to let him in deeper so that he can transform you by his love and power. He can help you become the new person that you long to be by changing the way that you think. The word of God was once spoken into a formless world over which the Spirit waited. On hearing the creative words spoken, light sprang into existence, Kingdom order and rule was seen, and new life appeared everywhere. Let the Holy Spirit go to work on you according to God's word, and you will be changed.

"For all creation is waiting eagerly for that future day when God will reveal who his children really are." (Rom 8:19)

That future day is still to come, when the creation itself "will join God's children in glorious freedom from death and decay" (Rom 8:21). But even now, the peoples of the world are calling out for the servants of Jesus to rise to their full potential, to do those "even greater works" (John 14:12) that Jesus promised, and to burst through our needless limitations into the full equipping that is available from the Lord. The Holy Spirit is hovering over us to bring us into the fullness of his power and to show us how mighty is the river that flows out of us. God's word is true, and "God uses (scripture) to prepare and equip his people to do every good work" (2 Tim 3:17). Jesus has sent ministries to help us grow: apostles, prophets, evangelists, pastors and teachers. These ministries have been sent to us so that we can be a people who are "growing in every way more and more like Christ" (Eph 4:15).

You are not stuck where you are in life or in ministry. Shake yourself up, and declare your hunger and thirst to the Lord, and he will transform you.

"(Christ) makes the whole body fit together perfectly. As each part does its own special work, it helps the other part grow, so that the whole body is healthy and growing and full of love." (Eph 4:16)

~~~~~~~

MEDITATE & MEMORIZE:

Memorize this scripture and speak it out loud as often as you can, taking time to meditate on it and asking the Holy Spirit to open it up for you. Let faith come as you hear your own voice declaring the true word of God.

"Let God transform you into a new person by changing the way you think." (Rom 12:2)

PRAY & PROCLAIM:

Pray for yourself that you will never stop short of Jesus' full intention for your life, that you will press on to maturity and fullness. Call on the Lord to change you, tell him that you are surrendered, and that you want to be continually renewed, completely restored by the workings of his Holy Spirit. Proclaim that you will not go it alone, but that you will be built together with all your sisters and brothers into the house of God. Pray for present day apostles, prophets, evangelists, pastors and teachers that the work of Christ might be fully established in the earth.

GIVE THANKS & WORSHIP:

Give thanks to the Lord that he has done this, that you are a new creation, a brand new person. Worship him for his great plan and purpose, that he has still more to pour into you, and that your new birth was only a beginning. Thank Jesus that you are changing the way you think under his gracious hand of blessing.

TESTIMONY

Have you heard what God is doing in Ottawa?

In March of 2015 my wife, Jen, found a lump in her breast. There were some tests and a biopsy, and then we met with a surgeon in late April. The surgeon told us that it was very serious. There were four high risk factors such as a large tumour, a very aggressive type of cancer, etc. Jen had surgery in late May and then started a regime of eight treatments of chemo with very aggressive drugs on the 26th of June. Regular chemo is on a three-week cycle but this was on a two-week cycle to increase the dosage and impact. Then four weeks after the last chemo treatment she would start twenty-five treatments of radiation: five days a week for five weeks.

I have become entirely convinced from my experiences as a Christian that all I need to know in any situation I face is what God wants me to do. He has been so faithful and acted absolutely miraculously so many times that I have no doubt of his love, grace and provision for me. After that meeting with the surgeon in April, I went off by myself and asked God "So what is happening here? What are we looking at?" I felt that God said to me, through the Holy Spirit "I have taken you around a lot of other obstacles in life. This time I am going to take you through it." And that is exactly what he did in an amazing way.

Jen and I both work from home offices. She is Director of Operations for a small software company, and I am a Project Manager in commercial construction. We are also both subcontractors and thus do not receive Employment Insurance benefits if we are out of work. At this point we had significant financial commitments and it was not an option to live on one salary and still make ends meet. Jen's company told her they would continue to pay her full time if she just did whatever she was able to. That was a blessing! Unfortunately, work had been slow for my company through the winter and spring and most of the other people were laid off. Then one week before Jen started chemo I too was laid off. I had worked with this company for nine years and never missed a pay. My boss was very regretful, but there was no work and he simply did not have any more money left to carry me. I had complete peace. The sense in my spirit, from the Lord, was that I was not to look for another job—that God was ordaining this time for me to be with Jen through chemo—and that He would take care of us. I believed that more work would come for the construction company (and thus me) in God's timing. So we took out a Line of Credit at the bank to meet financial demands. During the months ahead the people in our church also gave us some help with food and money.

The first four chemo treatments were very, very difficult. Apparently the chemicals chosen were unusually aggressive. We couldn't get nausea under control, there were drugs to control the side effects (with their own side effects), and then more drugs to try to control the side effects of those. At some points we were just trying to make it through one hour at a time. I have no idea how we would have managed if I had had my normal workload. A great blessing through this period was that our youngest daughter took six weeks off work to come and stay with us and help. Thankfully, treatments five to eight were different and (slightly) less difficult.

There had been a project on the horizon for the construction company I work with since earlier in the year. Construction was expected to start in late August. The only problem was that since there was no other work for the company, it would be necessary for me to go to Toronto and supervise on site full time. Once the Building Permit was issued I would have to start on site the following Monday. I did not know what I would do if the Permit was issued before chemo was over. I did not want to tell my boss I couldn't go, and I could not see leaving Jen (our daughter had by this time returned to her work in another province). As I walked with the Lord, I felt that I would just trust Him one day at a time to work this out. Through late August and into September, the Permit was delayed again and again as the Building Dept. questioned various aspects of the design. Finally on Friday, 9th October Jen had her last chemo. The following Wednesday the Building Permit was issued. I had been required to give her a needle for seven days after each treatment to boost her immune system, and so the last one was the following Saturday. Then on Monday, 19th October, two days after the last needle, I started on site in Toronto. Only God could arrange things this perfectly! On top of all that, on the Friday before I started in Toronto, my boss direct-deposited into our bank account all of the money I had not been paid over the last four months!

Jen and Dale Bright
Ottawa

Part Two:
JUMPING IN THE RIVER

DAY 5
Baptism in Water

"I am a voice shouting in the wilderness, 'Clear the way for the Lord's coming.'" (John 1:23)

John the Baptist gave these words as an answer to a question seeking to know who he believed himself to be. Prophets need to know that they are prophets in order to identify the one they serve as much as to define their purpose, and so it is with the wider body of believers. To serve as a prophetic people we must be able to give an answer to all those who inquire as to who we are, and to know our reason for being on earth and not in heaven. As his interrogators tried to categorize him, John delivered an emphatic denial to the three possibilities that had occurred to them. The prophets almost always face a determined attempt by onlookers to give them the wrong label; the crowd generally misreads the situation and the God-given purpose of the prophetic ministry. It's best just to be quiet and to listen to the Lord's servant. John then identified himself by his work. He was a loud voice calling the nation to prepare for Jesus' coming, as foreseen by Isaiah.

"Listen! It's the voice of someone shouting, 'Clear the way through the wilderness for the Lord! Make a straight highway through the wasteland for our God! Fill in the valleys, and level the mountains and hills. Straighten the curves and smooth out the rough places.' Then the glory of the Lord will be revealed and all people will see it together. The Lord has spoken!" (Isa 40:3-5)

The entire community of God is a loud voice, shouting. Like John, we call people to get ready for the arrival of Jesus into their lives. Anticipating the total transformation of lives that follows belief in Jesus, we call people to humble themselves and let him enter. We know better than to suggest that becoming a disciple of Christ will have little impact on new believers because he loves to make everything and everybody new. As Jesus explained to Nicodemus:

"I tell you the truth, unless you are born again, you cannot see the Kingdom of God." (John 3:3)

No amount of learning, trying hard to be better or pretending to be good enough will do it. Jesus declares that for every one of us, a new birth is needed. We must be born from heaven, born of the Spirit, because only "the Holy Spirit gives birth to spiritual life" (John 3:6). So, I urge you, clear a path in your life for Jesus to come in. Ask him to reveal himself, to save you from your sins, to make his home in you. Be born again and live that extraordinary spiritual life that the Holy Spirit will lead you into. John's call was for everyone to show sincere repentance and to get ready for Jesus, who was so much greater than he. If you are already his disciple, then stand before him and ask him to so inhabit your life and to anoint you so thoroughly that his glory will be revealed. Stand up, step forward, and dedicate your life not just to your own salvation, but to seeing the glory of the Lord revealed so clearly that everyone will see it together! The whole church seems to be permanently on tip-toe, yearning for the fullness of God's glory to be seen in our time. Isaiah knew how this would happen, and gives simple instructions to those who long to see God's presence intensify. To feel the full weight of his glory in our lives, we simply have to remove any obstacles that we are aware of, stop putting our own desires first, and ask Jesus to sweep in and take over. Then all will see his glory together. Crowds gathered in Jerusalem as the noise of Pentecost was heard for the first time, not the sound of loud music from a church meeting, but the awesome spectacle of the fiery birth of a new nation. A united group of believers in Jesus, with fire on their heads and in their bones, burst out into the public space, supernaturally declaring in many unlearned languages all the wonderful things that God had done. If that doesn't sound like your experience of church, then you have much to discover that will delight and amaze you. Don't ever settle for less! The crowd, who represents all the nations and languages of the world, hear this testimony of God's work in their own native tongues, and it stirs them to seek the experience for themselves. They don't want to remain as they are and be guilty of the death of God's appointed King. They want to be submerged in this mighty river of life in the Holy Spirit by placing their faith entirely in Jesus. If you have never asked Jesus to forgive you and come into your life, then you should join the crowd listening to Peter and cry out:

"Brothers, what should we do?" (Acts 2:37)

Peter's answer pointed them to the joys of two baptisms: in water so that our previous experience of life without knowing God could be dealt with and in the Holy Spirit so that the newly born Christian could live in the power and the glory of God.

"Each of you must repent of your sins and turn to God and be baptized in the name of Jesus Christ for the forgiveness of your sins. Then you will receive the gift of the Holy Spirit.

This promise is to you, to your children, and to those far away—all who have been called by the Lord our God." (Acts 2:38-39)

The idea of repentance highlights a complete turning around of our lives from reliance on what we can do to an acceptance with faith of what God has done. The two baptisms turn our hearts towards those closest to us, our children and grandchildren, and join us in covenant love to all those who are far away. Repentance breaks the chains of a life lived without God and begins a life of joyful dependence on Jesus. Believers in Christ are to repent and be baptized in water. Paul understood that baptism by immersion in water joins the new believer with Jesus in his death.

"Have you forgotten that when we were joined with Christ Jesus in baptism, we joined him in his death? For we died and were buried with Christ by baptism. And just as Christ was raised from the dead by the glorious power of the Father, now we also may live new lives." (Rom 6:3-4)

This generation longs to live new lives, nation-changing lives, in the glorious power of God. Such a resurrection-fuelled life is available only to those who have died to their old ways, sins forgiven, buried with Christ. If you have only recently put your faith in Jesus, then I urge you to obey the command of scripture voiced by Peter and be baptized by immersion in water as soon as you can. Let your old life be buried and let your new life begin. Water baptism makes Peter remember the great flood, and he sees Noah's boat as an image of Christ himself.

"And the water is a picture of baptism, which now saves you, not by removing dirt from your body, but as a response to God from a clear conscience. It is effective because of the resurrection of Jesus Christ." (1 Pet 3:21)

If you have been a follower of Jesus for a long time but have not been baptized by immersion in water following that decision to believe in Christ, then I urge you to bury your old life now. Be baptized in water, that "baptism, which now saves you" because of your faith in the resurrection of Jesus from the dead. Many Christians, though they have a true and sincere faith in Christ's offer of mercy and salvation, still feel the power of the old life holding them back from fullness in their spiritual walk. Habits, addictions, old attitudes, and problems seem still to have the power to spoil and distract the believer from their pilgrimage. Paul compared water baptism with the miraculous crossing of the Red Sea on dry ground, where a path was made for God's people to escape slavery. No path was available for those forces wishing to return the people to their old life of slavery. Israel passed through the waters of the sea, and we pass through the waters of baptism. They are baptized into the one who led the way from death to life (Moses), just as we are baptized into Christ.

"In the cloud and in the sea, all of them were baptized as followers of Moses." (1 Cor 10:2)

"We were joined with Christ Jesus in his death." (Rom 6:3)

Let us believe together that as we pass through death in the waters of burial with Christ our enemies will be unable to follow. The power of the old has ended and the new has come. The water of baptism has forever cut us off from the power of the devil to hold us in slavery. Neither old weakness, nor limitation of personality, nor shameful or embarrassing history, nor mistakes or false starts have the power to disqualify us from living the life Jesus died to give to us. Many Christians are consumed with a desire to live lives filled with power, to move in the gifting of the Holy Spirit, and to swim in a sea of miracles. There has always been a tendency to follow the man who can give us bread and fish without our having to work for it, or pay for our daily food.

Miracles caused some to bow before Jesus; healings were not just a welcome relief from sickness, but a powerful agent of change, a true revelation of whom Jesus is. But for too many others, miracles and healings became just the opposite; so attractive in themselves, the miracles became treasure enough for some, and the miracle-worker himself was obscured in their sight. We must beware of becoming addicted to the emotional impact of "spiritual" meetings that endlessly repeat themselves, giving us a temporary "high" while detaching us from our mission to glorify Christ by preaching him to the world. Soak in the Spirit, worship the Lamb with passion and spiritual songs, and then remember to share your food with the hungry, and to love the neighbour who looks different from you. The path to Pentecostal power passes first through the cross of Christ, and onwards to the tomb. The desire for miracles will always be a pure-hearted longing for those who humbly allow their old lives to be buried by immersion in the deadly waters of baptism. Resurrection life is, of course, available only to those who have died in Christ and risen with him.

At different times over the years, I have found an enthusiasm for the power and excitement of the Holy Spirit in the denominational groups around me, and yet have seen great resistance to water baptism in those same people. One dear, godly man in leadership of a local congregation once declared, with some emotion, that "if we accept the need for baptism in water following our first belief in Christ, then that will undermine the very foundation of this (denominational) church!" He was quite correct of course, as water baptism undermines, carries away, and totally buries for all time an entire life lived outside of faith in Jesus. But if we will act as dead as we claim to be, and let ourselves be buried in Christ's tomb, then nothing will ever be able to take away our freedom. No devil, no habit, no addiction, or wrong thought will ever again be able to take us back into slavery.

"Then the waters returned and covered all the chariots and charioteers—the entire army of Pharaoh…not a single one survived." (Exod 14:28)

The waters of baptism join us with Christ in his death and deliver us by his mighty resurrection into the life of the Spirit. And now we remember the promise made by Peter to those who were desperate to know what they must do in response to Christ: "Then you will receive the gift of the Holy Spirit" (Acts 2:38). This was a simple acceptance of the promise of Jesus that we "will receive power when the Holy

Spirit comes upon (us)" (Acts 1:8).

Peter's vision is that as we repent, burying our old lives in the waters of baptism, that we are then immediately baptized in the Holy Spirit. He believed the risen Lord that this would be the key to reaching the city, the region, and the ends of the earth. When the Holy Spirit fell on the church, the glory and power of God were evident. Jesus' assurance that as believers we would continue his work, seeing even greater expressions of the powerful love of God, is confirmed.

"Crowds come from the villages around Jerusalem, bringing their sick and those possessed by evil spirits, and they were all healed." (Acts 5:16)

The awesome experience of being baptized in the Holy Spirit produces a church that points the world to the glory of God in Christ and to an exciting outpouring of the supernatural. Healing, deliverance, salvation, mercy, and joy fill the streets, leading many to put their faith in Jesus.

"The news spread through the whole town and many believed in the Lord." (Acts 9:42)

~~~~~~~

MEDITATE & MEMORIZE:

Memorize this scripture and speak it out loud as often as you can, taking time to meditate on it and asking the Holy Spirit to open it up for you. Let faith come as you hear your own voice declaring the true word of God.

"Each of you must repent of your sins and turn to God, and be baptized in the name of Jesus Christ for the forgiveness of your sins. Then you will receive the gift of the Holy Spirit. This promise is to you, to your children, and to those far away – all who have been called by the Lord our God." (Acts 2:38-39)

PRAY & PROCLAIM:

Pray for yourself and for your family and friends that this promise might be fulfilled in their lives. If you have not been baptized by immersion in water since you believed in Jesus, tell the Lord that you will put that right immediately, and then do so. Proclaim that no enemy can catch you, and call on the Lord to mightily baptize you in his Holy Spirit.

GIVE THANKS & WORSHIP:

Give thanks to Jesus for burying your old life in his own tomb and for giving you his amazing Holy Spirit as empowerment for your new life! Worship the Lord of heaven and earth, and declare that all who are "far away" will soon feel the promise of his anointing in their own lives.

TESTIMONY

Have you heard what God has done in Wales?

Some of the most exciting times in my walk with the Lord have taken place at summer gatherings of many churches at Bible Weeks. So many lives were changed by powerful preaching, and so many saved or set free from addictions. There were healings and miracles, with adults and children alike encountering a living, loving God. At one of those weeks, I helped out with baptizing some new disciples in the local river near our campground in central Wales. We baptized people who came up wet but happy, and everyone on the riverbank cheered. It was great!

One lady came out of the water a little differently, though. She came up looking happy, and heard the cheers of the supporters, and then covered and uncovered one of her ears. "I've been healed," she declared with some amazement. She explained to us, while still in the river, that she had no hearing on one side, none at all, and now she had perfect hearing restored to her. She hadn't thought of it, and no one was aware of it to have faith for healing, but God knew. That lady left her old life and her deafness at the bottom of that river in Wales!

Mike Nicholson,
Builth Wells, Wales

DAY 6

If You Only Knew, You Would Ask: Baptism in the Spirit

"Jesus replied, 'If you only knew the gift God has for you and who you are talking to, you would ask me and I would give you living water." (John 4:10)

      Good people tried to avoid Samaria, and a godly man would not want to speak to a local woman unaccompanied. Samaria was a place of irredeemable mixture, and not at all a place where the pure of heart would be found visiting. This particular woman and her far from holy life would have been someone to avoid at all costs by those with a reputation to protect. And yet, the best and most pure man of all, God's own son, will go wherever he has to in order to find a single lost individual, so great is his love for the children of God. You may consider your life to be pretty good, or at least unremarkable. Or you may be convinced that your life has been lived so far from your Father in heaven that there is no hope for you. Whoever you are, one message of scripture is plain: "For everyone has sinned; we all fall short of God's glorious standard" (John 13:7). Every one of us needs help if we are to return to God's family. Don't hide behind your trumpeted goodness, or indeed your sinful excesses, from a loving Lord who has known all about you from before the beginning of time. Jesus is looking right at you, yes you, and he will give you healing, forgiving, merciful, living water if you will only ask.

"If you only knew…you would ask…"

      Turn from your sin, show your past life what your back looks like, and walk to your grave. Put your faith in Jesus, and join him in his tomb by obediently submitting yourself to the waters of baptism. With Jesus, such a death is not an end but a beginning. Though my childhood and young adulthood were lived quite placidly as an unrebellious good little churchgoer, I lived in the certain knowledge that I was in trouble and that a disappointed God would one day catch up with me. There was no assurance of ultimate salvation, no guarantee of a happy ending. Until I reached eighteen and responded to that invitation to a gospel meeting, no one had ever suggested that Jesus was here to help me. I assumed he was here to put me in jail where I belonged. When I heard that Jesus came into the world convinced that I was lost, that I needed to be rescued, and that he would be the one to save me through burial and resurrection to a brand new life, I was stunned! The thought that anyone had the power or inclination to end my old life and give me a genuine and complete new start as a brand new person was far removed from the religious message that had filled my life to that point. At the gospel meeting organized by the students of my university, the preacher simply asked, "who wants to know God?" and I put up my hand to say, "I do." That was all I agreed to, and I hadn't really understood anything else that went on that evening: strange songs, unchurchy musical instruments, odd language. Everyone else in that meeting seemed far more excited about what I had done than I was. Talk of there being "a party in heaven" because I had timidly raised my hand seemed over-the-top and a little bizarre. Heaven had never struck me before as being a party hot-spot, and waving my hand in the air seemed a poor excuse for celebration.

The next Sunday I went off as usual to my regular, always the same word-for-word church gathering, something that I had done since taking my first breath in the world. The hour of familiar prayer and responses were literally identical to every other time, and yet on this first attendance since my decision at the gospel meeting, I felt an almost physical pain at being there. If I had possessed an ounce more courage, I would have walked out. As it was, I endured to the end, silently asking God over and over again, "what have you done to me?" I was feeling new emotions, experiencing completely changed reactions to familiar things. I remember thinking, "this just isn't me!"

After a few days of worry, and after being shown the scriptures by my newfound Christian friends, I discovered that I had been exactly right. The old me had, indeed, gone, "passed away," as they say of the dear departed at funerals, with a brand new me having come seemingly out of nowhere. My understanding of those days has convinced me that the command from Jesus that we must be born again is based on the simple truth that God can make it happen. I thought that new birth was a kind of poetic illustration, but it turned out to be deeply, fundamentally real: a new birth of a brand new man. I followed the advice of my pastor and hastened to bury that old man before he began to decay, and appreciated the surprising truth that it was a new me that emerged from the water at my baptism. It took me a while, but I now understood that a party in heaven was an appropriate celebration of one more lost sheep rescued by the greatness of Christ, sprinkled and cleansed by his blood. The woman at the well, my unremarkable and uncertain life, both saved by a Jesus who declares, "if you only knew…you would ask."

What about you? Just ask him, and he will move in you right now to end the power and the flow of your old life, and cause you to be reborn as a child of the living God. And as you come up out of those burial waters of baptism, he will pour out his Holy Spirit on you. It won't matter anymore how great your sin was, for the old you will be dead and buried. And for the newly transformed, born again of the Spirit you, there is a fellowship with God and a fullness of the Spirit that will empower you to live a joyful, glorious life. No mere survivalism awaits you. No hiding away from life until heaven claims you at the end of your days. No, heaven claims you right now as you rise up as a citizen of a new nation, the Kingdom of God. The baptism in the Holy Spirit is a receiving of power to live by direct contact with God in the person of his Spirit, to be immersed in a continually flowing river of life. And this contact, this immersion in God, this baptism in the river of his Spirit, is for us all without exception.

"In the last days, God says, 'I will pour out my Spirit upon all people. Your sons and daughters will prophesy…I will pour out my Spirit even on my servants—men and women alike.'" (Acts 2:17-18)

This extraordinary outpouring in Acts is not the origin of Pentecostal denominationalism. It is the fulfillment of what the prophet John saw when he boldly declared, "He will baptize you with the Holy Spirit and with fire" (Luke 3:16). This is what Joel saw and Peter understood.

"What you see was predicted long ago by the prophet Joel … everyone who calls on the name of the Lord will be saved." (Acts 2:16, 21)

The Holy Spirit is poured out, and he has his eye on each individual who calls on Jesus, and on the ends of the earth. This is the realisation of Jesus' loudly shouted promise to all who believed, to all who received him as Lord and Saviour.

"Rivers of living water will flow from his heart." (John 7:38)

This is what Moses longed for, and Isaiah saw from afar.

"I wish that all the Lord's people were prophets and that the Lord would put his Spirit upon them all!" (Num 11:29)

"Until at last the Spirit is poured out on us from heaven." (Isa 32:15)

It is so important for new Christians, for all believers, to find death to the old life in water baptism and the power to live in baptism in the Holy Spirit. The first generation was commanded to wait for God's promised sending of the Spirit of power before trying to live the Christian life. Only the Spirit of Jesus living within you can live that life. You must wait, and he who is always faithful will send his Spirit to you. It is being full of his Spirit that puts fire on our heads and in our bones. It is that intimacy with the Spirit of the Lord that gets us to burst out of our rooms into the city streets. Jesus' disciples are always full of forgiveness, compassion, love, and mercy, constantly overflowing with the good news about Jesus. This baptism gives us the power to reach our neighbours to the ends of the earth with that same compassion, love, and with the name of Jesus.

No one expected to find a servant of God in Samaria, talking alone to a woman. But Jesus loved Samaria, had compassion for the woman as a valued sister, and carried within him the power and knowledge to save an entire village. As the church calls out to Jesus to pour out his Spirit upon us all, we too will find ourselves in unusual places, filled with love and encouragement for everyone we meet, and with the power of the Spirit to save whole communities.

Our generation will allow Jesus to stir in us again that love for the world that will drive us to reach out to the nations in the power of God. This will be a church generation that will not be ashamed to be compared with past heroes of faith who gave their lives to evangelize distant peoples and the nearest of neighbours. It is Jesus' plan that we, baptized to overflowing in his magnificent Holy Spirit, will preach the good news of Jesus, Saviour of the world, with supernatural signs following. If we only knew who it is that is offering, we would ask. But we do know. It is Jesus, who will baptise us in his Holy Spirit. And we do know what to ask for, and we will not rest until we have received the river of water that he promised, guaranteed, urged upon us.

"Suddenly, there was a sound from heaven like the roaring of a mighty windstorm, and it filled the house where they were sitting. Then, what looked like flames or tongues of fire appeared and settled on each of them. And everyone present was filled with the Holy Spirit and began speaking in other languages, as the Holy Spirit gave them this ability." (Acts 2:2-4)

The fulfilling of Jesus' promise changed everything. Men and women who believed were together, received together, and empowered from heaven together. The story of Acts and of the new testament church, it is not primarily about the work of elders, deacons, guitarists, children's workers, and greeters; it is certainly not about closed doors, rather predictable, repetitive church meetings that compete with Sunday sports and the chance to have a day off. No, this is the amazing true account of believers in Jesus being set on fire by the powerful, immediate presence of the Holy Spirit. It gets the church outside into the public arena in a way that brings heaven to the earth.

"Everyone came running, and they were bewildered to hear their own languages being spoken by the believers." (Acts 2:6)

A closed door church reaching no one new is suddenly exploded outwards into the heart of the city, supernaturally speaking the languages of foreigners and angels. A nervous church is suddenly filled with Holy Spirit boldness, and the whole city starts to buzz. Jesus' promise that this outpouring of the Spirit into and out of the hearts of every believer is kept as the work of reaching the ends of the earth is spectacularly begun. A river has begun to flow, powerful and unexpected, evangelistic and supernatural, Jesus-centred and believer-empowering. The church does not expect an unbelieving world to come to faith in Christ without evidence that he is the risen Lord. There is a river flowing through the earth full of the life of Jesus, producing fruit and transforming lives. The heavens are not cold towards the needs of humanity; fire is poured out on women and men. God is not dead, but mightily alive and concerned about us. His river of crystal-clear water transforms our land.

"A deep sense of awe came over them all, and the apostles performed many miraculous signs and wonders. And all the believers met together in one place and shared everything they had." (Acts 2:43-44)

~~~~~~

MEDITATE & MEMORIZE:

Memorize this scripture and speak it out loud as often as you can, taking time to meditate on it and asking the Holy Spirit to open it up for you. Let faith come as you hear your own voice declaring the true word of God.

"Suddenly, there was a sound from heaven like the roaring of a mighty windstorm, and it filled the house where they were sitting. Then, what looked like flames or tongues of fire appeared and settled on each of them. And everyone present was filled with the Holy Spirit and began speaking in other languages, as the Holy Spirit gave them this ability." (Acts 2:2-4)

PRAY & PROCLAIM:

Call out to God, asking him to bring sudden change into your life, your church, and your community. Proclaim that all your history, limitations, and mistakes are just not big enough to hold back the flood of living water that the Holy Spirit unleashes on us all. Ask Jesus for living water, and tell him loudly that you will live in the power of his Holy Spirit always!

GIVE THANKS & WORSHIP:

Give thanks to Jesus for going back to heaven so that the Holy Spirit would be poured out on all peoples, including you! Worship the Lord in his greatness, in his unstoppability. Worship the Lord of all the kingdoms, declaring that they are his to rule, his to bless.

TESTIMONY

Have you heard what God is doing in Ottawa?

Even though this happened back in 1993, it still feels like yesterday because it was the first time God used me in a miracle. I was a new Christian and just freshly baptized in the Holy Spirit. I worked as a morning show host at a small local radio station. I remember so clearly many mornings getting to work early just so I could spend some time alone in the studio praying in tongues and fellowshipping with God in the Spirit. Growth in my relationship with God was unforced, natural, and rapid. My heart was captured by his love, and my life ruined for anything else but His Kingdom purpose.

His joy would spill over into my four-hour show and permeate my interactions with people. I remember one particular morning our Admin Assistant coming into the studio to drop off some inter office mail. She was usually cheery so the sad look on her face stood out. When I asked what was wrong, the tears quickly flowed as she told me about the possibility of her daughter needing surgery to repair a birth defect affecting one of her kidneys. Doctors had known since she was young that a valve on one of her daughter's kidneys never developed properly. They had hoped that over time the valve would eventually grow and function would be restored, but it never did. She was now twelve years old, and she would now have to have a surgical intervention to permanently fix the valve in place. It was a Tuesday, and she was to have her last pre-OP appointment on Thursday with surgery soon to follow. Her Mom was a puddle of emotion as she poured her heart out.

Before I could think, out of my mouth came these words, "I will pray and Jesus will heal your daughter so that she will not need surgery." With a supernatural confidence, I hugged her and assured her everything was going to be ok. I was ok until she left and the words I said to her began to ring in my head. What had I just done? What had I just committed God to? What happens if she doesn't get healed? There was no way I could walk back or dumb down such a clear promise of God's healing to this woman's daughter. I didn't know what to do but I would not retract my declaration. I began to fast and pray, really more out of fear than anything else in an attempt to get God to hear me and save my reputation, trying to convince God to do something I was suddenly unsure He would now do. This attack of unbelief was quickly exhausting me.

Thursday came and went and I resigned myself to my fate. Monday morning rolled around and the studio door opened. There was our Admin Assistant's beaming face. She said, "You'll never guess what happened." She said that the final Pre-OP tests revealed that the deformed kidney valve had suddenly starting working normally and not only would her daughter not require surgery, but no more appointments would be necessary again for her previous kidney problems. In her Mom's hand was a small homemade card made by her daughter thanking me for praying for her and attributing her healing to Jesus. I was filled with a mix of praise and relief.

Afterwards, when I asked the Lord about this whole situation, I felt he confirmed in my heart that he had healed this young girl the day I declared to her Mom she would be healed and not require the surgery. It wasn't my panic or my desperate fear filled prayers that accomplished anything. Simply the words that came from compassion and the overflow of his Spirit out of me had healed her instantly. I learned so many lessons through this miracle. Miracles are not rewards for good behaviour or our trophies from uttering the exact right prayer. Miracles happen simply by yielding to God's Spirit and being determined to say what he says even when our minds argue.

Todd Pulsifer,
Ottawa

DAY 7
Living in the Light

"The Lord, my God, lights up my darkness." (Psa 18:28)

God loves light. In fact, "God is light, and in him there is no darkness at all" (1 John 1:5). The first words spoken by God in Genesis are, "Let there be light" (Gen 1:3). So the psalmist speaks with understanding when he rejoices in the light of God that lights up his life. John's gospel opens with an echo of the creation story, a fitting introduction to the announcement of a new creation from a God who makes all things new, including us. The creation of the universe itself turns out to be but one more seed now grown into a tree; a miraculous physical creation produced by the words of God, finding its fulfillment in the new creation wrought by King Jesus, the Word who was God!

I've always loved astronomy, and have appreciated the glory of God that is revealed in his creation. I have made a hobby, at a very amateur level, of trying to understand as much of science as I can. Every time I fly, I buy the current Scientific American to read on the plane in an attempt to keep up with new thought. I feel very proud of myself if I manage to get half way through most articles before they lose me, a little further for astronomy and physics pieces. I can understand the scientists that cannot believe in a God of creation, given what they know about the immensity of the universe and the complexity of the natural world. How could a God capable of creating all that is seen and unseen by speaking words over the nothingness possibly care about lives as insignificant as ours? The question is an excellent one. My answer would have to be, "I really don't know, but he does!" The only thought that seems to help me understand a God who keeps the galaxies spinning and yet still loves me as an individual is to acknowledge that the Father's love for his children is a familiar and powerful motivation. To him we are not just a random accident of biology located in a truly unremarkable part of a fairly average galaxy; we are his beloved children, his family.

I would suggest to you that if science and faith have been presented to you as enemies, and you have been told that you must choose sides, that you might want to question that approach. A modern proverb might read, "there are two ridiculous things in the world; scientists dismissing faith, and preachers dismissing science." He has shown us his glory in the world around us, so I guess that scientists know better than the rest of us just how great his glory really is! I would think that we should not tell our kids that they can believe in Jesus or dinosaurs, but not both. If we insist on a vote, I think we may lose the 5 to 8 years old demographic. God is light; he lights up our lives and brightens our darkness. He knows how consciousness emerges from our extraordinary brains, dark matter and dark energy are not at all dark to him, and he probably even likes math! End the war between science and faith, honour and appreciate the teachers and scientists around you, and see the glory of God everywhere!

"The Word gave life to everything that was created, and his life brought light to everyone." (John 1:4)

Baptism in water allows us to close our eyes on our old life without God, on a life which was, on reflection, lived in the darkness. Experiencing new birth by faith in Jesus, we are then baptized in the Holy Spirit and begin to live in the light.

"He has enabled you to share in the inheritance that belongs to his people, who live in the light. For he has rescued us from the kingdom of darkness and transferred us into the kingdom of his dear son." (Col 1:12, 13)

Out of darkness into the light in which we now live! Baptism in the Holy Spirit brings a revolution into our lives, as we find ourselves living in the river of God. We know that Jesus lived in the light, doing only those things that he saw his Father doing. Now we too can see and hear and know and understand the workings of the supernatural world with the help of the Holy Spirit. It's as if we were blind, and now we see—deaf and now we hear. The day will come when the whole earth will be aware of God's glory. By God's mercy and grace we are born again and filled with his Holy Spirit, living in the light, and we are already constantly aware of that glory, knowing that the good news about Jesus was a message filled with glorious light.

"For God, who said, 'Let there be light in the darkness,' has made this light shine in our hearts so we could know the glory of God that is seen in the face of Christ." (2 Cor 4:6)

It is vital that we hold on to Jesus' promise of the Holy Spirit, and receive him in all his fullness. Just as Elisha refused to leave Elijah at the end of his time on earth, so we must refuse to leave that upper room of prayer and seeking until the Spirit has fallen upon us. Elijah knew that the real issue was Elisha's ability to see. So we also know that the baptism in the Spirit will be an eye-opener for us, as the gifts of the Holy Spirit draw us into an understanding of the supernatural realities around us. God is a great God, and he is restoring all things. Be a willing part of his restoration endeavours by earnestly seeking the greater gifts of the Holy Spirit: those that are the most helpful to the world around you, and those that serve to make more people aware of the glory of the Lord as it fills the earth. Listen to the direction of the Lord in your own hearts; give yourself to the passions of the Kingdom; and spend your resources of time, money, and prayer on the most vulnerable in your communities. The Holy Spirit will open our eyes to see the workings of the Lord, and he will open our hearts to the needs of others. Jesus lived each day as a sacrifice, with a river of love and healing flowing out of him, living not for himself but for others. All of heaven flowed out of him to destroy the devil's works and to set the captives free. Being baptised in the Holy Spirit enables the Christ in all of us to be seen as the same today as he was yesterday; surrender yourself to be his devoted disciple, with your life laid down and a river of life, forgiveness and healing will burst out of you.

When Elisha was helping the king of Israel to be victorious against Aram, his help was based on his ability, God-given, to see and understand beyond the natural. The Arameans thought that they had gained the advantage when they surrounded the city where the prophet was with troops, horses and chariots. Elisha's young servant, seeing the strength of the enemy, was afraid in a way that Elisha could never be. Living in the light was the difference between them, and so Elisha prayed:

"O Lord, open his eyes and let him see! The Lord opened the young man's eyes, and when he looked up, he saw that the hillside around Elisha was filled with horses and chariots of fire." (2 Kings 6:17)

There had always been more help and support from heaven with Elisha then could ever be overcome by the forces that stood against him. His young servant was given an extraordinary insight into the experience of his master, a man of God. Elisha saw the supernatural more vividly than the natural, understanding the wisdom of the Lord, knowing things that only God knew because he walked with him. Wouldn't you love to share the reality of Elisha's life, or are you content to be more like his young servant? Elisha wasn't braver than his servant; he could just see better what the Spirit was doing. To us all, Jesus commands that we stay in the prayer-room until we see what Elisha could see. Jesus has promised supernatural power, wisdom, knowledge, faith, and discernment, not just to the few, but to all people, men and women, who belong to Jesus by their faith in his name.

The baptism in the Holy Spirit brings all believers into an understanding of what God is doing and saying around us. We can live in the light of Christ as the river of his Spirit flows out of us. A drinking that begins in response to our thirst for living water quickly becomes an outward flow, a river that waters the world around us. The first, bewildering miracle that amazed and puzzled the crowd following Pentecost was an outward flowing of the river, a gift of the Holy Spirit that enabled the believers to reach out to the nations. Jews from every nation and visitors to the city were included in the good news about Jesus.

"We all hear these people speaking in our own languages about the wonderful things God has done!" (Acts 2:11)

Paul later describes this gift of the Holy Spirit, so amazing to this diverse group, as "the languages of earth and of angels" (1 Cor 13:1), and declares, "I wish you could all speak in tongues" (1 Cor 14:5) and, "I thank God that I speak in tongues more than any of you" (14:18). He then declares that this supernatural gift of speaking unlearned languages is a sign for unbelievers, by comparing the gift to hearing foreign languages spoken in the streets by invading oppressors! As in Elisha's day, the gift of being able to see what God could see completely transforms our perception of the world and shows us that the resources of God are very great.

As we hear hundreds of voices in worship singing in "unknown language" given by the Holy Spirit, we can be certain that the armies of the Lord have not given up on the world. The other Spirit-given gift that Paul teaches as being for everyone is that of prophecy.

"Let love be your highest goal! But you should also desire the special abilities the Spirit gives – especially the gift of prophecy." (1 Cor 14:1)

Your neighbours and your friends all need to hear what God is saying to them, and the Spirit gives us the gift of speaking that word. Within our meetings, the word of the Lord can be heard: encouraging, comforting, and strengthening his people. Gifts of faith, miracles, and healing give substance to Jesus' promise that we would do even greater things than he did as the river bursts out into the world. In Jesus' ministry, the whole region brings the sick, the demon-oppressed, and the needy to receive the blessings of the Kingdom, and he healed, freed, and helped them all. The baptism in the Holy Spirit equips the church to continue Jesus' ministry in power. All that would have come to touch Jesus can now come to receive his touch through his mighty people, the saints of God. There is no war between faith and science; the gifts and abilities of a Holy Spirit filled church offer observable, repeated evidence of the real effects of an invisible, loving God in action.

Some are given by the Spirit the ability to understand and interpret messages in unknown languages, so that they can understand and be helped by the meaning of these miracle words. Others are gifted by the Spirit to know the Lord's wisdom, others to gain God-revealed knowledge, just as Elisha experienced. These gifts are given so that we can help each other and reach unbelievers, demonstrating that "we brought you the Good News…not only with words, but with power," with the result being that "the Holy Spirit gave you full assurance that what we said was true" (1 Thes 1:5).

We know that the enemy is real, and we must therefore be filled with all the available power of heavenly warfare from our experience of being baptized in the Holy Spirit. Jesus loved people, and destroyed the works of the devil. In the same way, this generation of believers is filled with love for the world; we are also utterly opposed to the cruel effects of the demonic on so many. Whenever we see acts of violence or terror, when we see women and girls oppressed, when we observe the gap between rich and poor widening, the gifts of the Spirit stir in us. The pouring out of the Spirit of Jesus moves us to faith-filled action on behalf of the voiceless. His gifts enable us to champion the cause of the poor and to preach the word with evidence of supernatural power.

God has brought us into the light and given us understanding, wisdom and powerful gifts. We exercise these gifts to help people, to demonstrate how God feels about sin and sickness, and to give him all the glory. When we allow the Spirit to flow out of us like a mighty river, everyone knows where all that good stuff comes from, a torrent that has its origin in heaven. The greatness of the Lord is revealed through the weakest, the most humble of his children.

"We now have this light shining in our hearts, but we ourselves are like fragile clay jars containing this great treasure. This makes it clear that our great power is from God, not from ourselves." (2 Cor 4:7)

~~~~~~~

MEDITATE & MEMORIZE:

Memorize this scripture and speak it out loud as often as you can, taking time to meditate on it and asking the Holy Spirit to open it up for you. Let faith come as you hear your own voice declaring the true word of God.

"O Lord, open his eyes and let him see! The Lord opened the young man's eyes, and when he looked up, he saw that the hillside around Elisha was filled with horses and chariots of fire." (2 Kings 6:17)

PRAY & PROCLAIM:

Pray first with humility and sincerity that the Lord might open your own eyes. Don't be overly impressed with your present grasp of bible truth and spiritual realities. Listen to John Robinson as he encourages the Pilgrim Fathers about to depart on the Mayflower for America in 1620: "I am verily persuaded the Lord hath more truth yet to break forth out of His Holy Word." Walk humbly with the Lord, and hold lightly to everything else but Jesus. Only then should you pray for your church and its faithful leaders, "O Lord, open their eyes too!"

GIVE THANKS & WORSHIP:
Worship the Lord who is able to change the course of events in any nation on earth by suddenly opening up heaven's doors and pouring out his powerful Holy Spirit. Thank him that he is always motivated by love and compassion for the poor.

TESTIMONY
Have you heard what God is doing in Ottawa?

I can't tell you how many times in the past three years that I tried to step out and start evangelizing in Ottawa. I would pray, then develop a detailed plan that included mapping potential areas to evangelize and a timeline to knock on every door in the capital city. Typically, I started planning in September and by March of the following year I would have come up with a plan ready to execute, but I also felt hindered in stepping out to carry out the plan. I knew that if people got saved that they would need a church that would build them up, and I was transitioning in search for a church that preached sound doctrine and demonstrated faith practically. I also felt that I needed to be married to have the stability and support necessary to undertake what God was placing in my heart; yes, I needed a wife.

In September 2015, God began to unfold a path for us in evangelism. Claire, my then fiancée, and I began to regularly attend All Nations Church Ottawa, a church that believes in the Ephesians 4 ministries. "So Christ himself gave the apostles, the prophets, the evangelists, the pastors and teachers, to equip his people for works of service, so that the body of Christ may be built up until we all reach unity in the faith and in the knowledge of the Son of God and become mature, attaining to the whole measure of the fullness of Christ" (Eph 4:11-13 NIV). In early 2016, Claire and I attended a weekday meeting led by an evangelist who was invited by the church. He spoke about his journey as an evangelist and God's desire for labourers in this day. At the end of the meeting, I approached the man of God asking for prayer. He prayed for me and after praying he encouraged me to focus on relationships when reaching out to the community for God's kingdom. However, Claire and I saw a turning point in our path towards evangelism after visiting a friend's home in the west of Ottawa. When sharing our heart for evangelism and desire to be part of an active ministry in that area (we still considered ourselves visitors at All Nations Church at that time), Hazel Nicholson prophesied over us. I will have to paraphrase what she said as I don't recall her exact words: "It is so beautiful to see the call of God for evangelism on both of you and whatever church you decide to join, don't be discouraged if you don't find an existing evangelism ministry. You are going to be the ones to start such a ministry there." She went on to say that our reason for being in Ottawa would become clear as we pursued God's heart for reaching lives in this city.

In the weeks to follow, I had an intense desire to wake up in the middle of the night to pray over the city. I would drive to a different location, find a quiet spot and plead with the Lord for the city. In March 2016 while visiting Claire at her apartment, I stood by the window stretching my hands to the adjacent and opposite buildings saying, "Lord, look at all these apartment buildings, how can we reach them?" The thought that came to me as a response was: "What about the one you are standing in right now?" It seemed so obvious but the thought had never crossed my mind before. And so the journey began. Easter was about three weeks away so Claire and I thought it would be a great opportunity to launch a discipleship group by welcoming residents in the building to meet for about an hour to fellowship and observe Lent. We would hold the meetings in the common room so as to make it inviting to anyone interested in joining. All this had to first be approved by the building's management. I told the Lord that if the management approved our request to make use of the common room for a Lent meeting, then it would be a sure sign that it was His will for us to start this group. Praise God, our request was approved and that group continues to meet regularly to this day. By God's grace, the ministry has expanded to five retirement homes and will soon include a local Christian secondary school. What had taken three years of starting and stalling, took off with in God's perfect timing and much prayer.

For the Father loves the Son and shows him all he does. Yes, and he will show him even greater works than these (John 5:20, NIV). Yet we read in Matthew 9:35 that "Jesus went through all the towns and villages, teaching in their synagogues, proclaiming the good news of the kingdom and healing every disease and sickness" (NIV). Could it be that what the Father is doing can only be experienced by those who are out there where the people are? Just a thought!

Fidele and Claire Bolton,
Ottawa

Part Three:
A RIVER OF JUSTICE

DAY 8

Why Aren't You Impressed?

"Yet (my people) act so pious! They come to the Temple every day and seem delighted to learn all about me. They act like a righteous nation that would never abandon the laws of its God.

They ask me to take action on their behalf, pretending they want to be near me. 'We have fasted before you!' they say. Why aren't you impressed? We have been very hard on ourselves, and you don't even notice it!'" (Isa 58:2, 3)

The man of God, sent by the Lord as a messenger to his people, was instructed to shout aloud at the nation around him. With the power and piercing clarity of a trumpet blast, the prophet was to confront this special nation with the reality of its sin and its shortcomings. The people were amazed at this, offended that anyone should shout at them and accuse them so hurtfully. I'm sure that many of them expressed doubt to one another about this man. "He calls himself a prophet, but he's so rude and discouraging! Can't he see how holy we are, how hard we try to please God?" Perhaps we can sympathize a little. Many congregations have also come to expect ministry that takes note of how wonderful we are and how well we are doing. We welcome being made to blush by the compliments and praise of those who speak softly to us. It takes a wise and humble people to open their hearts and minds to rebuke, delivered by faithful servants of the Lord.

I think that we have a choice to make in this area. Shall we seek out ministries that will praise us as we are or those that challenge us with a truth that will drive us on to maturity? Do we need to have our ears tickled, our egos fed, or are we disciples disciplined by a God who loves us as his children? Are we looking for a church that teaches what we already believe, confirming our strongly held conviction that we are the top of the tree in wisdom, or are we looking for Christ-given teachers who will be able to provoke us to greater growth and maturity?

If you honestly believe that there is no more light in God's word that you haven't already seen, and if you feel that the church is doing just great, then you may not be hungry for change to come to you or to your congregation. It may even be that you have been filled to overflowing with a theology that is end-times obsessed, and you have no faith for an effective, Holy Spirit empowered church capable of rescuing the lost and converting the most determined sinner. Whatever it is that has drained your batteries of hope for the nations, I plead with you to reconsider. We have been saved by faith in the grace of God in the person of Jesus Christ. Let us shake ourselves, shake off the dust that has slowed us down for long enough, and look for Godly preachers that will light us up once again, fanning into flames the love of the world that fills the Father's heart. Repentance got us into the kingdom of God's Son; it can help us again today to lift up our eyes to the horizon, and to have our faith restored in a nation-changing gospel. The saving power of Jesus that transformed your life can work mightily in the darkest of nations; we shall live to see the love of Jesus knock down the hatred and division that fills the headlines. If you think that news headlines are where we look to understand the times, then let us at the very least live such lives of power in the Holy Spirit that those headlines will have to speak of Jesus!

The first eighteen years of my life I lived in a religious environment, which somehow managed to be full of routinely delivered rebuke and correction, confirming repeatedly that God was disappointed with me. It was a message entirely devoid of hope. It was a strange and unhelpful combination, making me feel sorry for my many deficiencies, and yet unable to find anything that could help me change. I knew that God was deeply disappointed in me, and that my life fell far short of his expectations; I also searched in vain to find anyone who could show me a way out of my predicament. But even in this lack of gospel hope, even in this form of religion that denied the power of God to save me, there existed a profound church-wide concern for the poor. That church family did more to help the people with addictions and illnesses than many churches that I have seen since, and we were raised to have respect and compassion for those who struggled in life. If we spend all our energy on perfecting our meetings and building the ideal worship band while neglecting those around us who are in need, the Lord will not be impressed with us. Let us agree to turn our hearts towards the Lord and open ourselves to the cry of not only Isaiah the great prophet, but all of God's apostles and prophets. They will not flatter us—neither will they leave us without hope, as they lead the church forwards in a way that will bring God's favour upon us in even greater measure. The Ephesians 4 ministries, flowing in the river of God's Spirit and feeding us with his word, will turn us outwards to the work of preaching good news to all.

It will be the exciting rediscovery in our generation that the gospel really is very, very good news to us all that will take us deeper into the river of life. We will see the poor rejoicing, the prisoner going free, deaf ears hearing, blind eyes that see, the oppressed being lifted up by the love of God and the church living for the good of its neighbours. If we become Christians with a river of the Spirit flowing outwards to the world, not always inwardly to quench a seemingly endless personal thirst, then we will begin to witness miracles and healings that flow from the throne of the Lamb. However, we must always be sure to hold ourselves and each other to this higher standard.

The fact that Isaiah's crowd asked God "Why aren't you impressed?" strikes me as an enquiry filled with sadness and unreality. The thought that we, as the family of God, have reached such heights of perfection that God himself is applauding seems laughable. This self-satisfied assessment stands in stark contrast to Isaiah's own reaction when caught up into heaven. He is overwhelmed by the magnificence of the Lord's throne, his robe, and by the mighty seraphim who were shouting to each other:

"Holy, holy, holy is the Lord of Heaven's Armies! The whole earth is filled with his glory!"

"Then I said 'It's all over! I am doomed, for I am a sinful man. I have filthy lips, and I live among a people with filthy lips. Yet I have seen the King, the Lord of Heaven's Armies." (Isa 6:3, 5)

The good news here of course is that the needed change of heart-attitude is easy to see, and a joy to follow through on. We simply have to hang on to Isaiah's robes as we allow ourselves to be caught up into heaven to see the magnificence of our Father. We, too, will be moved to shout, "Holy, holy, holy!" When we allow God to hold us close to his throne we no longer see the filling of the earth with an awareness of God's glory as a distant prospect. When we see what the mighty seraphim see then we look with new eyes, new faith, at an earth filled to overflowing with the glory of Jesus.

Isaiah was stunned to see the Lord on his throne, but knew he shouldn't be there, knew that seeing the holy God in his sinful state meant death. His need for forgiveness of personal sin and for cleansing was met by a sovereign act of God's grace and provision. Anticipating the needs of his people, for every nation, and for all of us to be forgiven and cleansed, heaven acts.

"Then one of the seraphim flew to me with a burning coal he had taken from the altar with a pair of tongs. He touched by lips with it and said, 'See, this coal has touched your lips. Now your guilt is removed, and your sins are forgiven.'" (Isa 6:6, 7)

A sovereign action from heaven, undeserved and unearned by his servant, set him free. An act of love, grace, and commissioning from the sacrificial altar removed all guilt and guaranteed full pardon for sin. This makes all of us wonder if there is also a way for us into Heaven's throne room. Is there something greater than the burning coal, something that will touch our lips, our minds, and our hearts? The writer to the Hebrews shows us the way, forever opened by Jesus himself.

"Dear brothers and sisters, we can boldly enter Heaven's Most Holy Place because of the blood of Jesus. By his death, Jesus opened a new and life-giving way through the curtain into the Most Holy Place. And since we have a great High Priest who rules over God's House, let us go right into the presence of God with sincere hearts fully trusting him. For our guilty consciences have been sprinkled with Christ's blood to make us clean, and our bodies have been washed with pure water." (Heb 10:19-22)

The burning coal that brought the removal of guilt and forgiveness of sins pointed to a far greater altar. The Cross of Christ finished that salvation work, that rescue of our souls. The death of Christ opened up a way into eternal life for everyone who receives him, who puts his or her faith in his name. The river of blood that flowed from his side has made us clean, and the river of water that flowed with it has washed us with pure water. See yourself immersed in Christ's river of sacrifice; bury yourself in his love, mercy and grace. Enter into heaven's most holy place with the confidence and boldness that come from total dependence of the work of Jesus!

He experienced both death and separation from God his Father so that he could beat them both, forever robbing them of their power to hold us back from entering the house of the Lord, from uninterrupted friendship with our loving Father.

Isaiah's eyes were taken away from contemplating his own unworthiness and focused on the grace of God. Our eyes are taken away from trying to earn God's love and forgiveness and focused on the power of the cross, the power of the blood of Jesus. Similarly, the prophet is engaged in the difficult task of breaking the appreciative gaze of his nation in admiring its own goodness. He wants them to see their sin so that they too might return to God, and to his mercy.

"No, this is the kind of fasting I want: Free those who are wrongly imprisoned; lighten the burden of those who work for you. Let the oppressed go free, and remove the chains that bind people." (Isa 58:6)

When the people's question, "Why aren't you impressed?" reaches his ears, the Lord is ready to tell them why! His people are living, even fasting, to please themselves. Their apparent godliness and defense of the scriptures and laws have had no practical effect on how they treat people. They stand accused of oppression, fighting, and quarrelling. No amount of praying, fasting, bible reading, or attendance at church meetings will get them anywhere with God until they change. They are going through the rituals of holiness without being holy. They enjoy their own freedom but oppress and imprison others. Their definition of "brother" is getting ever narrower, with more and more of their neighbours being excluded from the place of favour. If your nation is divided, if you see yourselves as God's true defenders against other nations, different peoples, if you feel under siege and your greatest hope is to be raptured away from these sinful people, and if you no longer see the stranger as anything other than a threat to your way of life, then it is time to hear the prophets, and turn back to your loving Father. The words of God must penetrate deeply into our lives and produce fruit that is pleasing to our Father, or we will remain far from his rivers of blessing.

As we enjoy God's kindness towards us, we will remember to show great kindness to all God's children. As we bask in Christ's unfailing love and faithfulness, we will lay down our lives in love and faithfulness to others. When we spend time prostrate before the Lord to soak in his presence, we will remember to stand up and allow that presence to flow like a river out of our hearts into the world around us.

When our thirst is just a memory, we will live to end the thirst and hunger of others.

To please the Lord in the ways that Isaiah 58 suggests, we must identify ourselves with Christ, and also identify ourselves with the lonely, with the troubled and oppressed. We love to polish our doctrine and to handle the word of God accurately, which is vital for our health and effectiveness. This generation of believers seems to be particularly drawn to the beauties of worship and to its music and song. Singing together under the leadership of skilful, Holy Spirit musicians and songwriters has become a principal way in which many believers experience the presence of the Lord. Faithful prayer warriors do exist within the body of Christ; the power of prayer is, however, something that will benefit from the renewing of our love of the lively, faith-filled prayer meeting.

Costly prayer is neither easy nor popular; but as we respond to God's command to make his house a house of prayer, we will see strongholds fall and the river of life pour into many nations. To all of these things—teaching, worship in song, prayer—we must add our conviction that the heart of the gospel lies in the bringing of good news about Jesus to the people of our world without a shepherd. We are, at heart, born again into the work of Christ Jesus as he lifts burdens, sin, and sickness from every shoulder. It is as hope is revealed to those who have no hope that Christ is glorified. The church, well taught, singing loudly and praying our hearts out, will remember to love justice. We will visit the sick and see the unjustly imprisoned set free. We will bring the news of Jesus not just to the same saints every Sunday but also to the oppressed and downtrodden, whether in our own cities or in distant nations. The church of Christ will be like him, full of love and grace, preachers of mercy.

"Keep on loving each other as brothers and sisters. Don't forget to show hospitality to strangers, for some who have done this have entertained angels without realizing it! Remember those in prison, as if you were there yourself. Remember also those being mistreated, as if you felt their pain in your own bodies." (Heb 13:1-3)

We live our lives by faith, immersed in the river of life, under a tree whose leaves contain medicine that will heal nations. Being a Christian is such an amazing experience for an individual, full of joy and God's constant blessing. But there is so much to enter into beyond the level of individual blessing. I believe that this present generation will not ignore the plight of suffering people or rejoice in freedom while others face imprisonment. We will always be rooted in God's Word and fully apply that Word to God's world. Read the Bible, and watch the news. Read about God's glory and live to raise awareness of that glory across our communities. Tell your friends what you know; tell them about Jesus.

Fast the world: its food, its pleasures, its distractions, but feed on that which God gives you. Simplify your lives, and hold on to them lightly, holding onto God with all your strength! Do good to all your brothers and sisters, all people, everywhere, images of God. Perhaps then the prophets will begin shouting better things at the Lord's people!

~~~~~~

MEDITATE & MEMORIZE:

Memorize this scripture and speak it out loud as often as you can, taking time to meditate on it and asking the Holy Spirit to open it up for you. Let faith come as you hear your own voice declaring the true word of God.

"Keep on loving each other as brothers and sisters. Don't forget to show hospitality to strangers, for some who have done this have entertained angels without realizing it! Remember those in prison, as if you were there yourself. Remember also those being mistreated, as if you felt their pain in your own bodies." (Heb 13:1-3)

PRAY & PROCLAIM:

Stir yourself to pray for people who are not like you, but who are equally made in God's image. Proclaim that Jesus has set you free from anything that would separate you in any way from your neighbours because of political, religious, geographical, or any other differences. Remember those who are in prison, for whatever reason, as if you felt their pain in your own body. Pray for the healing of divisions in your nation, and proclaim that love is stronger than hate. Proclaim that any divisive attitude in your heart is ended; shout out loud that you love God and all his children!

GIVE THANKS & WORSHIP:

Worship your Father in heaven, telling him that you want to live every minute in a way that pleases him. Thank him for his love and for his correcting of you as his child; acknowledge that he rebukes those that he loves so that they may grow more like him. Thank Jesus that he died for all nations and not just your own. Worship him as the sovereign head over one body, and thank him for giving his precious blood to gather all the peoples together under his rule.

TESTIMONY
Have you heard what God is doing in his world?

Robyn Bright, a member of the church in Ottawa, is interested in issues of justice for all. She writes:

This is what I have come to believe in regard to our Heavenly Father and justice. First, the realization of justice—materially and socially—is a central feature of the kingdom of God. It is a core promise to all people, and in particular to those for whom the experience of dignity, opportunity, and equity is especially far off. Isaiah, amongst others, powerfully prophesied about the anointing that was to come, through Christ, to bring good news to the poor, to bind up the broken hearted, achieve freedom for the captives, and the release from darkness for the prisoners (Isaiah 61). It is a part of the nature of the kingdom that is both now and not yet: while the full realization of the justice for all people will only be achieved when Christ returns, it is a core mandate of all those that call Christ King to pursue justice as they pursue the kingdom of God.

Justice is featured in both the Old and New Testaments. Jesus specifically references the passage in Isaiah (Luke 4:18), signaling that it was being realized through him. That justice for all those who are broken down, beaten, and on the margins is central to the heart and mission of God is also reinforced in Jesus' sermon on the mount, as he speaks about those who are blessed as a result of the kingdom: blessed are the poor in spirit, for theirs is the kingdom of heaven. Blessed are those who mourn, for they will be comforted. Blessed are the meek, for they will inherit the earth (Mat 5:3-12).

Second, the realization of justice will be achieved through the active working of the bridegroom and the bride, the head and the body, Jesus and the church. I believe that the scripture, which describes our relationship with Christ as one of head and body, is meant to point to our empowered agency in seeing the kingdom realized and achieved. We were never called to be passive observers of God at work, cheering him on from our stadium seating. Rather, I believe that the Lord has given us an authority to work out his kingdom in partnership with him and with the power, insight, and wisdom required to do so.

Third, I believe God is seeking a church willing to employ all of its assets to see the poor set free. My own experience is that while material resources play a role in the eradication of poverty and inequality, it is supernatural healing, victorious mindsets, and path-breaking truths, deployed at all levels of society, which more definitively break the invisible chains of poverty. The drivers of poverty and injustice today often find their roots in systemic lies—be they about the dignity of women and girls, particular races or social groups, etc. Replacing worldviews that seek to limit and destroy with those that are full of hope and dignity can help to catapult whole communities forward and facilitate the discovery of all the blessings and resources the Lord of Heaven has made available for them. Jesus said "You will know the truth, and the truth will set you free" (John 8:32)—I believe that the truth he was referencing here was truly all encompassing—building on the power of the gospel message to include a full realization of who we have been created to be.

Fourth, I believe the full realization of the joy of the Lord comes with being an active participant in the building of his kingdom. As we pour out the joy, revelation, resources, and capacities the Lord has given us, we are rewarded with ever flowing fresh springs of living water, that not only allow us to continue serving, but also nourish our own souls. There is no more meaningful or powerful a way for us to use our lives than in his service and in seeking justice for those around us.

Robyn adds a moving story to her account at the end of the next chapter.

DAY 9

A Mighty Flood of Justice

"Away with your noisy hymns of praise! I will not listen to the music of your harps. Instead, I want to see a mighty flood of justice, an endless river of righteous living." (Amos 5:23, 24)

On second thought, perhaps the prophets aren't quite ready to shout our praises. Amos here expresses a similar judgement and solution to God's people. The Lord rejoices in our praises, of course, so don't give up on your noisy worship times. And don't let any of our beloved harpists be discouraged for a moment. But we should certainly acknowledge that a religious faith that doesn't help the cause of justice across this world is incomplete. Christian meetings of all kinds must be set in an atmosphere and a culture of righteousness and justice. We are lovers of righteousness, supporters of fairness, advocates for any who are mistreated or oppressed, pursuers of justice. We have been set free from the power of sin by the death and resurrection of Jesus, and so we no longer live for ourselves, or for "our kind of people;" our lives are laid down in the service of others. Jesus is filled with joy at the sight of individual believers who honestly are persuaded that the pursuit of greatness involves humbly serving everyone else's needs! We cry out for God's judge to save us, and he does. He then bands us together into an army whose only reason for still being on earth and not in heaven is that we are not satisfied until Christ's saving power has reached everyone who cries out for justice. Jesus tells us that "God blesses those who hunger and thirst for justice, for they will be satisfied" (Mat 5:6). Jesus framed his whole ministry in the context of justice and favour for the oppressed. He quoted his friend Isaiah the prophet:

"The Spirit of the Lord is upon me, for he has anointed me to bring Good News to the poor. He has sent me to proclaim that captives will be released, that the blind will see, that the oppressed will be set free, and that the time of the Lord's favour has come." (Luke 4:18, 19)

If any of us have ended up living almost all our lives in the sheltered confines of our church, sealed off from the woes of a troubled world, then it's hard to see how we got here. We are not a company that is made to be hidden away from the wicked world. No, we are specifically designed to love the world as our Father loves it and have a good news message about Jesus that will set the captives free. The Spirit of the Lord didn't come on Jesus to lead the meeting, announce the week's events, or to close in prayer. The river of the Spirit that flowed in Jesus to make the world a well-watered garden was a mighty flood of justice, a never-ending river of righteousness. Jesus wasn't here for those who thought that they were already good enough. He came as a physician for the sick, bringing freedom for the captives, and living hope for the hopeless. The more trouble you were in, the blacker your sin, the deeper your need, the better you appreciated the arrival of Jesus, the judge of all mankind. God has always sided with the defenceless and with the cause of justice.

"Then I will rejoice in the Lord. I will be glad because he rescues me. With every bone in my body I will praise him: 'Lord, who can compare with you? Who else rescues the helpless from the strong? Who else protects the helpless and poor from those who rob them?'" (Psalm 35:9-10)

It is of interest that Jesus' ministry was to the troubled, the captive, the oppressed, and the blind. Whatever your circumstance, whatever your need, Jesus is there for you. He loves justice, promotes righteousness, and shows loving kindness and mercy to all. He throws out demons, heals every sickness and disease, bringing comfort and joy to people who have nothing. We welcome Jesus into our lives as Saviour and Lord, recognizing that he is a king. If you haven't done that yet in your life, do it now. We have already listened to Peter, quoting the prophet Joel as an explanation for the outpouring of the river of the Spirit, and he shows us the way to be saved.

"Everyone who calls on the name of the Lord will be saved." (Acts 2:21)

Call on the name of Jesus right now. Ask him to forgive your sin, to wash you clean. Ask him to have mercy on you, to help you, and he will. Call out the name of Jesus and you will be saved. He will completely destroy the power of any habit, addiction, attitude, or life history that holds you in slavery. You will be driven along by the mighty floodwaters of the love of God, and you will never look back.

Jesus didn't come into the world to condemn you or me or any of us. He could see that we were all condemned already, and in need of help. He came as a rescuer, a saviour, and had the power necessary to break every chain. We have lost something of our appreciation and understanding of the gospel, forgetting what a revolutionary joy it brings into our lives. We react with more intensity to our sports teams winning the championship than to the incredible coming of Jesus into our world! This will change as the Holy Spirit continues to restore all things to us; he will restore our love of justice, cause us to break down dividing walls that have grown up between brothers and that only please the devil, and allow us to feel the pain of other peoples' suffering. Then he will restore the powerful weapons that tear down strongholds, bringing victory to the intercessors and freedom to the captives. The Holy Spirit is not terribly interested in restoring the extraordinary gifts of the Spirit if all we want to do is play with them while safely indoors. If we want the full list of the available gifts just to give some excitement in that part of our Sunday meetings that follows the singing, then we may be guilty of missing the point; we must be caught up in the war if we are to be granted use of world changing spiritual weapons. As we are compelled by love to have a concern for the communities outside of our church meetings, we will see a growing excitement at the effect of the amazingly good news that King Jesus is exercising his government in this world of ours. The church will begin to appear in all its strength, having gained more of its inheritance, with supernaturally gifted servant-shepherds advancing the kingdom and bringing justice to all who cry out.

His coming was not always great news for the powerful, rich, and comfortable. But for the captive, the disadvantaged, the marginalized, his coming was a breath of fresh air. He announced an ongoing time when the Lord's favour would be freely available to all who called on his name. The coming of Jesus was definitely bad news for demons and evil spirits. Such a spirit came to the meeting with the man he had possessed and knew Jesus right away to be the Holy One of God. Jesus set the man free, throwing the demon out with a clear order.

"Amazed, the people exclaimed, 'What authority and power this man's word possesses! Even evil spirits obey him, and they flee at his command!'" (Luke 4:36)

It's not right that any child of God should be dominated in this way, held captive and miserable. This evil spirit met with a flood of justice in Jesus, an endless river of righteousness. A whole village brought its sick to Jesus as the sun went down one day. "No matter what their diseases were, the touch of his hand healed every one" (Luke 4:40). Jesus treated every sickness not as a part of the plan of God, but as a work of the devil, and he knocked every sickness down. The sickness had a purpose, certainly. The purpose of pain and disease is to rob us of an experience of wellness, to destroy our health, and ultimately to shorten our lives and to end them. Purpose like this was always associated with Satan.

"The thief's purpose is to steal and kill and destroy. My purpose is to give them a rich and satisfying life." (John 10:16)

He was talking about his sheep. The crowd following Jesus didn't understand what he meant, and so he tried to give them a clear understanding of the two opposing purposes that they would see in the world every day. The thief has one purpose for your life: to steal from you, kill you, destroy you in any way he can physically, mentally, or by impoverishment or despair. The good shepherd has an opposing purpose: to save, feed, protect, and give his people a rich and satisfying life. I was saddened to hear from some close friends recently that their church has developed a different teaching from that of the gospel. Sickness comes to us from God, their preachers say, and furthers his purpose in our lives. They didn't get that from watching Jesus go to work, tearing down the devil's awful work and healing all who were sick. They seem able to believe in a loving Father God who has a purpose in giving people cancer; but those outside of the faith cannot accept such a travesty of justice, such a denial of decency from the Most High. Neither can I, as such a picture violates the revelation of who God is in the person of Jesus Christ. My friends decided that they could no longer stay in that church, couldn't bear to watch its light flicker and go out.

When faced with tragedy, difficult circumstances, or hard to understand events, people can often be heard to declare, "I believe everything has a purpose." I agree with that, but I am warned by Jesus' story about the sheep that there are at least two purposes on display in our world: the purpose of the thief and the purpose of the good shepherd, Jesus. Knowing which is at work is vital. You can be sure of this:

"The Son of God came to destroy the works of the devil." (1 John 3:8)

If you are oppressed by sickness, mental illness, poverty, violence, or injustice, recognize the purpose and modus operandi of the thief, your enemy the devil. Never, never, never, never be confused by the weak little lie that would suggest that God has some purpose in such suffering. If it is stealing health, peace, and freedom from you, if it is killing your body or your hope, and if it is destroying your full enjoyment of a rich and satisfying life, then a thief is at work. Close your eyes, call out the name of Jesus, and by faith, see him destroying the work of the devil and proclaiming the Lord's favour over you!

The many accounts of healing and deliverance are so astounding that we can skip from miracle to miracle and miss other issues of equal value. When asked by an expert in religious law what he should do to be certain of inheriting eternal life, Jesus answered his question with one of his own. What does the man's scripture say is the answer?

"The man answered, 'You must love the Lord your God with all your heart, all your soul, all your strength, and all your mind.' And, 'Love your neighbour as yourself.'" (Luke 10:27)

Jesus confirmed that this was the right answer, and then told a story about justice, righteousness, and love. The man delivered a follow-up question, asking who he should think of as his neighbour. It's a good question. Are we happy if God has placed us into a blessed country, a nation of freedom and strength? Is it enough that we are doing well, even if we are confronted every day by images of our brothers and sisters in distant countries who are not doing well at all? Does the Good News of the favour of the Lord end at my garden wall, at the city's edge or our national borders? Shall we build a wall so high that it will keep out not only those foreigners, but also any images of their plight, any news of their suffering? Perhaps God just meant to bless my life, my city, my nation.

The story Jesus told took down those walls, revealed those prejudices and the lack of responsibility for our neighbours. A Jewish man was attacked while traveling, was beaten and left for dead by the roadside. Those who knew better, who were without excuse, who were neighbours of this man, ignored his suffering and need and closed their eyes to it all. The one who went out of his way to help was described both as, "a despised Samaritan," and having "compassion" (Luke 10:33). The flood of justice, the endless river of righteous living water has nothing to do with healing, deliverance, or miracles in this case. When teaching us about the most important matters, Jesus draws our attention to meeting the needs of others who have fallen into trouble. We must wholeheartedly reject any notion that all we see has been allowed by God, and that those who have been beaten up in life must have deserved it somehow. Much of what we see around us is the work of the evil one and needs to be destroyed so that his children can go free; our response is the compassion of Jesus, not hard-hearted judgement. What is the Lord looking for in us? What does he say matters the most? Active compassion, involvement, reaching out, caring for others not quite like us. He loves to see us leaving our life and going out of our way to help another life. We are to soothe wounds, bandage injuries, use our own resources, and spend some money without hope of reward. Having been shown such great mercy, we are to be joyful showers of mercy to others. Whatever a brother or sister's circumstances, colour of skin, religion, nationality or life choices, if they are hurting, we must help.

Speak in other languages, prophesy to one another, and swim in the river of the spirit. Sing loudly and dance exuberantly in worship, and play your heart out on that harp! But, remember:

"O people, the Lord has told you what is good, and this is what he requires of you: to do what is right, to love mercy, and to walk humbly with your God." (Mic 6:8)

~~~~~~~

MEDITATE & MEMORIZE:

Memorize this scripture and speak it out loud as often as you can, taking time to meditate on it and asking the Holy Spirit to open it up for you. Let faith come as you hear your own voice declaring the true word of God.

"The Son of God came to destroy the works of the devil." (1 John 3:8)

PRAY & PROCLAIM:

Ask God to give you clear discernment about the works of the devil, so that you might join in the work of destroying them. Any anger, division, attitudes or judgement of others that cool your love for your brothers and sisters should be offered to God for burning. Pray that you might also discern the works of God, so that you can bless them.

GIVE THANKS & WORSHIP:

Worship the King of kings who destroys our enemy and pours out favour on his children. Give him thanks for the river of life that flows through us from heaven, and that flows out of us to others. Worship him as the God whose glory fills the earth with life, healing and hope.

TESTIMONY

Have you heard what God is doing in Liberia?

Robyn Bright continues her thoughts on God's justice by adding this story:
Here is one story that served to reinforce this revelation of God's heart for justice for me:

Menwoh was born in Liberia, in a small northern village, in the early '90s. While vigorous at birth, he was born with evident developmental disabilities, and members of the community spread rumours that his disabilities were the result of witchcraft, or worse, a curse on his family. They encouraged his parents to take their infant son out of the village, and to leave him to the vultures of the village dump. A missionary family living in a town nearby learned that a baby had been left to die at the garbage site, and they set out to rescue him. Unsure of what to do next, they decided to bring him in to their home, and eventually, to adopt him. Raising Menwoh was not easy; the family faced a steep learning curve in caring for him in a country whose worldview failed to see children with disabilities as worthy of love and dignity. But as they loved and raised their new son, he thrived, and mindsets in the surrounding villages began to change. They began to see in him a promising future, and a valuable present. And this in turn shaped their attitudes toward other child born with different abilities.

Menwoh went on to graduate from high school and to attend bible college, with a keen heart for evangelism and seeing other Liberians come to know Jesus. It seems clear that when Christ's body arose, they changed not only his life, but also the atmosphere in the village. I believe this is a snapshot of the kind of impact we as followers of Christ can have wherever we live and serve—changing lives and worldviews to align with the promises and characteristics of the kingdom.

Robyn Bright,
Ottawa

DAY 10
Trust In Your Money and Down You Go!

"Share your food with the hungry and give shelter to the homeless. Give clothes to those who need them, and do not hide from relatives who need your help." (Isa 58:7)

The recognition that all humanity is one family created in the likeness of God produces in the church an awareness of the lives of others. It fuels compassion for the suffering and a hunger and thirst for righteousness to prevail across the nations. The good news of Jesus and of the declaration of God's favour towards those who seek him is not a western thing, not a first-world but a whole-world promise. Injustice towards a brother or sister becomes our own injustice. If someone is suffering, we all feel their pain. If someone is wrongly imprisoned then we are all in prison with them. Just as Jesus laid down his life for us, so we will lay down our lives for others. We have a call to evangelize, and also to feed, to clothe, to share resources. The gospel is not a motivational message for believers aimed at ninety minutes every Sunday morning; it is the light of the whole world. If our basic world view is that the church has only a limited role in this evil world, and that our task is to ask Jesus to save us, to give us that personal relationship with God, and then to keep our heads down until the time comes for us to go home to heaven, we will have little faith for the kingdom of God to change the world. If the foundation of our thinking is that Jesus is a King who is destined to have all things under his feet, a shepherd filled with compassion and an active love for the lost, then our expectations will be different. The stories of healing and mighty miracles that we hear often emanate from developing nations, or from those whose governments restrict or oppose the preaching of Christ. Perhaps the supernatural power in those groups arises not only out of their greater dependence on God, or even because they face greater opposition, but because they feel that preaching Christ is worth it. That calling on the Lord to lift up the cross of the Lamb will in turn exalt the nation that turns in repentance to the Lord and begins to pursue righteousness. We don't need or want a world government outside of Christ's reign, but we do preach a world community, a multitude of diverse families that God promised Abraham would be blessed. Every woman on the planet is our sister, made in God's image, worthy of honour and justice and the favour of God. Every man is our brother, made in God's image, worthy of honour and justice and the blessings of heaven. When all the peoples feel like family, when their experience becomes of deep concern to all, then we can never hold back from joy-filled involvement in the lives of those loved by our Father.

"The godly are generous givers." (Psalm 37:21)

In this quality of course the psalmist is noting that the godly are like God, who is generous and giving to all who look to him in their need. We can try to avoid this topic of being generous, and focus more comfortably on memorizing the fruits of the Spirit or working endlessly on our character issues until the stars fall out of the sky. This has stupefied many Christians by causing them to allow their lifetimes to pass by as they make heroic but fruitless efforts to be better people, constantly living at the apprenticeship stage. Please, go on living a life dedicated to Jesus, and make every effort to be godly. But don't wait for perfection before throwing yourself into the work of Jesus; push outwards just as you are, and the Spirit will be well able to work on your character while you are running! Where should you get started in this new, more action-oriented time? Be just like God, and be a generous, joyful, faith-filled giver!

This principle of generosity as a trait of the Lord and his people can seem counter-intuitive in our materialistic age. Understand it, though, and you will feel as though a bright light has switched on in your head. Being lost in the river of God's glorious giving is a major aspect of our Kingdom freedom. Many of us are beginning to realise that even though we have conquered major and obvious sin in our lives with the help of Jesus that we can still be so easily enslaved to the material aspects of the world around us. Is there a deep reason for the lack of seriously supernatural Christian ministries around us, or is it simply that we have allowed ourselves to be distracted by stuff? Is our hunger and thirst for the miraculous being diluted by eating too much, spending too much time gazing at our phones, by the desperate need to buy the latest product? It would be fun to see a few Spirit-filled believers abandon their quest to finally reach level 147 in their video game and give their full attention to the Saviour of the world. Getting free from the world by living more simply, caring for the needs of others and for the health of our God-given planet can profitably begin by directing our finances differently. So let's begin to shake up our understanding.

"Give freely and become more wealthy; be stingy and lose everything. The generous will prosper; those who refresh others will themselves be refreshed…Trust in your money and down you go! But the godly flourish like leaves in spring." (Prov 11:24-25, 28)

Perhaps you can see why I described this as being counter-intuitive. Giving freely of our money, clothes, food, and shelter doesn't seem to be a sure-fire way of becoming wealthy, but there it is. It is the awareness of the involvement of a living God that makes all this work—faith, in other words. Those who fear the Lord don't fear anything else at all, because that awareness of God, putting him first, makes his people "generous, compassionate, and righteous" (Psalm 112:4). "They confidently trust the Lord to care for them" and "share freely and give generously to those in need" (Psalm 112: 7,9).

So, it is inescapable from our reading of Isaiah 58 that God gets upset with us when our religion becomes self-centred and self-serving, when all our money is used on ourselves, and he sends his prophets to shout loudly at us. The Lord is pleased with us when our desire to live for him turns us away from such selfishness and opens our hearts to those in need, identifying all people everywhere as our concern and our family. Fasting so as to look holy is not a great idea. Fasting and devoting ourselves to seeking the Lord so that chains can be broken pleases him greatly. The verse which introduces this chapter shows us how to proceed when our prayer and fasting is concluded. Praying for those in need and calling on the Lord to provide for them is an excellent thing to do. Reaching into our own pockets and food cupboards is even better. Being like God in our generosity and practical love pleases the Lord of Heaven. Laying our hands on the head of a hungry person should be followed, once the prayer is over, with a sandwich whenever possible. In this way, we can fast our food and clothes by sharing them, and we can be sure to use our money for more than our own needs. God, who has thought of everything, has definitely thought about this issue of money and other resources. Following Abram's victory over Kedorlaomer and his friends, Melchizedek, King of Salem, God's priest, comes out to meet him bringing bread and wine. Melchizedek blesses Abram in celebration of a God-given victory: "Blessed be God Most High, who has defeated your enemies for you"—remember that line! (Gen 14:20).

"Then Abram gave Melchizedek a tenth of all the goods he had recovered." (Gen 14:20)

This recognition of Melchizedek's superiority as a priest of God most high was expressed in the giving of a tenth of Abram's goods. Later, Abram's grandson Jacob reacted in just the same way when he encountered the Lord is an extraordinary way. As he slept on his journey he dreamed of a stairway joining earth to heaven.

"At the top of the stairway stood the Lord, and he said, "I am the Lord, the God of your grandfather Abraham, and the God of your father Isaac." (Gen 28:13)

When he awakens, Jacob recognizes the special nature of the place, and of his revelation that this is the house of God, the gateway to heaven. He makes a vow to God in covenant words that declare that the Lord is his God, and finishes with this statement:

"This memorial pillar I have set up will become a place for worshipping God, and I will present to God a tenth of everything he gives me." (Gen 28:22)

Oh God, please give us all dreams like that! If we can dream, even when we are awake, that our Father has forever joined heaven and earth through the sacrifice of his Son, then every breath that we breathe will be different. We will break free from the idea that the heavens are somehow distant from our lives, our Father living in unreachable glory, as if the gulf between us had not been closed by the blood of Christ. He has reconciled us to our Father; we are welcomed into his throne room as much-loved children, and the windows of heaven are thrown open upon us! Jacob understood that with heaven opened to him that he could give God a tenth and rely on an open heaven to supply his every need. This breaking away from feeling that our prosperity and security depend on our efforts and on our employer's payment, and knowing that we have free access to the storehouses of heaven is the beginning of wisdom, true freedom. "Read your bible and pray every day" is really good advice, and we should follow it wholeheartedly. But to walk with the Lord in the way that you long for, let Jesus also break you free from slavery to your money. Or lack of it! When you don't have much money, the slavery just gets you in a different way; you can have your heart tied up by the love of money, and your feet and hands manacled by the fear of not having enough! Break free by acknowledging that Jesus has put in a permanent connection to heaven for you and show you believe that by becoming a generous giver, like God. This practice of giving a tenth had a particular purpose in the lives of the people of God.

"This applies to your tithes of grain, new wine, olive oil, and the firstborn males of your flocks and herds. Doing this will teach you always to fear the Lord your God." (Deut 14:23)

A church that fears the Lord will be fearless and bold in its preaching, giving, and lifestyle. And in commanding his people to bring in the whole tithe, the needs of all were remembered. At the end of every third year, the entire tithe was to be stored in the nearest town.

"Give it to the Levites, who will receive no allotment of land among you, as well as the foreigners living among you, the orphans, and the widows in your towns, so that they can eat and be satisfied. Then the Lord your God will bless you in all your work." (Gen 14:29)

The outsiders, the vulnerable, those with no other provision, including the Levites were to be supported from the tithe. The prosperity message was that if I have two shirts and a visiting stranger has none, then between the two of us we have all we need! God blesses us in all our work if we have a loving, responsible sense of community and a generous heart for those who might not be doing as well as we are right now. This practice with other instructions about leaving a little of each harvest for the hungry, and a general compassion encouraged by the Lord, gave hope and dignity to those in need. Isaiah's instruction to share food, clothes, shelter, and resources was not a new command, but a reminder to return to the attitude of love and generosity found in God himself. Jesus, understanding that tithing pre-dated the law, reminded us of the practice and of the heart of tithing.

"For you are careful to tithe even the tiniest income from your herb gardens, but you ignore the more important aspects of the law—justice, mercy, and faith. You should tithe, yes, but do not neglect the more important things." (Mat 23:23)

So before you build up the wall of your property even higher, and before you raise the power of your electric fence to lethal levels to protect your possessions from those "other" people, ask yourself these questions. Do you give your full tithe to the Lord? Are you a giver of generous offerings? Having been shown such extraordinary justice, mercy, and love by Jesus, are you consumed with a desire to live outwardly as He did? The Old Testament closes with a tremendous promise to those who bring all their tithes into God's storehouse. In a most unusual exchange the Lord challenges his people to put him to the test.

"Bring all the tithes into the storehouse so there will be enough food in my Temple. If you do, says the Lord of Heaven's Armies, 'I will open the windows of heaven for you. I will pour out a blessing so great you won't have enough room to take it in! Try it! Put me to the test.'" (Mal 3:10)

If you have never learned to fear the Lord by giving him the tenth of your income that belongs to him, start today. If you have neglected this truth and become more fearful of poverty than of the Lord, begin again to bring your tithe faithfully. Test him in this and he will open the windows of heaven over you, and your crops will be super-sized! And the hungry will have food, the naked will have clothes, the homeless will have shelter, and even your relatives will be happy with you!

"'Then all nations will call you blessed, for your land will be such a delight,' says the Lord of Heaven's Armies." (Mal 3:12)

~~~~~~~

MEDITATE & MEMORIZE:

Memorize this scripture and speak it out loud as often as you can, taking time to meditate on it and asking the Holy Spirit to open it up for you. Let faith come as you hear your own voice declaring the true word of God.

"Give freely and become more wealthy; be stingy and lose everything. The generous will prosper; those who refresh others will themselves be refreshed…Trust in your money and down you go! But the godly flourish like leaves in spring." (Prov 11:24-25, 28)

PRAY & PROCLAIM:

Call out to the Lord to take you deeper into faith in His economy; confess any fears that you have but refuse to be in slavery to them anymore. Proclaim that from this moment you will give generously of your tithes and offerings, and that you will become wealthier because heaven's storehouses are open to you just as his word declares.

GIVE THANKS & WORSHIP:

See with Jacob the Christ who connects heaven and earth, and worship the one who paid the cost of your heavenly citizenship.

TESTIMONY
Have you heard what God is doing in Ottawa?

John's skin was dirty. Half of his teeth were missing. His clothes were old and he needed a haircut. He was the kind of man that many would disqualify quickly from being able to have a promising future, the kind of man who was easily dismissed and ignored. Yet, history has shown time and time again that God loves to use the unpredictable and to choose the unexpected. If the verse "people look at the outward appearance, but the LORD looks at the heart" (1 Sam 16:7) was referring to David in Scriptures, it could not ring truer for my husband and I. But we started to wonder if it could ring true for John as well, if this could become his testimony too.

As we walked by John that day, we knew that we had two options. We could either look at him with our natural eyes, or we could look at him the way God viewed him: as a chosen and called person to his kingdom. As a man who could carry the seed that would yield a crop thirty, sixty, and even a hundred times more than was sown. As a man that had the potential to heal the sick, set the captives free, and comfort those who mourn. But more importantly, as a man who needed to be loved just because he was a neighbour. Our paths had crossed. Our eyes had met. There was no walking away that could be done. His heart was what mattered. His broken soul was what needed to be restored. And as we kept looking at John with the heart that God had for him, and as we kept pondering on the desires and promises of the Father over his life, the dirt, missing teeth, and messy hair all became irrelevant.

And so we talked. With time, our conversations included laughter, and as our subjects deepened, sometimes tears. It was clear that this man panhandling by my office was no longer just a stranger on the corner. The preconceived notion my husband and I had that addressing or working with the homeless community would require a "special type" of training, as if they were a different category of people, now sounded so silly. All that was needed was some basic social skills: knowing how to listen, how to hold a conversation, knowing how not to judge quickly, and knowing how to love. Skills most of us successfully master with friends, family, and neighbours. There was no reason why this had to somehow be any different with John, or anyone else like him. And it came to a point where it wasn't.

We talked about each other's day, about pets, and about plans for the weekend. And sometimes we had deeper conversations, discussing life disappointments, hurt from the past, and internal struggles. Eventually, he became a frequent guest over for dinner. His enthusiasm while watching a football game surely became contagious to us. And as we got closer, he started attending church with our family, and the message of Christ easily made its way to his heart as it was consistent with the love he had received. Eventually, he surrendered. His heart got captured, his soul got saved. And I knew in my heart that this was just the beginning.

The harvest is indeed plentiful, and the gospel is just as powerful. And that gospel was becoming to us personally less and less of just a theory in a book, but a tangible message, a compelling reality that was meant to be shared with the world, no matter how poor that world looked like.

Sandie Morency,
Ottawa

DAY 11
Rivers of Light: Being the Light of the World

"Feed the hungry, and help those in trouble. Then your light will shine out from the darkness, and the darkness around you will be as bright as noon." (Isa 58:10)

The prophet emphasizes again and again that to please the Lord we must remember all who need our loving support, and assist all that we encounter who are in trouble. We are caught up in the work of Jesus, who came in such great love to lift heavy burdens from so many who were wearied by them, and to set captives free. It is important to live holy lives, and to run away from sin. It is wonderful to be lost in worship, to be attentive to the preaching of God's word, to give generously. But to do all of these things while ignoring the plight of our brothers and sisters in our own communities and around the world is not acceptable to our loving Father.

Our longing is not for extravagant blessing for ourselves while others struggle; our prosperity message from scripture is that all may know the Lord and enjoy his great care. This is the foundation of our pilgrim spirit, that we cannot rest until we have brought many others into the great blessing of knowing Jesus. When our time comes to face judgement, it will, praise God, be based less on our weaknesses and more on our selfless focus on helping others. We sometimes seem a little obsessed with the details of our many imperfections, causing us to be inward-looking and self-critical, when the Lord wants our eyes to be on our neighbours. If you thought bad thoughts about your uncle when his dog chased your cat, repent quickly and get over it. There are hungry people who need some food, lonely people who need some faithful friendship. We are to join together under the leadership of Jesus, to come together as one people and concentrate on the bigger issues so as to make a difference in the world. Get this wrong and we will always be focused on ourselves and our failures to be holy. Get it right, and we won't have time to worry about our own lives! We will be overwhelmed by the beauty of Christ and by our own love for the world. Isaiah goes on to encourage God's people to look outwards, to live with a river of light flowing out of them for everyone to enjoy.

"Arise, Jerusalem! Let your light shine for all to see. For the glory of the Lord rises to shine on you." (Isa 60:1)

You may be reflecting on the fact that the world is a hard place to live in, and that so many people seem to live under appalling oppression. How can this little light of ours make a difference in such an unhappy world? God knows the need more than we do, and prophets always speak into the real world.

"Darkness as black as night covers all the nations of the earth, but the glory of the Lord rises and appears over you. All nations will come to your light; mighty kings will come to see your radiance." (Isa 60:2-3)

We must not allow church meetings to become our refuge from a world that needs our involvement. Meetings with other Christians are a vital part of our lives, and they are to be cherished. Meetings are not, however, to be a place to hide from the troubles of our lives or a way of meeting our own needs while ignoring the plight of others. Soaking in the presence of God, bathing in his love and nearness, is not only to keep us strong; it results always in a flowing outwards of a river of God's glory to others. Fellowship with the Lord and other Christians is not an oasis in the desert that keeps us alive in a wicked world. It is living in the light of his glorious presence so that rivers of light might flow out of us towards others. When the Lord started to speak to me and to my wife about coming to Canada, we joyfully accepted the challenge to work for Jesus in a new place. We arrived in the middle of an extraordinary outpouring of the Holy Spirit centred in Toronto. Those gatherings were an important indication to us that the power of God has been poured out on the nations, a gospel of words, truth and power, all working together to exalt the name of Jesus. We joined thousands of our brothers and sisters in enjoying laughter, peace and true joy in the Holy Spirit. The touch of God was unmistakeable; my legs failed me on many occasions as the greatness of the Lord drew close to us all. Out of those years, and out of that amazing experience and others like it around the globe will surely rise a generation of saints whose light will shine brightly into the darkest parts of the world. Darkness is not destined to lead to ever-greater darkness; God has given no glory to the darkness, no permanence. The light of the saints of God, gathered as we were into a communal experience of revival joy in Canada's biggest city will certainly result in a brightness like the dawn shining on all of God's world. He gave us a wonderful time of drinking in his glorious presence that continues of course to this day; just try to imagine the mighty flood of salvation, healing and power that must be the result of such an investment of his grace! This is the kind of drinking that does not result in a sorrowful headache, but it does result in something. The river that flowed in is now beginning to flow out like a river of light, and the world is waking up to a new dawn in the church of Christ. We have all learned how to drink in; now we are learning how to pour out into a thirsty world! Jesus says to us:

"You are the light of the world – like a city on a hilltop that cannot be hidden. No one lights a lamp and then puts it under a basket. Instead, a lamp is placed on a stand, where it gives light to everyone in the house. In the same way, let your good deeds shine out for all to see, so that everyone will praise your heavenly Father." (Mat 5:14-16)

Jesus is our light and our life. He fills us so completely, sends his Holy Spirit into us so readily, that we shine brightly with irresistible light. This makes me want to shake off any thought that Jesus did all that he did just to make our lives a little better, while we patiently wait for a better time in heaven. He lit up his people with such an extraordinary brightness that he can light up his entire continents-wide house by placing us on a stand. We can spend hours in worship of the king simply by declaring "Oh, Jesus, you are the light of the world, and you have filled us with your river so completely that you now call us the light of the world!" The nations of the earth are all covered in darkness, but the light of the glory of our God shines out of that darkness, through his people. This brightness is visible, it's real, and it is powerful enough to change nations. The promise of the prophet is that world leaders will come towards that light; people of influence will come to enquire as they see a radiant church, a glorious community. Good news to the poor is not just about economic need; it is the active shining of the light of Jesus in us that is like the brightest of all dawns into the darkness of all people, everywhere. We have never seen a light so great as the one that fills Jesus and now spills out of his sisters and brothers. The light of heaven illuminates the preaching of the good news that

Jesus has come to save us; we declare the word boldly and also serve as a powerful reading lamp so that all God's truth is illuminated by the brightness of the lives of his kingdom people.

You will have noticed that Jesus seamlessly links the rivers of light that flow out of you with the good deeds that you constantly pursue. Good deeds, bright light. Care for the oppressed and troubled, and a light that shines in the darkness. Not just a little light, but enough to turn night into day, darkness into noontime. If we are to be God's community, a true kingdom, then we will live our lives with the Holy Spirit flowing out of us in a way that means good news for all. The peoples of the earth are troubled by the growing gap between rich and poor, by the consumption of so much by so few. It is a shameful truth, a sign of a world gone wrong. The growth of a Holy Spirit filled Christian community that understands that the river of life flows out, not in, will reverse this selfish trend. Let the river of life flow out to those around you from your innermost being, and see those around you helped and transformed.

It can be a subtle trap for Christians today, the thought that receiving from the Lord just to satisfy our own needs is the most important thing. It seems to be the understanding of some believers that they must hear all the preaching, never miss a worship time, get their needs met Sunday after Sunday, conference after conference, never taking time out to humbly serve others. If the world is filled with terror, with hatred and darkness, perhaps we should retreat behind church walls and keep the world away. If the world is full of hungry people, perhaps we should fill our own cupboards and tables and lock our doors, guarding our supplies with our guns. Or, we could let the prophet speak to us, and let our lives be changed by his words. Isaiah wants us to share our food, to help people out of trouble, to clothe the naked and welcome strangers. He wants us to live outwardly for others, not just inwardly for ourselves. Then, he asserts with confidence, the lights will come on. Darkness will be dispelled by the rivers of light flowing from God's people. He knows that if we live our lives facing outwards, that rivers of light will change the whole world; that the glory of our great God will rise upon us all. David sang this song to his Lord:

"O Lord, you are my lamp. The Lord lights up my darkness. In your strength I can crush an army; with my God I can scale any wall." (2 Sam 22:29-30)

David lived in a time when there were real armies to crush and tremendous obstacles to be faced. And so, of course, do we. To help those who are in trouble on a global scale requires a church that has come into its full inheritance. If we are to fill the world with light, then we must have a faith that matches the needs of the oppressed and troubled in many nations. We must read our bibles, pray our prayers, and sing our songs. But we must also produce leaders who have the maturity and stature to take on those who would keep the nations in darkness. We need leaders and ministers, servants of Christ who can take back the world from violent men not by violence, but by the power of the Spirit.

"We are human, but we don't wage war as humans do. We use God's mighty weapons, not worldly weapons, to knock down the strongholds of human reasoning and to destroy fake arguments." (2 Cor 10:3-4)

We would be able to shrink from this Kingdom task of freeing the peoples from trouble, if our God has grown old and weak, and is not able to accomplish such a victory. But another prophet, Habakkuk, sees how great is the light of the Lord of Hosts.

"I see God moving across the deserts from Edom, the Holy One coming from Mount Paran. His brilliant splendour fills the heavens, and the earth is filled with his praise. His coming is as brilliant as the sunrise. Rays of light flash from his hands, where his awesome power is hidden." (Hab 3:3-4)

God is not our emergency lighting, coming on to keep us safe only because the church has lost its power. No, his coming is as brilliant as the sunrise, and he has lifted up his church to light up every corner of his house. God loves you very much, but the gospel is not all about you or me. He meets our needs, great and small, yet his eyes are set on the needs of the whole world. Let us not get too caught up in our own lives, but allow our hearts to be lifted up higher, to feel and meet the needs of all peoples. Are you ready to ask God to use your life for a greater purpose, so that the whole earth might become aware of his glory? Are you stirred up to love your neighbours, to build bridges rather than walls? Then feed the hungry, visit the sick, help people in their troubles, and do it all in God's mighty power. He will help us.

"For the Lord your God is living among you. He is a mighty saviour." (Zeph 3:17)

"It is not by force nor by strength, but by my spirit, says the Lord of heaven's Armies." (Zech 4:6)

MEDITATE & MEMORIZE:
Memorize this scripture and speak it out loud as often as you can, taking time to meditate on it and asking the Holy Spirit to open it up for you. Let faith come as you hear your own voice declaring the true word of God.

"O Lord, you are my lamp. The Lord lights up my darkness. In your strength I can crush an army; with my God I can scale any wall." (2 Sam 22:29-30)

PRAY & PROCLAIM:
Proclaim that the Lord Jesus is your source of light and that he is very bright; then proclaim that his plan has worked in you, and that the light that fills you and your church to overflowing is as brilliant as the dawn. You are proud of Jesus' victory, not yourself, so don't hold back on this. Then ask him prayerfully to lift you up onto a stand today, so that your light can light up the lives and experience of others. Pray also that your light will flow out of you brightly enough that someone will get saved through your witness this week.

GIVE THANKS & WORSHIP:
Give thanks to God for saving you out of the darkness and for bringing you into the bright light of his Son Jesus. Worship God for his creation, for only having to say "let there be light" for the whole universe to light up! Worship the God who lights the galaxies and brightens your life, all with the same heavenly brilliance.

TESTIMONY
Have you heard what God is doing in India and the United States?

In November 2015 the Lord had put in my heart to give money to a lady I know who has a healing anointing. She runs a local restaurant and uses the money gained to support an orphanage for girls in India to save them from a life of prostitution. That last week of November I went to see her, and told her that in my spirit I felt I should give her some money, which I gave to her in an envelope and left. Three weeks later I visited her again, and she thanked me for my gift, saying, "that was the exact amount that I needed for the rent in the orphanage in India." I was blessed when she told me, and I was glad that I had obeyed the word of God in my heart.

On another occasion, having no work, I was looking to God to help me. A man from the United States was in town so I went to listen to his preaching. He began to prophesy, and I received one of his prophetic words as being for me. He said, "in two weeks someone will phone you and give you a job that you have not applied for". Two weeks later I was given a job on a Tuesday, and two days later sent to Tennessee for a month of training.

Maurice "Mo" Caron,
Ottawa

Part Four:

A RIVER OF HELP IN TIMES OF NEED

DAY 12

Trumpet Blast: Let the World Hear Us!

"Shout with the voice of a trumpet blast. Shout aloud! Don't be timid." (Isa 58:1)

We have been thinking about the river, flowing out from the throne of heaven, the throne of God and of the Lamb. It is full of life, crystal-clear flowing water, and produces fruit to eat and leaves that heal. It is a city river, flowing right through the centre of town. It seems that the river flows out of heaven and into us to take away our thirst, and flows mightily out of us to turn other lives into well-watered gardens. Our old lives are dead and buried, and we are brand new people, filled to bursting with God himself: the Holy Spirit. We are part of a thriving church, built on the foundation of apostles and prophets, with Christ Jesus himself as the cornerstone. It makes us want to shout! I remember years ago, at one of those Bible Week gatherings with thousands of saints together in one vast space, a preacher encouraged us to hear the sound of a united church shouting. It seemed a little strange to me at the time. I was used to having predictable, repetitive unexciting church meetings, where making noise was not encouraged. In fact our decision to move on from one church in the English Midlands was confirmed when one lady turned around in her seat to chide my very young daughter for clapping her hands to the song that we were singing. "We don't clap in this church," was her uninvited counsel to my daughter, and she was, of course, quite correct. Knowing that if we kept silent that the rocks would shout out God's praise, and that if we stopped applauding Jesus that the trees of the field would clap their hands, and suspecting that if we silenced our prophetic voices that a donkey might well take over, we set off in search of a more demonstrative body of saints.

And so, months later, here we were with a preacher encouraging us to abandon our British reserve and shout out to God. I thought that this might be fun, but when the people raised up their mighty trumpet voices I was actually quite shaken, in a good way. I think that the Lord of my terribly shy, reserved, northern-English, unused-to-expressing-emotion little soul thought that I could benefit from a little shaking, and that's what the shout did for me. The volunteers counting the offering behind industrial sized double doors, completely taken by surprise by the sudden shout, later described their near-death experiences as the doors shook violently, and these worthy volunteers felt as if they were trapped inside God's very own big bass drum! And something in my Spirit understood for the first time what a passionate church united in heart can do when they raise a trumpet to their lips. It was as if Jesus was saying to me by way of instruction, "Mike, my boy, shout aloud, and don't even think about being timid." Whatever spirit I had, of shyness, fear, and timidity hadn't been given to me by God, and as I had asked Jesus to be Lord of my life he wasn't willing to share accommodation with a different spirit from his own. So the shout shook inside of me something that was shakeable, and not of his kingdom.

Prophets are given big voices, loud enough to be heard by governments, and they are to shout out the truth of God with a trumpet blast. The whole earth will one day be aware of God's glory, and so must first be filled with the noise of bold preaching, powerful testimony, and unrestrained praise. Not just the prophets, but all God's people will learn to shout out for all to hear the good news that Jesus is alive. His blood shouts out 'forgiveness,' not 'vengeance,' and that voice will be heard above all the chaos of the nations.

I was never quite the same after that meeting, and I'm not as timid as I used to be! The church is throwing off its spirit of quietness as we realize that we aren't here to play hide and seek, hoping that the devil won't find us. Being prophetic as a church does include having a clear message, delivered loudly enough that the word of the Lord is heard by all the people of the earth.

The crushing, heart-breaking disappointment at the execution of Jesus had silenced his disciples. Mary Magdalene stood outside his tomb weeping at Jesus' death and at the added cruelty of not knowing why his body had been taken, or where. Tragedy and disappointment will do that to you. It will silence you and fill you with unanswered confusions, unresolved questions. The appearance of Jesus, risen from the dead having conquered the power of the grave, turned her silence into a shout.

"She turned to him and cried out, 'Rabboni' (which is Hebrew for 'Teacher')." (John 20:16)

If your voice as a Christian has been silenced by tragedy, disappointment, sadness or apparent failure, be sure of this: Jesus knows your name. He knows who you are, how you feel and where you've been. Hear him speak your name, just as Mary did, and turn your silence into a shout. You have seen the Lord earlier in your life, and known his great love, his amazing sacrifice to give you life. Cling to him again as Mary did, and tell your friends that you have seen Jesus afresh.

One debilitating factor for many people of faith is the dominant view that says, "God must have had a purpose in this," in the face of terrible, tragic events. No matter what happens, so many presume that a faith response must be based on the accepted truth that whatever happens, God has a purpose in it. The opposite response is also commonly heard, as hurting individuals proclaim, "I cannot believe in a God of love who would ever have allowed this to happen." The truth is there are at least two opposing purposes at work in our world. Perhaps both responses need to look again at the ministry of Jesus, who could distinguish easily between the purposes of his good and loving Father and the work of the evil one. When hate-filled terrorists harm the innocent with unrestrained violence, we can know that here is a work of the evil one, and we are to do all in our power to oppose such heartless people. When the infant and the elderly are both afflicted with pain or disease, think about the Jesus who shows us the Father's heart by healing, and compare it to the heart of wickedness that loves only to steal and kill and destroy. The trumpet blast of faith and praise can be made louder when we know what God does, and when we are stirred as the army of God against the forces of evil that would hurt us and rob our loved ones of their God-given health and freedom.

Perhaps your declaration of love for Jesus has been silenced by scepticism and doubt that has come creeping into your life, little by little. The cares of life have dragged you down; everyday worries have robbed you of your joy and your peace. Thomas felt that way. He was so devastated by the violence and finality of the torture and cruelty that took the life of the man whom he had believed in, that those images dominated his thinking.

"I won't believe it unless I see the nail wounds in his hands, put my fingers into them, and place my hand into the wound in his side." (John 20:25)

It was the very wounds laid on Jesus, so horrific, so final, that kept Thomas from renewing his faith. Only when Jesus came close to him and invited him to do the very things that he said were necessary to finding faith was his silence turned into a shout.

"'My Lord and my God!' Thomas exclaimed." (John 20:28)

It is so moving that Thomas, who was held back from faith in Christ by the deadly horror of his wounds, found faith once more at the sight of Jesus' hands and his wounded side. Isaiah the prophet foresaw that an appreciation of the wounds of Jesus lead all us to have faith in him, and to be healed.

"That evening many demon-possessed people were brought to Jesus. He cast out the evil spirits with a simple command, and he healed all the sick. This fulfilled the word of the Lord through the prophet Isaiah, who said, 'He took our sicknesses and removed our diseases.'" (Matt 8:16, 17; Isa 53:4)

Peter adds, "by his wounds you are healed" (1 Peter 2:24). Thomas' understandable difficulties in believing, disturbed as he was by the suffering of Jesus, were put right by those very wounds. There is power in the blood of Jesus!

Whatever it takes, the church of Jesus must get back its voice and raise up a mighty shout. Whatever has silenced us must be recognised and repented of, and we must set off once again with hearts and minds focused anew on pilgrimage. The saints of the Lord can find that trumpet sound, that unreserved thankfulness and unrestrained joy that is our birthright as the new creation people of God. We sometimes get there in worship, but we need a loud voice at other times. The prophet is commanded by God to shout like the blast of a trumpet: a loud sound, a clear signal. Isaiah knew that the day would come when the Lord would gather his people, calling them back to worship him on his holy mountain.

"In that day the great trumpet will sound." (Isa 27:13)

I believe that the Lord is right now calling multitudes to faith in his name, to return to God's holy mountain to worship. The river of living water that rushes out of the believer's heart has this trumpet sound, calling all the nations to worship the king. That day of the great trumpet sound will come as he has promised, but how about some music practice right now as that day gets ever closer! Don't let yourself imagine that the sound of the great trumpet will come on a silent, rainy Wednesday when we are all sleeping, and that it will make us jump up with complete surprise. Imagine instead that the clear prophetic voice of the church will continually increase in volume, to be heard in more and more places, that the orchestra of the saints will raise up a mighty tune until God's great trumpeter is provoked to bring the house down!

Call on the prophets that minister to your church to prophesy the word of the Lord with the piercing sound of a trumpet blast! You will have noticed that Isaiah 58:1 doesn't call us to remind unbelievers about their sin. It is to God's own people that the trumpet call is directed, that we might be put back on track so as to please God and transform the world. Let the church be humble and quick to welcome the prophet and respond to the word of the lord. We can influence the unfolding of history simply by being sincerely responsive to the words of God through his holy prophets, and by not ignoring or rejecting this intervention from the Lord. Shout, and don't be timid is our instruction from heaven.

The effect of the first pouring out of the Holy Spirit upon the one hundred and twenty men and women gathered together to pray was to end their timidity. They were all, every one of them, filled with the Holy Spirit and all began speaking together in unlearned languages. Because of the time and location, Jerusalem was filled with devout Jews gathered from every nation. What did they hear?

"When they heard the loud voice, everyone came running, and they were bewildered to hear their own languages being spoken by the believers." (Acts 2:6)

Timidity has gone, and the newly-born church is very loud, and able, from the first, to speak into every nation. This is the way that your Father God chose to introduce the promised Holy Spirit, loudly and with international impact. The divisions at Babel were undone by a unifying Spirit spilling out of noisy, bold, baptized in the Holy Spirit believers. This noisy, brave group saw many people added to the church until they numbered about five thousand (Acts 4:4). The city leaders, wanting to know what was happening, just had to ask:

"By what power, or in whose name, have you done this?" (Acts 4:7)

When given the answer that Jesus Christ of Nazareth was at the heart of all that was happening, and that his was the only name that could save us, they were stunned.

"The members of the council were amazed when they saw the boldness of Peter and John." (Acts 4:13)

Oh, wouldn't it be good to see the people of God so noisy, sounding like a trumpet blast, filled with boldness? To be accused (wrongly!) of being drunk, bewildering visitors to our cities by the miraculous, supernatural gifts of the Holy Spirit? Wouldn't it be great to impress our nation's leaders with our boldness in declaring the good news about Jesus? There are a lot more of us than one hundred and twenty, and we have sisters and brothers in every nation. How do you think it will go when this crowd bursts out into the city squares of the world? In the book of the acts of the Holy Spirit through God's mightily anointed servants, boldness seems to be almost as much a gift of the Spirit as prophecy and unknown languages. When Peter and John were set free from prison and reported to the church, the saints seemed unafraid of opposition and were deeply impressed by the confidence demonstrated in front of the council. They prayed like a trumpet blast!

"And now, O Lord, hear their threats, and give us, your servants, great boldness in preaching your word. Stretch out your hand with healing power; may miraculous signs and wonders be done through the name of your holy servant, Jesus. After this prayer, the meeting place shook, and they were all filled with the Holy Spirit. Then they preached the Word of God with boldness." (Acts 4:29-31)

~~~~~~~

MEDITATE & MEMORIZE:

Memorize this scripture and speak it out loud as often as you can, taking time to meditate on it and asking the Holy Spirit to open it up for you. Let faith come as you hear your own voice declaring the true word of God.

Stretch out your hand with healing power; may miraculous signs and wonders be done through the name of your holy servant, Jesus. After this prayer, the meeting place shook, and they were all filled with the Holy Spirit. Then they preached the Word of God with boldness." (Acts 4:29-31)

PRAY & PROCLAIM:

Adopt this mighty prayer of the early believers as your own; pray it with fire, pray like you mean it! Proclaim that God's word is the word of a God of covenant, that he does not lie, and that his Holy Spirit is at work in you to make you bold and effective. Call out to the Lord to bring revival to your nation, and tell him that you are fully surrendered to his word and to his work.

GIVE THANKS & WORSHIP:

Keep reading Acts chapter five, and let it feed into your thanksgiving and worship of such a great God. Worship the Lord who heals the sick. Call on God to anoint the women and men of God in your region that miracles will break out like a river in flood, and that many people will raise their voices in praise of the King of heaven and earth.

TESTIMONY
Have you heard what God is doing in Ottawa?

It took my husband, Ben, and I ten months to conceive our first child, Isaac. Those ten months seemed like a very long time. I thought I could plan when I was going to have a baby, down to the very month he would be born. I wasn't prepared for the emotions of finding out each month I wasn't pregnant, wondering why I couldn't control this part of my life, and feeling inadequate, like something was terribly wrong with us.

When our son was just over one year old we decided it was time for baby #2 to come along. It took us a year and a half to conceive. Around the time we requested a referral to a fertility specialist, I got the long-anticipated positive pregnancy test.

At the end of my first trimester, we shared our baby news with our son, our family, workplaces and social media. A week later we found out the baby had stopped developing and no longer had a heartbeat. The miscarriage was a drawn-out, complicated process that ended a month later with haemorrhaging and an emergency room visit.

In a season of infertility and waiting on a promise, I knew the Holy Spirit as my comforter and my counselor. Although I look back at it as a time that was difficult and heartbreaking, in the midst of it I knew God's goodness. Since most people knew about my miscarriage, quite regularly close friends brought me words of encouragement and faith to counter hopelessness and discouragement. I thought it would be difficult that people knew we were having trouble conceiving, but in the end the Holy Spirit was able to work through the church community because, quite simply, they knew what we were going through. Chris Gore's writing on not taking offense at God, and Bill Johnson's teaching on disappointment, helped center my faith - God wasn't the author of miscarriage or infertility. I didn't know why we were waiting for this baby but I could turn the waiting into a time to strengthen my faith and passionately pray for others who were facing infertility too.

About a year after my miscarriage, two church leaders from Cuba, Noel and Leno, travelled to our church. On a Sunday morning, they asked to pray for people who wanted to grow in sharing Jesus with others. I went up for prayer. They didn't know me and I hadn't told them about our son or our challenges conceiving. While they were praying, Leno gave me a prophetic word: "Don't be afraid to have more children." He told me he saw me holding a baby girl. I had thought my heartbreak and desires were too small for the Lord but God saw me where I was. In that moment, one of my fleeting thoughts was that I wasn't afraid to have more children… I wanted more children! But God's word was sharp. I ended up speaking that Holy Spirit message to myself many times over the next couple of years – in every ultrasound when my heart beat quickly in fear, when I had negative pregnancy tests, when we visited our fertility specialist. The Holy Spirit reminded me, "Don't be afraid." He carried me on that word.

I had a second miscarriage about a year and a half after my first. My natural mind thought, Here goes another year, at least, of waiting to conceive again… Soon afterwards, we met with two church leaders, Steve and Sarah Wilkins, and, again, we received counsel and comfort from the Holy Spirit. Steve told us He felt God saying we had waited a long time for a second baby but that it would happen quickly now. We would look back on this season that seemed very long and it would be like a brief thing of the past. I thought the opportunity for a miracle had passed since we had waited so long, but I conceived a baby three months after that second miscarriage. This was incredible compared to our previous experiences of waiting ten to eighteen months to conceive.

Now we have a one-year old baby girl, Mavis. Her name means "songbird" or "joy." Noel and Leno, from Cuba, visited again when she was just a couple months old and I was able to introduce Leno to her - fulfillment of the prophetic word spoken two years before. And now that five-year period of waiting really does feel like a time long ago, buried in the past. God is good!

Maryann Roebuck
Ottawa

DAY 13

Rivers of Difficulty

"But now, O Jacob, listen to the Lord who created you. O Israel, the one who formed you says, 'Do not be afraid, for I have ransomed you. I have called you by name; you are mine. When you go through deep waters, I will be with you. When you do through rivers of difficulty, you will not drown. When you walk through the fire of oppression, you will not be burned up; the flames will not consume you.'" (Isa 43:1, 2)

Jesus revealed to the world that the Lord is a God who is with us, not against us. He comes into our lives as a saviour, determined to reach us with his love, rescuing us from our weaknesses and sin by giving himself as a sacrifice. He is a God of covenant, a promise keeper, faithful to us always. The idea that he is our God and we are his people is foundational to our understanding of scripture, an unshakeable statement of unfailing love. Jesus came into our world looking for the lost, so that he could take them home to safety. He came as a physician, actively offering understanding, love and healing to all who were sick in body or mind, and he healed them all. Jesus came to tell us that our sad days of separation from God were over, and to lift heavy burdens from our weary shoulders. To all who thought that they were doing fine, the 'no, not for me, thanks' crowd, he had no words to say. But the sinners who knew they were sinners found a true friend in Jesus; he had no message for those who considered themselves righteous. He came to a hurting, messed up, difficult world in search of those who would freely acknowledge their need of his help and receive him as a saviour. It is strange to see so many people keeping their distance from Jesus because they are, in their own judgement, too bad, or too messed up to be helped. It's just too late for them they say. There is a lie that persists in our thinking that makes us believe that we need to be good to be saved. The reality is that Jesus comes looking for you when you are lost and in trouble. Jesus understands that the lives we live in this world are so often filled with difficulties, disappointments and despair. To the many whose faith in God has been tested, even destroyed, by the cruel challenges of life, Jesus comes to stir renewed hope. So many of us have struggled with physical or mental illnesses, or love the family and friends who even now continue to struggle in the darkness of such miseries, that our need of a Saviour who loves us and can help us into the light is clear. The Lord certainly knows that in our lives we have not been destined to fail, to suffer without hope of relief, or to lose our faith.

"You have been chosen to know me, believe in me, and understand that I alone am God." (Isa 43:10)

Your life is not an accident, and it has a distinct purpose. God has chosen you so that you might know him as an intimate, faithful friend. He has decided to show his favour to you, to bless you, by stirring you to believe in him. Knowing how insecure we can be in such relationships, he also emphasizes that there is no one like him, no other God who can undo or challenge his choosing of you. He has decided to love you, and he cannot be diverted. Knowing his own power to keep you he declares that "no one can snatch anyone out of my hand. No one can undo what I have done" (Isa 43:13). All you have to do is call out the name of Jesus, and he will save you and keep you. Not even your past actions, history of godlessness, sin or unbelief have any power to keep him away. Just believe, and hide in his loving kindness.

The first two verses of Isaiah 43 convince us that the Lord of our lives truly understands what our daily experiences can be like. He knows that often we are afraid, that we pass through deep waters where life's troubles threaten to overwhelm us. In the deepest of waters he promises to be with us, to see us through. When difficulties conspire against us, when we feel that we are going to drown under their relentless weight, he rescues us. The heat of oppression will not be allowed to consume us, because he never abandons us to them. Would you allow me to say to you that any thought that God has somehow allowed your suffering, mental, financial, physical or emotional, or that he has decided to burden you with pain and despair should be immediately and forcefully dismissed? That any shadow of a belief that God has done this to you for his own mysterious purpose is a despicable lie that attempts to deny the clear purpose of Christ's work among us? We all rightly think of the courageous men and women who fight fires in our communities as heroes, running towards the fire that threatens us while the rest of us run away from the inferno. We would feel differently if we discovered that a fire-fighter had deliberately put us in danger by starting the fire that he now rushed to put out! How then can we deal with a God who we believe makes us suffer, or who allows such suffering, and then rushes in to rescue us? We should try to simplify our thoughts. Fire fighters are heroes, as are all first responders who come running into our crises. In the same way, Jesus is a courageous, heroic Saviour who gave His very life to save us from sin, sickness and the despicable burdens that are the devil's work.

    I remember being greatly humbled one afternoon during a bible school teaching day. The teacher asked all the participants to describe the heaviest issues that affected the members of their various churches. Some were from the United Kingdom, others from the United States, while others worked in churches in Africa and South Asia. The Brits and Americans listed financial and relationship pressures, along with disagreements on doctrine. The others talked about brutal violence, extreme poverty, demonic practices and imprisonment for their faith. The leaders from western churches blushed to hear about the truly oppressive circumstances faced by their brothers and sisters. All God's servants, indeed all of God's children, must reorient themselves to be nation-changers, breakers of chains and lifters of oppression; in this we will catch the winds of the caring Holy Spirit, and move deeper into the river of God's mighty love. I felt a great weight of sadness years ago when a revival among the young people in a local church was stopped when the original members decided to hang on to their traditional church pews rather than change the space to accommodate the fired-up just-saved youth placed in their care; the new converts left, and the fires of revival, long prayed for, died quickly away. The Spirit is passionate about releasing people from their rivers of difficulty, setting them free to swim in the river of life flowing from God's throne room. Let's catch his heart, raise our sights to consider more important issues than empty tradition and the colour of the carpet in our meeting rooms, and see the fire fall!

    Whatever it is that has kept you from faith in God, or robbed you of it, turn now to the Lord who loves you, and has pursued you with his grace. Waste no more time. Don't give another minute to doubt or feelings of unworthiness. Trust in Jesus with all your heart and mind, and leave the rest to him.

"Then your salvation will come like the dawn, and your wounds will heal. Your godliness will lead you forward, and the glory of the Lord will protect you from behind." (Isa 58:8)

The difficulties and set-backs of life can make our experience seem very dark, and hope fades in the gloom of our circumstances. Being ill in body, or facing the relentlessness of mental illness or depression, makes many sufferers unwilling to make things even worse by being weak enough to allow false hope of deliverance from such dire challenges. Into such darkness salvation comes like a great light, like the dawn, transforming everything. Zechariah, John the Baptist's dad, filled with the Holy Spirit, began to prophesy:

"Because of God's tender mercy, the morning light from heaven is about to break upon us, to give light to those who sit in darkness and in the shadow of death, and to guide us to the path of peace." (Luke 1:78, 79)

When Jesus saves us the result is no small change, but a total transformation. Darkness into light, night into day. Even if you have been a Christian for decades, you can still allow this truth to change you, to transform your life even now. Is your life too dark for God's light to reach you? Or have you lived a long life as a believer, and feel it's too late for you to receive transforming light? I once encountered an excellent man of God who was robbed of hope in a time of refreshment in the Holy Spirit. He had taught for decades in several parts of the world against the baptism in the Holy Spirit. He felt disqualified, and too far on in his life for this new light to reach him. Job knew better:

"See how he spreads the lightning around him, and how it lights up the depths of the sea." (Job 36:30)

If the light of Jesus can illuminate the depths of the ocean, then he can lighten your darkness also. David knew this truth, saying, "O Lord, you are my Lamp. The Lord lights up my darkness" (2 Samuel 22:29). This dear servant of God that I had the honour to know, had diligently instructed thousands of Christians that speaking in unknown languages by the power of the Holy Spirit was demonic. How could the new light of God reach the abyssal ocean depths of his life after decades of preaching against that very light? He felt that if we were correct in preaching Holy Spirit baptism, then he had devoted his life to saying that the work of God was the deceit of the devil. This servant of Christ said, 'God will have to hit me like a truck if he is to change me now!' A few days later, as pastors from across the city laid hands on another brother for prayer, the Lord answered that challenge. The Holy Spirit came powerfully upon that dear man, in his eighties, and he fell to the floor, sliding away from the group, and ending up with his head under a stack of plastic chairs. I thought for a moment that God had killed him! Eyes closed and deeply surprised, this fine servant of God was reduced to a simple, "wow!"

At about that same time a young woman in the church led her unbelieving grandfather to Jesus. He had been disappointed and upset at his church as a young man, and abandoned his faith. He was a long-time determined atheist, and resisted all attempts to remind him of God's powerful love. At the age of 100 years old he came to Jesus, and spent his time from that moment on loudly singing hymns to the Lord. You may be held back by disappointments, mistakes, wrong turns, offense and other rivers of difficulty. Decide now not to be held back for a moment longer, but to let your life be transformed by the Lord who waits to rescue you.

The waters of life's hurts can be very deep, and drowning in your despair may have seemed a likely outcome for you more than once. The rivers of difficulty can run powerfully and threaten to knock you off your feet. The heat of oppression, whatever form it may have taken for you, can be so great that it seems ready to burn you up, to consume you. In the face of it all, something Winston Churchill said can keep you hanging on until help arrives. He said, "Never give in, never, never, never." And as you hang on, refusing to surrender your life, your hopes and dreams, I promise you a powerful, faithful helper will rescue you. Jesus has ransomed us all, called us by name, taken us home into his own family. Reach out your hand to Jesus, right now, and ask him to rescue you. Thrown into a fiery furnace, three children of God were rescued by the Lord. Death was not allowed to touch them, and the heat of oppression was defeated by God's loving protection. They were delivered from a fire so hot that it killed those who threw them into the furnace.

"Then the princes, prefects, governors, and advisers crowded around them and saw that the fire had not touched them. Not a hair on their heads was singed, and their clothing was not scorched. They didn't even smell of smoke! … He sent his angel to rescue his servants who trusted in him." (Dan 3:27-28)

MEDITATE & MEMORIZE:

Memorize this scripture and speak it out loud as often as you can, taking time to meditate on it and asking the Holy Spirit to open it up for you. Let faith come as you hear your own voice declaring the true word of God.

"Because of God's tender mercy, the morning light from heaven is about to break upon us, to give light to those who sit in darkness and in the shadow of death, and to guide us to the path of peace." (Luke 1:78, 79)

PRAY & PROCLAIM:

If you are experiencing "rivers of difficulty" in your life, then use the scripture above as your proclamation, over and over again, saying "break upon me." Ask the Lord to let his light break over you, to heal you and set you free. Pray for others that you know who need to receive his wonderful, compassionate help.

GIVE THANKS & WORSHIP:

Worship God for who he really is, for his love for the lost and for sacrificing his own beloved Son so that your sins, sicknesses and rivers of difficulty could be buried in Christ's tomb. Thank him that Jesus could not be held by mere death but that, leaving all your troubles behind him in the ground, he rose again into a resurrection life that includes you and me!

TESTIMONY
Have you heard what God is doing in Ottawa?

My dad calls me anti-fragile. He says it's an economic term. It means something like things that are better or stronger and more resilient because of brokenness, shock, and failure. Isn't that how things are, though? Haven't we all heard that where a bone heals after a break it becomes the strongest part of the bone? It doesn't mean I'm not fragile or emotional or weak sometimes. It just means that where I once endured a break or a loss, I am now stronger than I was before. By the Grace of God, that's me. Anti-fragile.

"This is not a sad story of sickness, but a testimony of God's goodness … This journal is a testimony of victory, grace and the power of God in my life and the life of my family" (a quotation from my journal in the summer of 1999).

I had no idea how true this would be. But in the spring of 1999 I was paralyzed on my left side and legally blind in my left eye. They said it was MS. I initially didn't know what that was except that people went on MS bike rides and walks to help those stricken with it. So it couldn't be good.
As confident as I was when I wrote those words of victory in my journal, I was also scared. I felt like a ticking time bomb. That at any moment, things would get worse. Sometimes we think that there can't be faith mixed with fear. Sometimes we are told by well-meaning people that fear will undo any possibility of healing as if my constant state of absolute faith is the only way for things to get better. I thankfully don't believe that anymore.

Even as the paralysis improved over the late spring of 1999 and the eye was suddenly clear during a church meeting in the spring of 2000, I was reminded often that an MS flare up could strike at any moment. My battle became not against a crazy hyperactive immune system ready to attack, but against breathtaking, paralyzing fear.

I found the verse, "The Lord is my strength and my song; he has given me victory" (Psa 118:14 NLT) at some point early in this time. I remember repeating it to myself and being determined to make this true. I knew the Lord was my strength to not collapse under this weight of sickness and fear, knew periods of joy along the way, and was almost afraid to hope that I might actually be okay in the long run.

In the years that soon followed, I returned to teaching and had my first child, and still I remember driving when suddenly this fear of sickness would overwhelm me. Often, I would glance at my toddler in the rear view mirror and state, "Honey, once mommy was blind but now she can see." I needed to hear myself say that. My body was doing fine. No flare ups, just irrational fear of any feelings of pins and needles if I sat on my foot for too long, or if lost my balance, or my hand was shaking. I lived like this for years.

I had a second child and was reminded once again that pregnancy can keep MS symptoms at bay, but they can be worse after you have the baby. My active imagination did not need this information. It only compounded my pretend-symptoms. By pretend-symptoms I mean that I could convince myself I was feeling something strange only to have the feelings disappear when I got my mind on something else. The mind is an amazing machine. No symptoms followed the second pregnancy, or the third. But still, this fear plagued me that at any moment IT could strike.

I can remember trying so hard to not be afraid and at the same time knowing that faith was not about trying harder. But I was trying nonetheless to wind up faith so that I would be healthy. That sort of "faith" is just so exhausting. But that's how I was living. One Sunday morning, someone kindly introduced me to a lady visiting the church because this very nice visitor had MS and the gentlemen probably thought we could compare notes. She began to ask me if I had this symptom and that problem. I began to panic, my heart was pounding in my ears, and I needed to get out of that situation. I didn't know that people with MS could have THOSE symptoms. I didn't want to know. The kind man who had introduced us probably thought that I was so strong and could help this lady. I hid this fear well from most people. I managed to finish the conversation with some excuse that I had to go.

Lesley Ford's story is continued at the end of the next chapter...

DAY 14

Faithfulness

"So the Word became human and made his home among us. He was full of unfailing love and faithfulness. And we have seen his glory, the glory of the Father's one and only Son." (John 1:14)

Over the years I have come to honour faithfulness more highly than any other attribute. Love is so vital, so important in our lives, and yet it is unfailing love that is our anchor. Love that fails, weakens, and ultimately abandons us is the root of so much disappointment and heartbreak. How many families and nations have been wounded by the unfaithfulness of a partner, parent or neighbour? One of the lies of the enemy is that we are alone and without help in this world, that it is 'every person for himself.' Those who are without resources, those who are weak or vulnerable, are at risk of oppression from the strong and the greedy. Loneliness attacks the hearts and minds of so many. Isolation seems to be a common fate even in the midst of our largest communities. Believing that our brothers and sisters across the world are less important than 'we' are can so often lead to division, violence and suspicion. God does not recognise such comparisons. He hates divorce, division, discrimination, and denomination. He loves all the peoples of the world equally, and commands us to do the same.

"When God created human beings, he made them to be like himself." (Gen 5:1)

It's hard to see how we can believe that the whole universe is a result of God's work of creation and yet deny that all the peoples of the earth are made in God's image, all one family. The question, "Who is my neighbour?" can only generate the answer, "all who are made in the likeness of God." To claim that my family, my people, or my nation enjoy God's favour in a way denied to others is to deny God's creation, as well as his pleasure in it. In talking about the poor, James declares:

"How can you claim to have faith in our glorious Lord Jesus Christ if you favour some people over others?" (James 2:1)

Any attitude that shows preference for one nation over another that is influenced by wealth, colour of skin, ethnic heritage, or any other difference is not the attitude of Christ. James continues by saying:

"Doesn't this discrimination show that your judgements are guided by evil motives?" (James 2:4)

It is certain that the unfailing love and faithfulness revealed in the person of Christ is not for the few, but for all the world to consider. We often hear shouts of praise in our worship times, shouts of "glory, glory to Jesus." John would perhaps have shouted, "glory, unfailing love and faithfulness" as he considered the wonder of Jesus making his home among us. To be hungry for God's glory is also to be consumed by unfailing love and faithfulness for every people, every brother and sister, every neighbour. If your heart is bursting with an expectation of experiencing the presence of the Lord in your lives, then know that he will display his glorious presence to the loving, the faithful, and the righteous. Paul encourages us in this.

"Let the Spirit renew your thoughts and attitudes. Put on your new nature, created to be like God – truly righteous and holy. So stop telling lies. Let us tell our neighbours the truth, for we are all parts of the same body." (Eph 4:23-25)

Our unfailing love and faithfulness is not a small thing, not a sprinkling, but a mighty river that touches every individual that we encounter. James sums up this inclusiveness in a familiar way:

"Yes indeed, it is good when you obey the royal law found in the Scriptures: 'Love your neighbour as yourself.' But if you favour some people over others, you are committing a sin." (James 2:8-9)

In looking towards his own death, Jesus also expressed that the river of his unfailing love and faithfulness was offered to all who received him with faith. His gaze was not fixed on a few; his arms were spread wide to welcome all who believe.

"As Moses lifted up the bronze snake on a pole in the wilderness, so the Son of Man must be lifted up, so that everyone who believes in him will have eternal life. For this is how God loved the world: He gave his one and only Son, so that everyone who believes in him will not perish but have eternal life." (John 3:14-16)

Jesus came to live with us and to call us home, to live in the glorious love of our Father. Enduring the greatest of personal costs, at the expense of his own life sacrificed for us, with the shedding of his own blood, he has saved us. His great love and faithfulness caused him to take action by reaching out to help us all. He had you in mind, and he had a plan to bless your family and your nation. But he is a great God, and his faithfulness encompasses all the families of the earth and every nation. We experience the full flowing of the river of the Spirit within us when we understand his love for the whole world and share in it. We are compelled to turn our backs forever on division, on prejudice, on tribalism, on nationalism that derides other nations. If you declare that God is your Father then you acknowledge that all men are your brothers and that all women are your sisters. Our faith for the salvation of all peoples knows no limitation when we comprehend the true extent of the river of faithfulness that flows out of heaven and into the whole earth. The river of God is mighty, and the waters of life are not in short supply.

"You are the hope of everyone on earth ... those how live at the ends of the earth stand in awe of your wonders. From where the sun rises to where it sets, you inspire shouts of joy. You take care of the earth and water it, making it rich and fertile. The river of God has plenty of water." (Psa 65:5, 8-9)

The river that flows out of heaven from the throne of God, of the Lamb, and then out of your believing heart has plenty of water. The flow of the Spirit that comes out of you has enough life and vitality to water the whole world. The river of life isn't meant to flow in to your life only, as if its task was to water only you in your dryness. God's blessing is certainly on you as an individual, and the river of unfailing love and faithfulness to you will never run dry. You will never be forgotten, never abandoned even for a moment. But always remember that this mighty river flows out of you to water a thirsty world. God is unfailingly loving and faithful, and expressed this perfectly in Jesus. He is now expressing his unfailing love and faithfulness through the pouring out of "the Spirit of Jesus" (Acts 16:7) through his people. It is exciting to be alive today, when a generation of saints is welcoming the Spirit of Jesus to flow unhindered out of our hearts. This generation, shaped by obedience to Christ and to his word, is discovering that the river of God has plenty of water for every person who declares that they are thirsty. We are throwing off apathy, fighting the spirit of violence as it seeks to terrorize nations, and acknowledging the worldwide family of God. Filled with Christ, we are consumed by passion for God's house and driven by unfailing love and faithfulness. We will not be discouraged. And we will not rest until the whole earth is aware of God's glory in Jesus. The Spirit is urging us to fear the Lord, love the people of the world, and to cherish faithfulness.

"Unfailing love and faithfulness make atonement for sin. By fearing the Lord, people avoid evil." (Prov 16:6)

I have enjoyed the privilege of learning faithfulness from the very best. When the Holy Spirit unexpectedly began to speak to my wife and me about restoration, and to encourage us to have a greater vision for the church, he quickly led us to men and women who knew far more about "the restoration of all things" (Acts 3:21) than we did. The Spirit joined us with a growing company of believers who declared that God loved the world and that he loved his children with unfailing faithfulness, with covenant love. This idea of covenant love, demonstrated in God's unshakeable love for the world, could also be expected of our love for each other as God's offspring. Our Father relates to us out of his own perfect goodness, and the strength of that loving bond is owed entirely to his own unchanging character. He delights to see his own children living with each other in that same quality of faithfulness, brothers and sisters bound together by covenant love. The value of this expectation of unshakeable covenant love between brothers and sisters in Jesus has only been increased in my estimation by its frequent failure. Covenantal relationships that were tested to breaking point under the intense heat of life's situations and challenges only serve to highlight the beauty of faithfulness that endures. When the intense flames finally pass away, as they always do, then that which remains is truly precious.

"Anyone who builds on that foundation (Jesus Christ) may use a variety of materials- gold, silver, jewels, wood, hay, or straw. But on the judgment day, fire will reveal what kind of work each builder has done. The fire will show if a person's work has any value." (1 Cor 3:12-13)

Sometimes in life we have to endure the disappointment of failed friendships, abandoned partnerships, marriages that are broken and robbed of life and joy. So many individuals seem to carry lengthy hurts sustained in their church experience, and most find it hard to try again, to get back into meaningful fellowship. Ministers of the good news about Jesus do not appear to be exempt from this testing to failure, as disciples joined in the work of God become separated by circumstances that overwhelm the bonds of brotherly love. Two things seem clear. One is that when the fires that destroy friendship pass away, diamonds of faithfulness remain, and jewels of enduring covenant love are there to be seen. Look for those diamonds; be encouraged by the jewels of lasting, tested, life-long relationships. How sad it would be if our attention stayed for too long on that which is lost rather than on the faithful family and friends that remain. A second truth is that God is truly the restorer of all things. Broken hearts can be mended, giving fresh hope for the future; brothers that have been swept apart by the inferno can find each other again in the grace of Jesus.

In my own life I have enjoyed the unfailing love of a wonderful wife, four amazing children who fill me with awe and pride, and six (so far!) delightful grandchildren who are very loving and very noisy. He has also given me faithful friends who understand and live out covenant relationships. Two men of God in particular, faithful mentors to so many, have taught me the most. My brother Keri Jones has, for thirty-five years now, shown unshakeable friendship and support to me: wise advice and Godly direction, all given in integrity and faithfulness from a man who loves to live his bible. His brother Bryn, certainly the most excellent and passionate of skilful preachers that I have had the pleasure to listen to, was once asked about those who walk away from faithful, covenant relationships. After a little thought, he offered the observation that although someone may break covenant with you in life, no one can ever stop you from being a person of covenant in your own heart. Others may have the power to break a partnership but never to break the deep faithfulness that is your own foundation. Treasure faithfulness in your own life, and let disappointments only make you even stronger in your own covenant love for the Lord and for all those that you touch. Say yes to the prayer of Jesus:

"May they experience such perfect unity that the world will know that you sent me and that you love them as much as you love me." (John 17:23)

~~~~~~~

MEDITATE & MEMORIZE:
Memorize this scripture and speak it out loud as often as you can, taking time to meditate on it and asking the Holy Spirit to open it up for you. Let faith come as you hear your own voice declaring the true word of God.

"Unfailing love and faithfulness make atonement for sin. By fearing the Lord, people avoid evil." (Prov 16:6)

PRAY & PROCLAIM:
Pray fervently that unfailing love and faithfulness will be found in you. Proclaim that you forgive all those that have sinned against you; let go of any desire for vengeance. Let your fear of the Lord in you be clean; let it strengthen your soul, and pray that he will keep that fear alive and healthy in you.

GIVE THANKS & WORSHIP:
Give thanks to the Lord that his love for you is unfailing, a covenant love that cannot be shaken. Worship him with joyful abandon, from close to his throne, because he has reconciled you to himself thoroughly! Worship him as a faithful Lord in prayer, in song, and by being faithful to all who are in your life.

TESTIMONY

Have you heard what God is doing in Ottawa?

Lesley Ford's story continued…

It was after 7 years without any flare-ups that I moved to Ottawa and a friend suggested that I find a neurologist here in order to track my health for insurance purposes. It sounds like a very practical thing to do. Funny. Even after eight years without any problems fear had a firm hold, and through the 6 weeks between a routine MRI and the follow up appointment, I could barely breathe. I remember standing by my kitchen window waiting for the kettle to boil and singing, "Breathe, just breathe," by Faith Hill over and over because I felt that's all I could do as I waited for the weeks to pass. I now laugh and tell people, "What was I expecting in the MRI results? That I was actually paralyzed so I should really stop with all this walking?" The mind is a crazy thing. It is irrational.

As Christians we can have so many "shoulds" in our lives. I shouldn't be scared. I needn't be scared. Jesus said, "Do not be afraid." But I was. Terribly afraid and could tell no one. Or felt that I could not. My world felt very small. This fear isolated me. It was always in the back of my mind. It was hard to think about the future because maybe I wouldn't have one.

Those MRI results I waited for were fine. "Looks stable" my neurologist would say. And despite the good news that I was not going to suddenly need a wheelchair, I was only slightly relieved. This was strange to me. If eight years symptom free and a positive word from a MS neurologist and researcher did not alleviate the fear, what could?

I'm not sure if I was beginning to get fed up with feeling this way or what, but I was in a home decor shop shortly after and saw a sign that read, "BE THANKFUL." I knew that I needed those words in my house. I began to think about how amazing it was that now eight years later, I am walking, driving, have 3 children, and no symptoms. "BE THANKFUL" was a key to get my eyes off myself, off those things that I cannot control, and onto the Lord. Somehow being THANKFUL unlocked fear. This was miraculous. This gradual change felt like a weight of fear gradually falling off.

In 1999 I trained and ran a 10K race with a dear friend to celebrate 10 years of health. I cried for the last 2 kilometres just thanking the Lord for my healthy and strong body. So grateful.

It is so wonderful that this all happened in the timing it did because it was in (about) 2011 during another routine MS neurologist appointment and after several other routine MRIs that she said, "Well, I don't usually say this until 20 years symptom free, but…" and then she wrote "BENIGN???" in my chart (she double underlined it). I responded, "I will help with the next 10 years." I can still picture her writing. Amazing.

I love that the fear had already dissipated before the doctor declared me "BENIGN?" I'm so grateful for the goodness of God to help me see that "BE THANKFUL" sign and the transformation that followed in my mind. This changed my life. Sometimes now, I forget that fear had had such a tremendous impact on my thinking of my life and my future. I tell this story and it feels like it happened to someone else. Fear of any flare up is no longer part of my thinking.

The "BENIGN?" diagnosis has been such a gift to me in the years that have followed; life has brought other challenges and I am so grateful that the chapter of sickness and fear was over before the next began. Sometimes I'm not sure what was more of a miracle in my life, being free from fear, and from the shame of feeling so fearful, or being free of MS. Indeed it has been true that "The Lord is my strength and my song; he has given me victory" (Psa 118:14 NLT). He has been my strength through great brokenness and has been my song of hope through the journey into the victory that only He could give me.

And so I am free. Free to no longer need to prove I'm okay. To know His faithfulness is not dependent on my strength and faith. I am not trying really hard to have faith. I'm just standing, or falling and crying out, and clinging to the deep, deep knowing that the Lord really has got me. I don't even need to hold on. He's got this too. He's always had me. He is faithful. He has made me stronger where I was once broken. He has made me anti-fragile.

Lesley Ford,
Ottawa

DAY 15

The God Who Answers

"Then, when you call, the Lord will answer. 'Yes, I am here,' he will quickly reply." (Isa 58:9)

This promise from the Lord is at the very heart of our lives of faith. Isaiah 58 has called on us to live noble lives that are worthy of our calling as children of God. We are not to live superficially; attending Sunday meetings and conferences but neglecting the poor and living for ourselves is not an option for us. We are to give clear evidence of our transformed hearts and minds by having the attitude of a servant. The pursuit of righteousness for all and a love of justice consume us. Our understanding of baptism in the Holy Spirit is founded on the belief that the power of God is being released like a flood into a waiting world, filled with the cries of multitudes that need God to be the God who answers with power. The gifts of the Spirit, once fully released from the meeting place into our city streets will be seen for what they truly are; the liberating weapons of a powerful family of compassionate saints engaged in meeting the needs of others. It will be a glorious day indeed when so many disciples of Christ take a short break from yet one more 'getting the saints ready for action' study course, and leap boldly out through the church doors to take the God who answers into the community. Our love for the world must be evident to all, as we pray, fast and take action on behalf of the oppressed, the wrongly imprisoned. If women and girls are taken captive in Nigeria, then their cause is our cause, and we cannot rest until they are returned to our families. If minorities are treated shamefully in their own nations, then our voices must be raised in their defence; we must find a way to share our food with the hungry, our clothes with the naked, our money with those in poverty, whatever their faith, nationality or location. When the Lord is delighted with our love for our brothers and sisters, when he sees his people in pursuit of justice, "then, when you call, the Lord will answer."

A God who does not answer when we call is no God at all. I remember (with a little shame) a time when my wife and I were members of a great congregation in a Church of England setting in the East Midlands of England. They were great people, wonderful leaders who possessed both zeal and integrity, and a warm, loving group of true friends. One of the best was a deacon, affectionately known as Trev the Rev, who tried hard to avoid our gaze when his turn came to sing a Psalm at evensong. The old English version of scripture, the fact that my wife and I were quite unruly Anglicans, and the slightly surreal reality of evensong in a tough mining area led to scenes that we found funny, but Trev the Rev did not. The most hilarious occasion occurred when my friend had to sing of false gods that "have ears, but hear not; noses, but smell not" to a solemn melody. We lost it, Trev made eye contact with us at just the wrong moment, and the holiness of evensong that Sunday night was lost forever. The words he sang rang true. What's the good of a god like that? We must not allow faith to be defined as believing in a god who doesn't hear us, never answers our prayers, and seems busy elsewhere. He is revealed to us in scripture as a brave and victorious saviour, as a loving father. When Daniel and his friends found themselves in exile, far from home, they decided to cling to the Lord no matter what the cost. The trust they had was placed in a God who is real, a God who answers when we call. King Nebuchadnezzar of Babylon had a dream that troubled him, and demanded to know its meaning, without telling anyone what he had dreamt! Anyone who failed to tell him the dream and to reveal its meaning would be torn apart, and their houses demolished. The magicians and astrologers had no idea what the king had dreamt, and declared the task to be impossible. Daniel alone had a relationship with a God who heard him, and who would answer the cry for help. In a dream of his own, Daniel was shown the secret content of another man's dream, and its meaning. When Daniel awoke he praised the God who answers, saying,

> "Praise the name of God forever and ever, for he alone has all wisdom and power. He determines the course of world events; he removes kings and sets others on the throne." (Dan 2:20, 21)

If Daniel's God remained silent, then Daniel's life would be over. Because his God was listening and involved in the real world with his servant, a mighty miracle was seen by all. Christians will never fear the power of Babylon when its king is so moved by the God who answers that he declares, "truly, your God is the

God of gods, the Lord over kings, a revealer of mysteries, for you have been able to reveal this secret" (Daniel 2:4-7). As servants of Christ we cannot ignore the suffering of so many people around the world, all of whom are created in the image of God. Neither can we ever feel helpless in the face of violence, terror, hatred and greed. Our God is simply too great, and when we call out to him, he is the one who can change the course of world events.

As Christians who are made to be like Jesus, we can't just ignore the news. Nor can we pretend that it is someone else's news, or even the judgement of God on the wicked. The self-centred ignorance found in the generation visited by the first coming of Jesus was demonstrated in their questions about those around them. "Why is this man blind? Is it because of his own sin, or his parents'?" If we, without truly thinking it through, begin to think of our brothers and sisters in other lands as being somehow deserving of whatever war, brutality or hatred that is poured out on their heads, that it is all part of God's inscrutable plan, that "there is a purpose in everything," then we will be as guilty as that generation that misunderstood Jesus. If we understand that every situation is one in which the power and mercy of God can be seen, then our prayer rooms will be full and all the saints will spring into action on behalf of our oppressed family around the globe. Our God is the God who loves us, who hears and answers our cries to him. The church is one of the instruments that he uses to powerfully spread the news of Jesus, and to demonstrate the he is a God of action. No, we can't turn away from the distress of others, we can only be like Jesus, who loved the people of the world and laid down his life for us. The sicknesses, the violence and terror, the hunger and suffering that we see are not the judgements of God, but the work of the evil one. Jesus came to knock down the devil's work and to rescue mankind. Shall we not do the same?

"But the Son of God came to destroy the works of the devil." (1 John 3:8)

This generation of believers is being stirred by the Holy Spirit to be bold, confronting the evils of this world with courageous faith. We have received the poured out Holy Spirit not just to make our meetings more interesting, but to receive power to reach and rescue the nations. We surely understand that God is a great God. He is looking for more than the next great worship song. He is looking to flood the nations with grace and mercy, to raise up Jesus as a saviour for multitudes, to fill all the earth with an awareness of his glory. It would be too small a thing for any of us to want to be a worship leader, or a pastor or preacher to other saints only. Our hope must be for a world set free from injustice by a God who answers the cry of the oppressed. Which is greater? The love of God and his people? Or the hatred of violent men? Whose god will answer?

Elijah the prophet put his life on the line on this very issue of the God who answers prayer. Confronted by the false prophets of a baseless religion, he staged an open-air competition. The prophets of Baal tried for hours to call on their God to set fire to their sacrifice, a bull cut into pieces and laid on an altar. No one answered, though they called to their god all morning. Elijah soaked his offering and the wood beneath with gallons of water, and then began to call on the Lord of miracles.

"O Lord, answer me! Answer me so these people will know that you, O Lord, are God and that you have brought them back to yourself. Immediately the fire of the Lord flashed down from heaven and burned up the young bull, the wood, the stones, and the dust ... and when the people saw it, they fell on their faces and cried out, 'The Lord is God! The Lord is God!'" (1 Kings 19:37-39)

The test had been a simple one. The God who could hear the cry of his servant and answer by fire from heaven would be the only true God. The same truth applies today. Our Christian faith is an evidence-based experience, with a God who loves us and answers from heaven. We do not require people to believe in a silent, unhearing Lord, or they will all begin asking, 'where was God when I needed him?' No, our God is real, mighty in power, filled with unfailing covenant love. Pentecost isn't the story of the origin of some denominations. Pentecost is the Lord of Heaven answering by fire poured out on the heads, hearts and bones of all God's people.

God is not far from us or hard to please. He has not aged or become deaf to our cries, and he loves us so much that he didn't hold back the life of his own son. He is our God and he is always with us. He is faithful and quick to answer. Pray for the smallest things that you need in life, and he will provide for you. Pray for the largest things, for the nations to be at peace, and he will give that to you also. Above all, pray for the poor, the oppressed, the downtrodden, and he will answer you. Just be prepared to do what he tells you!

"I will walk among you; I will be your God, and you will be my people." (Lev 26:12)

MEDITATE & MEMORIZE:

Memorize this scripture and speak it out loud as often as you can, taking time to meditate on it and asking the Holy Spirit to open it up for you. Let faith come as you hear your own voice declaring the true word of God.

"But the Son of God came to destroy the works of the devil." (1 John 3:8)

PRAY & PROCLAIM:

Pray that the Lord will open your eyes to understand what is going on in the world, and ask the Holy Spirit to give you the gift of being able to discern different spirits. Set yourself to pray that the will of God should be done everywhere, and that all the works of the devil should be seen, recognised, and knocked down by the power of God and the faith of his people.

GIVE THANKS & WORSHIP:

Worship the Lord and thank him for being the God who answers. Thank him for convincing you that he always hears and answers the cries of his people, and worship him for his goodness and grace to all who look to him for refuge.

TESTIMONY
Have you heard what God is doing in Ottawa?

Since a young age, I've struggled with mental illness in various forms, such as depression. At its most severe, I was diagnosed by doctors with dissociative identity disorder and schizophrenia. For years, I never spoke to others about how I struggled with my mental health because of shame and an intense fear of being rejected. During this time, I often experienced feelings of low self-worth, hopelessness and suicidal thoughts. I knew there was an element of this problem that was medical, and needed to be treated medically. But sadly, no amount of counseling or any other effort to be healed had ever worked. Almost all seemed to be just a band-aid solution for the problem and wasn't life changing or sustainable.

Thankfully, I met Jesus and "declare[d] with [my] mouth, 'Jesus is Lord," and believe[d] in [my] heart that God raised him from the dead," (Romans 10:9) and I was saved. Just this past year I experienced tremendous breakthrough in the area of my mental health. I started to think and speak the truth and stop believing lies about myself and what my life would be. God gave me a revelation that "The tongue has the power of life and death, and those who love it will eat its fruit," (Prov 18:21) and "for as [a man] thinks in his heart, so is he" (Prov 23:7). For example, I spent two weeks in the hospital being treated medically for depression and schizophrenia. But during that time, instead of viewing myself as someone who is ailed by a disease in my mind or someone struggling with mental health, I made a firm decision to focus on my words, how I speak and what I believe, as my identity was to be firmly established and rooted in the truth of God's word, not in the label I had been given by the hospital.

I decided to trust God as the one who gives life to the dead and calls nonexistent things into existence (Romans 4:17). I agreed, believed and declared the truth of God that I was healthy, strong, had a sound mind, that I had the mind of Christ, that I was fully healed, full of love and full of His peace. Once I began to declare out loud and focus on believing truth, I began to change the way I think. Even though my circumstances spoke to me something different at the time, I knew that "by his wounds [I was] healed" (Isa 53:5). Jesus said, "It is finished" (John 19:30) and He truly won the victory. I now have known a sustained victory over mental illness for almost two years, to God be the all the glory.

2017, Ottawa

Part Five:
THE RIVER IN FLOOD

DAY 16

Water for the Thirsty, Strength for the Weak

"The Lord will guide you continually, giving you water when you are dry and restoring your strength." (Isa 58:11)

Isaiah now begins to contemplate the consequences for the people of God when they live to please him. What will life be like when we remember the poor and oppressed, when we feed the hungry and help those who are in trouble? How will our experience change when we love justice and pursue righteousness for all? The thought that 'the Lord helps those who help themselves' has been supplanted by, 'the Lord helps those who help others,' and results flow out of this transformation. Three fruits are visible here: guidance, water and strength. This is good news indeed for the lost, the thirsty, and the weak. So it seems that the path to a closer walk with God, to having him provide all that we need, takes us first to meet the needs of others; to love the stranger, to be hospitable and friendly. We see Jesus come to earth to live as a servant of all, to remove burdens, and to offer his life and his death as a willing sacrifice. So by faith we decide that we will live in the same way, swimmers in the same river that flows out of Jesus. Asking the Lord for his continual guidance is something that he welcomes, and encourages in his children. Saul got this, and many other things, quite wrong.

"So Saul died because he was unfaithful to the Lord. He failed to obey the Lord's command, and he even consulted a medium instead of asking the Lord for guidance." (1 Chron 10:13-14)

It may seem obvious to say that to witness people consulting mediums is abhorrent to God, but it's best to be clear. God's people should never consult psychics, horoscopes or any occult method of finding answers. Even Saul knew this truth.

"Saul had banned from the land of Israel all mediums and those who consult the spirits of the dead." (1 Sam 28:3)

And yet, despite being convicted of the foolishness of consulting such people, under the influence of fear and when failing to hear the Lord, he consulted a medium. When at his request Samuel appears, the condemnation is swift, and he learns that God has become Saul's enemy. God's people seek only his guidance, and put no value in occult or psychic sources. If, like Saul, you once knew this but have slipped back into this unhelpful and dangerous practice, then call on God now with sincere repentance. Turn away from words that spring out of darkness, and live in the light of God's holy word.

"For the word of God is alive and powerful. It is sharper than the sharpest two-edged sword, cutting between soul and spirit, between joint and marrow. It exposed our innermost thoughts and desires." (Heb 4:12)

Love your bible, and read it every day, regarding it as essential, healthy food. Love the words of the Holy Spirit in your life and be convinced that the Spirit and the Word are always in agreement. The guidance of the Lord over your life is continuous, and is to be welcomed and trusted. I have found that my own confidence in following the leading of the Spirit has grown whenever I have been careful to declare his faithfulness out loud. I used to say to myself quite often that I was unsure about what the next step was, and to worry that I might take a wrong step, a wrong turn on the road. As a pastor I found that many other believers also had persistent concerns as to their ability to hear God clearly enough to keep them walking in a straight line. Eventually I realised that this whole approach maximised the need for me to get things right in life, and minimised the Spirit's ability to keep me safe and on the right track. Maybe it's just me, and everyone else has discovered this years ago. But have you noticed that many of our worst days arise from self-doubt, and all of the best days come out of the realization that He is in control?

Everything gets better when the light of heaven shines on me, and I realise once again that I'm not in the right place because of my amazing wilderness survival skills, but because even this directionally-challenged soul has the covenant keeping God as a travel guide! Talking to myself is a good habit, and I don't want to suppress it; so I'm working to say much better things about God's continual, loving guidance in my everyday life. The preaching you listen to most often by far is your own thoughts and words, so be a great preacher! If I pray, "Jesus, please give me enough for today, and let something happen before I go to sleep tonight that will glorify your name," then I guess I will follow it up by training myself to think and speak in agreement with that prayer. When I finish talking with Jesus, and start talking to myself, I'm going to say, "I'm going to have more than enough to meet my needs today, and some left over for others, and God is going to glorify Jesus through me!"

He will also give you water whenever you are dry. It is a comfort to know that being dry isn't a sin, just a need that Jesus loves to help us with. Jeremiah mirrors the thoughts of Isaiah when he speaks of the Lord's covenant love for his people, for his joy in restoring their lives, and in giving them abundant supplies of water.

"'In that day,' says the Lord, 'I will be the God of all the families of Israel, and they will be my people.'" (Jer 31:1)

This is a simple statement of God's covenant love for all who belong to him, for all the richly blessed families of faith.

"I have loved you, my people, with an everlasting love…I will rebuild you, my virgin Israel…tears of joy will stream down their faces, and I will lead them home with great care." (Jer 31:3, 4, 9)

The Lord is a loving, faithful God, who rejoices over all his people, bringing them home and owning them as his family. The result, as both prophets could see from afar, was that:

"Their life will be like a watered garden, and all their sorrows will be gone." (Jer 31:12)

When we are dry, Jeremiah knows that water will flow from the Lord to end our drought and wash away our sorrows. The prophet also understands that intercessors can themselves let water flow towards the Lord as they come before him with the needs of others. This kind of prayer poured out to the Lord has often been seen in times of great need, with intercessors learning how to break through into the heavens as they seek God's intervention on the earth.

"Cry aloud before the Lord…let your tears flow like a river day and night. Give yourselves no rest…rise during the night and cry out. Pour out your hearts like water to the Lord." (Lam 2:18-19)

Heaven and earth are joined as rivers of tearful prayer rise up to God on behalf of the children of this troubled world, and rivers of life flow from God's throne to the earth. In the season ahead, the Lord will raise up an army of believers who will rise up during the night hours to intercede for their neighbours and for the nations. Our hearts will turn to water and our tears will flow, and a river of prayer will flow back into heaven. When the rivers of prayerful intercession mingle with the waters of life flowing from the throne then no work of the evil one will stand up to the flood of God's blessing, and nations will go free. The emotions that come on individuals caught up in the Holy Spirit in this way can sometimes seem overwhelming; but let the river flow and God will hear you from heaven. I am being woken in the night more often these days, and so are many of my friends, with a heart filled with tears that come from an awareness of the needs of so many around the world. Satellites and 24 hour news feeds have brought the circumstances of every life into our homes, but only the Spirit of Christ can turn that knowledge into deliverance from evil for his children, by turning us to prayer.

Another consequence of living for others is that he will restore our strength. Living for ourselves weakens us; making wealth the main purpose of our lives weakens our friendship with God. Isaiah is convinced that remembering the hungry, helping the troubled and counting everyone as our neighbour pleases God, who will strengthen us when we are weak. Jesus told a parable about a rich man. The rich man would have been fine if he had acknowledged the Lord as the source of his blessing. He would have won God's favour by using some of his wealth to lift the burdens of others. But no, he put his faith in wealth itself, and saw it as his own resource, for his own selfish consumption. He would talk to himself about his security being in his abundant crops.

"And I'll sit back and say to myself, 'My friend, you have enough stored away for years to come. Now take it easy! Eat, drink and be merry!'" (Luke 12:19)

I guess you should know that you're in trouble when you start addressing yourself as "my friend!" Such a focus on self, combined with a love of wealth and a security in riches, ruined his ability to know and serve the Lord. It's not that God loves the poor and hates the rich. He loves us all equally. But he has made us in his image, and, like any father, looks for his children to be like him. So all of us can please our Father in heaven by imitating him and caring for our neighbours and remembering everyone who cries out to him. You can make your relationship with

God richer by forgetting yourself a little more, and by calling more people your friend. There are hate-filled forces in this world of ours, but we must not use that fact to close down our circle of friends until we only trust ourselves and those who look like us. Look again at the folks on the other side of town; look at the nation next door, and at those across the ocean. Think of them as your concern, your friends, all potential fellow-citizens of the kingdom of Jesus, and watch your prayer life grow stronger.

"Yes (says Jesus), a person is a fool to store up earthly wealth but not have a rich relationship with God." (Luke 12:21)

Living for self weakens us. Living for others pleases the Lord, who restores our strength and helps us to prosper. That is why Timothy received this instruction:

"Teach those who are rich in this world not to be proud and not to trust in their money, which is so unreliable. Their trust should be in God, who richly gives us all we need for our enjoyment. Tell them to use their money to do good. They should be rich in good works and generous to those in need, always being ready to share with others." (1 Tim 6:17-18)

God is a great God, and he is restoring all things. He wants us to grow in trust and to be stronger, and provides for us richly so that our enjoyment of life lived under his rule might be complete. He wants us to turn from our own riches, abandon our own efforts, and surrender to his guidance without reservation. He is giving us an abundant water supply by immersing his saints in the river of life flowing over us from heaven, and he is restoring our strength. Shall we not dare to believe that the church of Christ will be a strong church, strong enough with his provision to take on a whole world? He does not strengthen us in order that we might retreat, abandoning the lost to their fate. He strengthens us in order that we might boldly advance, filled with Jesus' love, boldly declaring the power of the blood of the Lamb who was slain. Dare to imagine your city becoming ever more aware of the church of Jesus living among them, filled with the light, love and strength of the gospel of the Messiah. God is restoring his church so that once more the sick, the sinner and the lost will turn to the disciples of Jesus for aid. The prophet Isaiah is clear in his vision of God as a restorer of all things, and it is to the vital concept of restoration that he turns next.

MEDITATE & MEMORIZE:

Memorize this scripture and speak it out loud as often as you can, taking time to meditate on it and asking the Holy Spirit to open it up for you. Let faith come as you hear your own voice declaring the true word of God.

"The Lord will guide you continually, giving you water when you are dry and restoring your strength." (Isa 58:11)

PRAY & PROCLAIM:

Proclaim over yourself that "the Lord will guide me continually, giving me water when I am dry and restoring my strength." When you feel an assurance of faith on this truth, then proclaim over someone you are praying for, then a part of your city, and finally for your nation, "the Lord will guide you continually, giving you water when you are dry and restoring your strength. "Pray that the work of Jesus will go forward without delay into your own community.

GIVE THANKS & WORSHIP:

Worship the Lord for his everlasting goodness and for his nature as a loving Father. Thank him for always being there for you, for sharing with you his mighty river of life, his wisdom and his strength.

TESTIMONY
Have you heard what God is doing in Ottawa?

In the early nineties there was a significant economic recession. We had started in business in construction a few years earlier and the recession had drained our resources. It was early December and we had no work and no money. We literally did not know what we would do for food in the weeks ahead, let alone other expenses. On top of that, in residential and commercial construction the month of December is the most unlikely time in the whole year for anyone to start a construction project. Nobody wants you working in their house or business at Christmas.

I had previously been fixing up the attic of our home into bedrooms for our children and had some materials on hand for taping the drywall. So, one day I decided to finish the taping. A young man that had worked for us occasionally agreed to help me. He was not a Christian but I had talked with him about Jesus. As we ate our lunch I shared with him our financial situation and lack of work. As we talked I was moved by the Holy Spirit to declare to him that even though this was the most unlikely time of the year for anyone to call me to start a project, I believed that God was going to provide work for us in the days ahead. He was clearly not convinced but acknowledged he would watch what happened. Less than two hours later the phone rang. A young couple had seen our company name "randomly" in the phone book. They needed a large attic in an old house fixed up immediately into a living space for several students that were due to move in during January. There was a stairway to be constructed and walls on the second floor to relocate plus all the work in the unfinished attic. All they wanted to know was how soon we could start. The young man helping me clearly saw God's miraculous provision! On top of that, we were able to hire him as one of the workers on the project!

Dale Bright
Ottawa

DAY 17

The Restoration of All Things

"The Lord will guide you continually, giving you water when you are dry and restoring your strength." (Isa 58:11)

We have looked at the message of this chapter, seeing that the Lord wants a people who are not religious in an empty way, but who are overflowing with compassion. We have upgraded our faith in the brightness of his light, and have allowed the Spirit to raise us up and to use us for his own purposes, so that the river of light that flows from the church is starting to light up the world. We are able to believe that the church of Christ is of a stature sufficient to take on the evils that hold so many of our sisters and brothers in slavery to fear and deprivation, and that the victory of the cross of Jesus has the power to save nations in a day. All this means that we are no longer hiding, no longer unsure of ourselves. We are so certain of the eternal power of His precious blood that we are determined to see the full harvest of souls brought in to the glory of Jesus Christ. Our loving Father responds by blessing us and constantly restores our strength.

It is good to know that when we are weak or running on empty that the Lord restores our strength. There is something particularly healthy about exhausting our resources in service to others, to those who need God's help, and having him refill our tanks. But there is more to think of here than just the restoration of our individual energy. When the New Testament church is revealed and the Holy Spirit is poured out not on a few individuals but on everyone, Peter preaches to the crowd and thousands are saved and added to their number. Miracles begin to flow as the supernatural origins of the church are revealed, and a lame man is healed at The

Beautiful Gate. As the transformed man dances off into the temple with them, Peter sees a good opportunity to speak to the witnesses. The healing should not be attributed to Peter or John, but to the God of Abraham, Isaac and Jacob. He points them as always to Jesus, encouraging them to express their own faith in his name. Then he declares:

"Now repent of your sins and turn to God, so that your sins may be wiped away. Then times of refreshment will come from the presence of the Lord, and he will again send you Jesus, your appointed Messiah. For he must remain in heaven until the time for the final restoration of all things, as God promised long ago through the prophets." (Acts 3:19-21)

God renews us and restores our strength when we grow weary, weak or discouraged. Peter, though, is speaking at a different level. He is considering here not only the individual but also heaven itself. Not simply the restoration of our stamina, but the restoration of all things. He has in mind the whole of creation and the entirety of time. He is thinking, you might say, of the end of the world as we know it. He is looking up, way up, and seeing the future return of the King. He has deeply convicted his listeners, by telling them that they have killed God's Messiah. Now he tells them that the time will come when God will again send Jesus to a waiting world. Before this happens, we will experience times of refreshing and the restoration of all things. God has promised! We can join our brother Peter in raising our heads and believing for greater things, crying out to the Lord to renew his wonders in our own time. We are not encouraged if the reality is that the church was exciting and powerful only while Jesus was on the planet, and for a short period afterwards. It is not good enough for us to believe that we have all missed the good stuff, that the golden days were millennia ago and that we can only envy that long-ago generation. Neither are we so slow as to blame our own smallness of faith, or foolish enough to think that God has abandoned us because of our sin, or our nation's errors. We have always known that if it has been left up to us that we will always find a way to lose; but because it has always been up to Jesus then the victory is already won! No, the cross of Christ is too powerful to be negated by foolish men, and the blood of Christ is too irresistible to be brought to nothing by our inadequacies. So let us all shout glory to the King and lift our faces to the heavens, expecting nothing less than the restoration of the supernatural impact of the church of Jesus. Look around you. Will anything less be enough?

God is great, and he is in every way good. He only does good things, and works through Jesus and his church to destroy the terrible works of the devil. The evidence of the influence of the evil one is seen in every evil thought and action, with the exaltation of violence, war and division. God hates hatred, and will not allow the success of violent men and women in our time. Jesus destroys pain, sickness, sin and despair, and restores the health, hope and lives of everyone he touches. God loves love, and commands us to recognize all men and women as made in his image, to be our brothers and sisters. God loves us all, and restores us completely, body, soul, mind and spirit. Jude reminds us of this truth.

"God the Father, who loves you and keeps you safe in the care of Jesus Christ. May God give you more and more mercy, peace, and love." (Jude 1:1-2)

He will oppose the proud and take down every brick of every wall that seeks to separate us from his love or from the rest of his world-wide family of faith. He will anoint the peacemakers, encourage the merciful and promote those who live as sacrifices because they are compelled to do so by the mighty love of our Saviour. He will grow our stature by constantly adding more and more mercy, peace, love, forgiveness, faith and kindness to all who look to him. God is good and kind to all, and so we, his children, will be good and kind to all. The world has tried to destroy our unity, to make us afraid and suspicious of strangers. But, with God's help, we are overcoming the world and renewing our hope in the good news that Jesus has come into the world to fill it with himself. God has perfectly revealed himself in his Son Jesus, and shown us his heart by the work that Jesus did. God is great, and he is restoring his people. We are finally remembering in our generation not to accept everything that happens as the will of God. We are waking up to the fact that there is a destroyer at work in our world, and that the church is here to oppose him. It may be that we want to say, "everything happens for a purpose" in life. But, oh, how exciting it is to see a church that is coming into greater maturity so that we can discern the purposes and works of God and reject the purposes and works of the evil one. When lamenting the lack of progress in his readers' lives, the writer to the Hebrews says:

"Solid food is for those who are mature, who through training have the skill to recognize the difference between right and wrong." (Heb 5:14)

So, if God is waking us up, let's all become fully awake. If Jesus had believed that everything happening around him was God's will, and somehow advanced his Father's purpose, then he would have had no work to do. He would have spoken pleasant little sermons, stirring up no opposition and avoiding the final battle at the cross. But Jesus comes in a different understanding, comes to establish the will of his Father on earth as in heaven. He builds up and tears down. He cherishes the will of his Father, and opposes the affects of sin and destroys the works of the devil. Every sick person is restored to health. Dying embers of faith are lovingly fanned into flames. Troubled minds are set free to enjoy peace, and hope shines brightly in the nation. The poor have the good news preached to them, and the outcast is restored to the community.

God is restoring all things, and he is teaching us, calling us, to be involved in ministry that restores lives, minds and bodies. He is continually sending us times of refreshing, not once or twice in a generation, but refreshing that flows like a river. There is indeed a river of life that makes the city of God, and his church, a joyful place. We sincerely sing his praises because he has made us glad, refreshing us by his Holy Spirit. As we look out at a world so often in the grip of violence, fear, poverty and hopelessness, we are not helpless, or without supernaturally potent resources. We are a company of saints who are well able to rebuild, renew and restore our world in the power of the Spirit of Jesus. The apostles who were with Jesus were restoration-minded men, and it is in this light that Jesus looks forward to the powerful outpouring of God the Holy Spirit.

"When the apostles were with Jesus, they kept asking him, 'Lord, has the time come for you to free Israel and restore our kingdom?' (Jesus) replied ... 'you will receive power when the Holy Spirit comes upon you. And you will be my witnesses, telling people about me everywhere ... to the ends of the earth.'" (Acts 1:6-8)

Everyone understood that Jesus wasn't here to arrange the flowers or preach little inspirational messages. The Messiah had come to knock down everything not built by God, and to bring the kingdom of heaven down to earth. God's rule appeared among us when Jesus burst on the scene, his help freely offered, with salvation freely given to all who received Jesus as Lord. Baptism in the Holy Spirit is all about equipping with power a church that is involved in the restoration of our planet. Receive the Holy Spirit into your life and get to work. As the river flows out of you, lives will be restored, walls of salvation will be built, and the valleys will sing with his praise!

~~~~~~~

MEDITATE & MEMORIZE:

Memorize this scripture and speak it out loud as often as you can, taking time to meditate on it and asking the Holy Spirit to open it up for you. Let faith come as you hear your own voice declaring the true word of God.

"Now repent of your sins and turn to God, so that your sins may be wiped away. Then times of refreshment will come from the presence of the Lord, and he will again send you Jesus, your appointed Messiah. For he must remain in heaven until the time for the final restoration of all things, as God promised long ago through the prophets." (Acts 3:19-21)

PRAY & PROCLAIM:

Stand unshakeably in your decision to repent from works that lead to death; turn from sin and put your faith entirely in Jesus alone. Pray that God will bring us into times of refreshing in the fullness of his Holy Spirit that will glorify Jesus and provoke his return. Ask him to revive and restore his people in supernatural power, making us rivers of peace, joy and hope for the nations.

GIVE THANKS & WORSHIP:

Give thanks to God for his servants the prophets, and ask him to embolden those women and men who serve as Christ's prophets today. Worship the Lord who has destined us to live in his glory, bringing the rule of heaven down to earth.

TESTIMONY
Have you heard what God is doing in Ottawa?

A few years after my wife and I moved to Toronto, I found that I was starting to suffer from extreme back pain. At first, we thought it was an injury or some other temporary condition, but it grew progressively worse. Within a year, it got so bad that when I got up in the morning, I had to roll out of bed and crawl to a bath and soak until the pain died down enough to get dressed and go to work. My mobility was severely compromised, and I was unable to bend forward or backwards more than a few degrees. A simple activity like putting on my shoes was an exercise in ingenuity and agony as I attempted to put my shoes on without bending my back. I could not bend my back far enough to scratch my knee from a standing position. I occasionally awoke screaming in pain at night, and developed associated nerve pain that made climbing stairs difficult and painful. Sitting or lying down for longer than a few minutes would aggravate things until I could think of nothing but the pain.

Being quite young, it took a couple years of testing and various medication attempts before I was diagnosed with ankylosing spondylitis, a type of arthritis in the spine. It just hadn't really been considered because of my age. I was referred to a rheumatologist and started treatment and exercises to control the problem. Unfortunately, all of the medications and treatments failed until I was placed on a medication of last resort: a new bio-drug that disables a portion of the immune system. The medication proved effective, and within a couple of months, pain had decreased dramatically. I still had restricted mobility due to fused and damaged vertebrae, but I was nonetheless thanking God for pain free days.

In 2006, we moved from Toronto to Ottawa. I don't really know when or how, but shortly after the move, I noticed that my mobility was completely restored. We had been praying for restoration, but I can't pinpoint a specific time or date for the change. All I knew is that I had gone from being barely capable of scratching my own knees to being able to touch my toes!

A few months after the move, I hurt my back lifting something silly. I went to see my family doctor, and he ordered some X-rays as he was concerned that there was the possibility of further spinal damage due to my history of spondylitis. When the X-rays came back, I went back for a follow-up. By this point, the injury had healed, but the doctor was somewhat shocked and perplexed. He asked me to confirm that I had been diagnosed with ankylosing spondylitis as my medical charts had not yet been transferred from Toronto. I confirmed this again.

The doctor shook his head and said that there was nothing wrong with my spine. At first, I thought that he simply meant that I had not injured it seriously with my lift, which seemed reasonable since it was already feeling better. But he went on. He said that not only was there no sign of any arthritic activity, but there was absolutely none of the old damage and no sign that I had ever had the condition! The bio-drug I had been using has proven highly effective in halting the progress of certain types of arthritis, but what I had experienced was not a halt. It was a complete restoration! I regained all that I had lost, and even the scars and damage that had already occurred were wiped away. My doctor had no explanation, but I know that this was the healing power of Jesus. This was the kind of work that only God can do. I wasn't merely healed. This portion of my body had been restored.

Wesley Roebuck
Ottawa

DAY 18

All the Families on Earth

"Some of you will rebuild the deserted ruins of your cities. Then you will be known as a rebuilder of walls and a restorer of homes." (Isa 58:11)

If we are interested in finding God in our lives, then we should go looking for him in our cities. If it would seem good to you to better understand the heart motivation of your Father in heaven, then we should consider the importance of families: all of them, throughout God's earth. God is big enough and loving enough to keep all the families on earth in his heart, and to have a glorious plan for the future for all creation. When trying to build the community, Paul rebuked false teachers because of the terrible effect they were having on local families.

"They must be silenced, because they are turning whole families away from the truth by their false teaching." (Titus 1:11)

We must fully acknowledge that the Lord of heaven is not content to be allowed free movement only on Sundays, behind the walls of our churches and chapels. He is not a religious God, and we have already seen that he cares more about our living for others than he does about our Sunday morning programs. He is looking to catch us up into his chariot of fire so that we can pick up the pace of revival in the earth, seeing everything through his eyes. As we gain an appreciation for the brightness of the light that he has lit within us, and as we earnestly seek the greater gifts of the Spirit that will build up the church, then we will be an effective means of blessing to every family that we touch. The Spirit of God roams over the whole earth, every day, and his blessing is directed at our homes. In one of the most pivotal passages in all of scripture, God makes a promise to a man described as the father of all who believe, Abram.

"I will make you into a great nation. I will bless you and make you famous, and you will be a blessing to others. I will bless those who bless you and curse those who treat you with contempt. All the families on earth will be blessed through you." (Gen 12:2-3)

Our God is the Lord of heaven and earth, and loves equally all of humanity. He has no respect for division or denomination, is unimpressed by boundaries and borders, and never applies for a visa. He is the breaker of chains, a lover and source of justice and the lifter of the heads of all who are oppressed. He is stunningly good news for those who need him, giving full and satisfying lives to all who call out his name. Everyone on the planet has been made in the image of God, and God promised Abram that you and your family and every family would be blessed.

"For you are all children of God through faith in Christ Jesus. And all who have been united with Christ in baptism have put on Christ, like putting on new clothes. There is no longer Jew or Gentile, slave or free, male and female. For you are all one in Christ Jesus … true children of Abraham … God's promise to Abraham belongs to you." (Gal 3:26-29)

So Jesus came to save all mankind, loving all women and men equally. The promise he made to Abram touches every family, every nation. Abram's promise has been inherited by all who put their faith in Jesus, to all who call out his name to save and help. Isaiah knew that when all of God's people are united into one body, one kingdom, one family—when we all live to please him—restoration will be seen. A world broken and damaged by sin would be rebuilt by the Holy Spirit empowered people of Christ. Renewal would touch and refresh all of society. Everyone hurt by hatred and violence would be healed, restored by the faithful service of Spirit-directed people. The Lord is not directing his power to hide people from the world until they get to heaven. He is sending us out into every part of our world to be its light. The gifts of the Holy Spirit, and the ministries of Christ, are God's method and plan to rebuild broken walls, to restore families. If your life has experienced great loss, know that God has remembered you; Christ has come looking for you; the Holy Spirit will transform and restore your life.

"For this is how God loved the world: He gave his one and only Son, so that everyone who believes in Him will not perish but have eternal life. God sent his Son into the world not to judge the world, but to save the world through him." (John 3:16-17)

Our Father in heaven loves us all and he loves the world we live in. He has held back nothing from us in his desire to help and heal and save us, not even the life of his own Son. You will notice that he is intent on saving each one of us individually ("everyone who believes in Him"), and has his eyes on the whole world ("to save the world through him"). No one is forgotten; no one will be left behind. And yet God's plan for the world has more to it than to save each of us, one at a time. His mighty, loving heart is one of restoration of our homes. Whole communities, every nation can be rebuilt and made whole again. You may worry that this seems impossible when we hear so much about terrible hatred expressed in violent acts. How can the nations be healed? Paul acknowledges the depth of the problem.

"Our lives were full of evil and envy, and we hated each other." (Titus 3:3)

Paul sees the love and mercy of God, expressed in the sacrificial life of Jesus, as a more than sufficient answer.

"He saved us, not because of the righteous things that we had done, but because of his mercy. He washed away our sins, giving us a new birth and new life through the Holy Spirit." (Titus 3:5)

Every one of us can have a completely fresh start, a new birth into a fulfilling life, by putting our faith in God's son Jesus. Make room for him, receive him as your rescuer, and ask him to let his forgiveness and mercy touch you. As to the world, the nations, Jesus gives us hope for the transformation of every society.

The world has access to this same powerful grace, as the nations are healed by the flowing from heaven of the river of life. Don't be concerned about who you are, what you look like, where you live, or whether your thoughts, words or actions have somehow disqualified you. God's mercy is great, and his saving arms are long!

"Put on your new nature, and be renewed as you learn to know your creator and become like him. In this new life, it doesn't matter if you are a Jew or a Gentile, circumcised or

uncircumcised, barbaric, uncivilized, slave or free. Christ is all that matters, and he lives in all of us." (Col 3:10-11)

God is great, and he is restoring all things. He is healing the sick, bringing peace to troubled minds. He is setting us free from slavery to sin. He is banishing hate, refusing to give hateful and divisive beliefs victory, and causing us to love one another faithfully. He has poured out his Spirit and equipped his people with powerful gifts and abilities that their empowered spiritual service might save the nations. He has given us apostles and prophets to be a foundation to a society based on faith and truth in Jesus. He has sent us pastors, teachers and evangelists so that no one will be left unsupported by the Word and the Spirit. The Lord is determined to rebuild broken cities and to restore our love for him and for our neighbours, reversing hate's plan to divide us. Not only the heavens but the earth also will be renewed. Believe with passion in restoration as the overwhelming force in our world. See what the prophets have always seen, and you will be lifted up by the irresistible love, power and mercy of our great God.

"Then I saw a new heaven and a new earth … and I saw the holy city, the new Jerusalem coming down from God out of heaven like a bride beautifully dressed for her husband…And the one sitting on the throne said, 'Look, I am making everything new!'" (Rev 21:1, 2, 5)

~~~~~~

MEDITATE & MEMORIZE:

Memorize this scripture and speak it out loud as often as you can, taking time to meditate on it and asking the Holy Spirit to open it up for you. Let faith come as you hear your own voice declaring the true word of God.

"For you are all children of God through faith in Christ Jesus. And all who have been united with Christ in baptism have put on Christ, like putting on new clothes. There is no longer Jew or Gentile, slave or free, male and female. For you are all one in Christ Jesus … true children of Abraham … God's promise to Abraham belongs to you." (Gal 3:26-29)

PRAY & PROCLAIM:

Proclaim from your heart that God has made one new family out of the many, and that we are without division and full of precious diversity. Pray God's blessing on all your sisters and brothers, all one in Christ Jesus. Claim the promise of God to our father of faith, Abraham, as your own.

GIVE THANKS & WORSHIP:
Worship God as our Father in heaven, and thank him for his covenant love and never-ending grace towards our families.

TESTIMONY

Have you heard what God did in the skies over Eastern Ontario?

Of all the things that have happened to us as believers, nothing has strengthened our convictions and faith in God as much as raising children. As soon as you bring your little helpless baby home, you realize that you are responsible for their care and well-being. However, as most parents soon realize, there are times in which you have very little control over what is happening to your little ones. It's a recipe for some frightening moments and is ultimately a test of what we truly believe about God and, in particular, His sovereignty and love towards us.

This past summer our family had the opportunity to serve at a camp near Bancroft, Ontario. During the day we as parents had responsibilities to develop the staff and oversee the program, so our youngest child (four at the time) was being watched by an amazing young lady whom we trusted wholeheartedly.

One morning, just as the day camp was about to begin, one of our children rushed up to us exclaiming that our youngest hit her head and was now 'sleeping.' We rushed up to the room to find her lying on her back, groggy and disoriented. Apparently the kids were playing on bunk beds in our bedroom and she accidentally smashed her head on the bunk above her. After a few moments of getting her to stay awake, she continued to get worse until we decided we needed to get her to a nearby hospital. From the time we strapped her until about 20 minutes later, she lost consciousness and began to breathe irregularly. Scary stuff. We pulled over and called 911.

A few minutes later the ambulance attendants we examining her. Her eyes were unfocused and pointing in different directions. Her breathing was shallow and laboured. "It doesn't look good" was all they really told us. The head attendant initiated ORNGE, which meant the Ontario Health ambulatory helicopter would meet us at the hospital to fly her to Ottawa for immediate attention.

It was at this point that we had to make some key decisions, the first being, "Do we panic in fear, or do we rest in faith in our Father who has demonstrated time after time His faithfulness?" The second: "Who else do we bring in on this journey?" There are some people who tend to withdraw or hide that bad things are happening to them. I think it is because we never wish to look weak to others: "I'll pull myself together and then share with others my success." We, however, are extremely thankful that we belong to a body of believers with whom we feel free to be vulnerable and can invite to join in faith when things are rough. So in those brief moments, when our little girl was being strapped to a spinal board, unresponsive and in medical crisis, we quickly prayed and then began texting everyone we knew.

When we arrived at the hospital her condition remained unchanged and now all we had to do was wait for the helicopter. Texts began to flood in almost immediately from people everywhere (literally around the world!) who were joining us in faith. Instead of hand-wringing and knotted stomachs, it was restful, an amazing place to be really while on the table in front of you, all the evidence was pointing to things like 'serious head trauma' or 'brain damage.' But that's the bizarreness and beauty of faith; it is handling evidence in a way that lives in your hope in God, with complete confidence in things you can't see.

It was also in that hour of waiting that we received a text from a friend from Norway. Apparently there was an international meeting of leaders which, when they heard the story, stopped and spent a few moments praying together for "this little girl from Canada." That's also a beautiful part of being a believer: our worldwide community of faith which may be separated by geography, language and culture, but stands united on the solid foundation of Jesus' work in all our lives.

The helicopter came (and took mother and daughter to the children's hospital in Ottawa. I am happy to say that as one of us drove back to the camp and the other was enjoying a scenic trip over Eastern Ontario, both of us as parents were resting in what has become our mantra: faith over fear. Our minds could easily have wandered into the murky realm of "what ifs" or doubts, but there was an above-normal peace that took over and governed our thoughts: It's going to be OK; she's going to be just fine.

Once the helicopter safely touched down in Ottawa they were greeted by a crowd of people from the church, which prompted the response from the air ambulance crew, "Are they all here for you?"

Absolutely! When the doctors checked her out she was still a bit groggy but definitely showing signs of improvement. At one point she opened her eyes and proclaimed, "No pain." Within hours she was up and moving around and finally, after the doctors did some tests, she was cleared to go home - and all this in one day! By the next day, our little girl was back at camp, playing happily as if nothing had ever happened, and to this day, there has been no sign that anything that traumatic had happened to her.

Jon and Janie Tenthorey,
Ottawa

DAY 19

A River of Favour: God is on Your Side

"The Spirit of the Sovereign Lord is upon me, for the Lord has anointed me to bring good news to the poor. He has sent me to comfort the broken hearted and to proclaim that captives will be released and prisoners will be freed." (Isa 61:1-2)

"He has sent me to tell those who mourn that the time of the Lord's favour has come." (Luke 4:18-19)

Jesus read this passage from a scroll of Isaiah the prophet handed to him in his hometown synagogue. He told them what he knew to be true of himself - that these words were fulfilled that very day. The Lord had anointed Jesus with a ministry of restoration, and it was good news for those who had nothing. Great news also for the broken hearted, the captive, the prisoner and for those who mourn. The message delivered that day was applied to all people for all time, and is your promise to take hold of. If you have nothing, or feel that your life is empty, then Jesus has come with a message that will satisfy your every need. If your heart is broken, even if you have wondered, 'where is God,' when you needed him, you should know that Jesus has a comfort for you that can bring healing. If you are a captive of a terrible domestic situation, or a prisoner of addiction, or isolated by loneliness and despair, then Jesus has come to snap your chains and set you free.

It may be that you have belonged to God for some time now, having already surrendered your life to Jesus as your Lord and saviour, and life is pretty good. To you also Jesus presents himself as a bringer of continuing good news, that you might live your life in an ever-deepening river of glory. Christians in general are a little hesitant about saying out loud that they had hoped for more than this in life, as they don't want to appear ungrateful after all that Jesus has done. Many of us were quite stunned by the experience of salvation, as it dawned on us that Jesus had totally transformed us as people, granting us the incomparable treasure of becoming children of God! We felt the warm glow of new birth for a while; sometimes, well-meaning people fussed over us, advising us to calm down, or we would be disappointed as the ordinariness of Christian living kicked in. But that was a disservice, and our advisors would have done better to tell us that though salvation is an outstanding experience to go through, that we ain't seen nothing yet! Let's begin to give different advice to new converts. "Get saved by believing in Jesus; get baptized by immersion in water quickly; then the Holy Spirit will fall on you immediately and powerfully; you will receive great power as Jesus' witnesses and the river in flood that is the God of favour will fill every day of your life with the fire of heaven!" We have at times reduced the greatest news in all of history to a scripted rule book, and robbed salvation of its awesomeness. But no more; too many of us have had our eyes opened to the incredible reality of God's freedom poured out on our heads. To all who need him, to all who will believe in him as saviour, good news has arrived: The time of the Lord's favour has come!

Isaiah goes on to speak about God's anger against his enemies, but Jesus stopped before this point. He did this because he knew about the power of restoration that he carried in his body.

"For since our friendship with God was restored by the death of his Son while we were still his enemies, we will certainly be saved through the life of his Son." (Rom 5:10)

Isaiah's message ended with anger for God's enemies. Jesus reading of Isaiah ends with the restoration of friendship with God for his enemies. He didn't come to judge us, or to wreak vengeance on his enemies, because that was all of us, without exception. I have heard some people say that the good news is just too good to be true. But if the good news about Jesus was any less than it is, anger would remain for us all. Allow the fact that the Father's heart is so much greater than yours, and that the river of his mercy is unstoppable, to inspire you and not hold you back any longer. Jesus lived with a restoring anointing, transforming lives and making everyone and everything new.

The prophet continues to describe this glorious restoration of all, this absolute transformation and reversal of fortunes: a beautiful crown instead of death; blessings of joy and praise instead of sadness; the poor rising up like strong trees. Once we were poor, lost, far from God. Now we are like the Lord's own garden, putting down roots into righteousness and bearing fruit that gives him glory. We must never settle for less than this complete transformation wrought by our new birth in the Spirit. God isn't going to improve you a little; he's going to end one life and give you the free gift of a new life in Christ: a new heart, new thinking filled with his word and his Holy Spirit, nation-changers raised up into priestly service by his hand. When I became a Christian it was an exit from a life of religion into a relationship with Jesus, and it took me by surprise. The transformation was a radical one, and I found it to be much more thorough than anything I had experienced in my previous faith life. The power of God to make me his child was revealed, and I was a little unnerved by it, simply because it took a while for me to understand what had happened. I'm glad that it proved to be an encounter with a living, active God now of course, as it leaves my life in the hands of a God who knows what he is doing, and who has unlimited power to keep moving that transformation forward. If you are yet to begin, then I encourage you to go for it. Surrender your old life to him with sincere repentance and faith, and, after he has separated you from the power of your old life through water baptism, he will fill you with his own Holy Spirit and take you on an adventure. He will give you a brand new life; he will then live it with you at a bewildering pace, all to the glory of Jesus.

Again the prophet declares that those restored and renewed by Jesus, born again of the Spirit, will themselves be caught up in the work of restoration.

"They will rebuild the ancient ruins, repairing cities destroyed long ago. They will revive them, though they have been deserted for many generations." (Isa 61:4)

This new life that God gives to everyone who receives his Son transforms us into skilled rebuilders of ruined communities, bringing the genuine hope of a fresh start to all that we talk to about Jesus. The God of revival makes us to be like him, revivers of cities long deserted. How inspiring is it to you, as you see violent men and women destroying communities, killing the innocent and erasing culture, to be caught up in a saving work of restoration? Cities emptied of people and hope will be busy again with new life as the church of Christ goes about the work of rebuilding, renewing and revival! Don't give the devil one second of hope that his destruction will go unopposed—the army of God is on the move against him. A new life has begun, and Jesus people will live that life to the full!

"*This means that anyone who belongs to Christ has become a new person. The old life is gone; a new life has begun!*" (2 Cor 5:17)

Jesus restores our friendship with God by taking our old lives with him into the tomb. Our old lives aren't improved a bit; they are gone! The lives we live now are new lives, newly begun, and lived by the power of the Spirit of Jesus. If we will put our faith in Jesus in this way, then he will give us the power to reach the whole world with this same transformative message about Christ. All of us will be called priests and ministers of God, as we live not for ourselves, but for him. The whole world will see it.

"*Everyone will realise that they are a people the Lord has blessed.*" (Isa 61:9)

The whole earth will become aware of the glory of the Lord, as the rivers of life flowing out of God's people soak the earth as do the waters that cover the oceans. Let the river of his Spirit flow freely in your life, and join with all your brothers and sisters in soaking all peoples with God's transforming love. Don't hold back on the floodwaters that fill you. Give the Lord a mighty shout of praise and let the rivers of the water of life flow out of you to all around you. Live your life joyfully, in recognition of how much he has blessed us all, and that very joy will be infectious. The good news has turned out to be even better than we were told; build a road in your life that Jesus can walk on, a highway of holiness that he can use to bring freedom to every captive and renewed hope to those who have no hope. Above all else let your life be filled to overflowing with the immense love of our Father in heaven. We must worship God and pray without ceasing, growing daily in faith in his every word. But it is our love for each other and for our neighbours, even our enemies, which will let the nations know that Jesus is truly Lord of all. An absence of anger and suspicion is not enough to show God's glory to all; we must be understood and received as unstoppable rivers of love to everyone that looks at the church of Jesus.

When Jesus finished reading and rolled up the scroll, he looked piercingly at those attending that day. He told them, as they looked at him, that the word of God had been fulfilled! I have, on several occasions, heard Christians who were disgruntled over various things quote their favourite proverb:

"*Hope deferred makes the heart sick.*" (Pro 13:12)

I have heard that scripture applied so often, too often, and it now tends to make my heart sick just to hear it. The truth is, that as soon as Jesus declared that the scripture about the Lord's favour being available to all had been fulfilled, everything changed. The ending of the proverb has now come into our world; His coming changed everything and ushered a jubilee year that will never end.

"But a dream fulfilled is a tree of life." (Prov 13:12)

Everything is really about Jesus, the beginning, middle and end. He has fulfilled all the righteous dreams of humanity in himself, and given us renewed access to the tree of life. All the scriptures are about him, and his is the only name by which we can be saved. He is a courageous saviour whose love is covenantal, unfailing. He is righteous and good and wins justice for the oppressed. He has reconciled us to our Father, and he will never leave us again. He is faithful and true. And in the coming of Jesus into this broken world, filled so often with greed, guilt and selfishness, a transformation has been achieved. Jesus in this world is a dream come true, a dream fulfilled that is a tree of life to us. The river of God is flowing from God's throne, and beside it grows that very tree whose leaves are sufficient for the healing of the nations.

So don't live for yourself any longer. Jesus has come into your life, and he is a dream of good news fulfilled. Let his Spirit lead you into his ministry of love, encouragement and the restoration of friendship with God, your perfect Father.

~~~~~~~

MEDITATE & MEMORIZE:

Memorize this scripture and speak it out loud as often as you can, taking time to meditate on it and asking the Holy Spirit to open it up for you. Let faith come as you hear your own voice declaring the true word of God.

"They will rebuild the ancient ruins, repairing cities destroyed long ago. They will revive them, though they have been deserted for many generations." (Isa 61:4)

PRAY & PROCLAIM:

Take some time to ask God to put particular people, situations and places on your heart; now begin to pray restoration, rebuilding and revival over them. Proclaim that you have been empowered as a rebuilder of ancient ruins, and given authority from heaven to lift up the oppressed and remove chains from the captives.

GIVE THANKS & WORSHIP:

Thank your Father for never giving up on anyone, for refusing to give ground to the enemy. Thank him that he is Lord of all the nations, and that all families of the earth are in his care. Worship him as the true God who loves his children unceasingly.

TESTIMONY
Have you heard what God is doing in Ottawa?

The church in Ottawa to which I belong has a number of song writers and an exceptional spirit of worship in the people. One song, written by my friend Noah Bright, has always helped me to feel close to God. The song words are given here, with an introduction from the composer.

MY GLORIOUS KING

I know the Lord is always with me
I will not be shaken
For He is right beside me
(repeat)

No wonder my heart is filled with joy
No wonder my life is filled with peace
No wonder I'm overcome with love

For the King of kings
My mouth will shout His praise
He's the Lord of Glory
 Zion will proclaim,
"He's alive forever"
My hope now rests in Him
My Glorious King

Written by: Noah Patrick Bright (2002) (noahpatrick@rogers.com)

This song arose when a friend of mine emailed me a scripture: Psalm 16:8-11 (NLT). It resonated deeply with me at the time (and still does). I had heard the phrase "I know the Lord is always with me" several times throughout my life and the profound importance of that truth had become a bit stale. It was the first line of verse 9 that really opened my eyes again. It was David's response to this truth that truly gripped my heart,"No wonder my heart is glad, and I rejoice". No wonder. As if there could be any other response to

His promise. That is the foundation of this song. That no matter what happens, the Lord is with me. Therefore, no wonder my heart is filled with joy even in the face of tragic situations. No wonder my life is filled with peace even in the midst of stressful circumstances. No wonder I'm overcome with love for my King when the world around me is in chaos. No wonder I have hope in the face of impossible looking situations. No wonder I am confident when the storms of life arise. No wonder. For if my God is for me, then who could ever be against me? He is alive and in control of all things. He is alive and He reigns on high. My mouth will shout His praise.

Noah Bright
Ottawa

DAY 20

The River in Flood

"In the west, people will respect the name of the Lord; in the east, they will glorify him. For he will come like a raging flood tide driven by the breath of the Lord." (Isa 59:19)

    The context of Isaiah 58 is not a particularly happy one as the prophet once again chides the people about their inexcusable sinfulness. He declares the unchangeable nature of God, who is strong enough, present enough, loving enough to save his people; it is their sin that has cut them off from the river of God. He has not ceased to care, though he has turned his back on them. He has not grown old or deaf, though he has stopped listening to their prayers. Their hands are dirty, and their mouths are filled with lies. Once again Isaiah laments the falling away of a love of righteousness in what should be a holy people. But in this verse he is lifted by the vision of God himself coming to rescue the lost, raising up his own trumpet voice in defence of the oppressed. If no one else will respond to his chastisement and change their ways, then God will do the work himself.

    In our own days we are hearing remarkable accounts from around the world of people who are seeing visions of Jesus, come to preach the good news about himself! We hear recounted extraordinary stories of Jesus suddenly appearing in the bedrooms and kitchens of people who live in countries closed to the free preaching of the good news. We can allow ourselves to be provoked in at least two different ways by these accounts: We can jump up and shout our praise to our loving Father, a great God who will reach out with his grace and mercy directly from his throne, with his own mighty arm. We can also jump up and shout, "Here I am, send me, I'll come with you!" This heaven-centred activity is of course pointing to the central moment of history, when heaven opened above our heads and our good Father, consumed with love for the world, sent his own beloved Son to take the initiative to save us all.

God is not restricted by the action or inaction of his church in setting the world free from its slavery to sin. He does not stay out of the fight when we lose our way and fail to heal, deliver, raise the dead, or preach Jesus with boldness. If we are a little busy at our meetings and programs, pursuing our own personal sanctification and hoping for more excitement in our gatherings, then he will shake himself and step in to save those who cry out for help. But I do not for a second believe that this will be our fate, as I see so many saints rising up with the same passion that God clothes himself in, stepping forward and dedicating their lives to serving Jesus in the fullness of the power of the Holy Spirit. We have in our own hearts that deep desire to see God glorified in the west and in the east; it is the passion of God to see his Son Jesus respected throughout the earth, with all being aware of his Kingly glory, and he has given that same passion to his servants. I believe that this is a generation that is capable of being set on fire with the word of God, motivated not by selfish ambition but by the need to see God exalted across the planet. And because we realize that Jesus isn't revealed to us as a celebrity, but as a sacrificial saviour, we will know what our work is to be. Jesus is a giver of sight to the blind; he restores hope to the hopeless, freedom to every captive, justice to the down-trodden. He doesn't need his name in lights, but he has come to save us from sin, to remove chains, to break our captive bonds, to heal our minds and bodies, and to take us safely home. The saints of God, driven along by the strong currents of the river of the Holy Spirit, will do the same works, and greater. In our opening verse, Isaiah almost seems to be describing the most troubling aspects of our own time when he declares:

"All their activity is filled with sin, and violence is their trademark." (Isa 59:6)

In our own generation the daily news seems to be so often dominated by sinful, hateful activity and merciless, godless violence. Despots cling to personal power at terrible cost to their own people. Nations fail as cities crumble and basic services come to an end. Rulers lead their people into division and war while making themselves rich. Strong nations use their strength to dominate weaker ones rather than to shelter them, and military power is exalted over mercy. The peaceful lives of the innocent are shattered by bombs and bullets, and whole communities fall into suspicion and fear.

God has given us big hearts; the devil is trying to get us to trade them in for hearts so tiny that the Grinch begins to look compassionate by comparison! So, will you get out of this evil river of division and leap into God's river of life, with its copious supply of food and life enough for all, and with leaves that will heal our nations? Where are the lovers of righteousness? Where can we find justice for all inhabitants of the earth? Who will provide refuge to the widow, the orphan, the dispossessed? The joy of living has been taken from too many, and the dream of restoration has been reversed. For so many women and girls around the world, freedom has been exchanged for captivity, abuse has replaced the honouring that they deserve. The poor are exploited, not helped, as the rich seek salvation in ever-increasing riches. All these sins and more keep us from swimming in God's river of life, and he is displeased with his world.

"We have turned our backs on our God, and we know how oppressive we have been." (Isa 59:13)

The first thing that God does is to judge our lack of care, or inaction as a society. The second thing he does is to stir himself and all his saints who are willing to intervene.

"He was amazed to see that no one intervened to help the oppressed. So he himself stepped in to save them with his strong arm, and his justice sustained him." (Isa 59:16)

The church is on the earth to show an expression of how God rules among his people. We are a kingdom people, a holy nation, and we belong to God. We reveal his nature to the world by showing unfailing love, by promoting justice, and by helping all people in their troubles. Our goal is not to be raptured out of a hurting world, but to see the nations filled with God's glory, saved by the righteous actions of Jesus the King. This generation wants to see God amazed at our godly actions, not our failure to intervene. We want to hear shouts from heaven as the kingdom people of God stir themselves to greater faith for the nations. We will not sit back, shaking our heads at terrorism and the rise of hatefulness. We will stand up and get involved, using our Spirit-given gifts not only to bless the saints in private, but to change the flow of history so that everyone can join in singing praises to God. Jesus Christ has come to save the lost, not abandon them, and that is why he has saved us and poured out his Spirit upon us. God himself has stepped in to help and to save, and all who believe are swept along by his mighty outpouring. The Lord cares; God is love.

"He (has) wrapped himself in a cloak of divine passion." (Isa 59:17)

So don't underestimate the Lord's determination to promote righteousness. We are not waiting for heaven, but many oppressed people are waiting for the church to stir itself on their behalf. The prophet declares that all will see his glorious strength and come to respect his zealous power. When God is on the move he is unstoppable. When the church is stirred we are a formidable foe to the enemy of our souls. And when the river of the waters of life flow unhindered out of our hearts, we are a hope to the oppressed, a relief for the downtrodden. God is stirring himself to intervene in our time, and the floodwaters are taking his people with him.

"For he will come like a raging flood tide, driven by the breath of the Lord." (Isa 59:19)

God made a covenant promise, an unbreakable agreement, that no flood would ever again destroy the earth. He made this promise to Noah, and confirmed it by giving the sign of the rainbow to all the creatures on earth. God has once again in our day flooded the earth, and the result will be life, not death. He has poured out his Spirit upon all people, and the waters are rising. This deluge of the Spirit across the world is driven along by God's own breath – and the bible tells us exactly what that breath is.

"All Scripture is inspired by God (literally 'God-breathed') and is useful to teach us what is true, and to make us realize what is wrong in our lives. It corrects us when we are wrong and teaches us to do what is right. God use it to prepare and equip his people to do every good work." (2 Tim 3:16-17)

The Lord is intervening directly in our world by his Spirit, and through his Spirit-filled people. Moved by the Spirit, we are driven along by God's breathed-out word, the scriptures. Nahum stood on firm ground when he declared the goodness of God and the power of his flood.

"The Lord is good, a strong refuge when trouble comes. He is close to those who trust in him. But he will sweep away his enemies in an overwhelming flood." (Nahum 1:7-8)

Rise up, people of God, and remember the victims of hate, violence, hunger, and poverty in the world that the Father loves. Sense the stirring of an intervening God, and get caught up in the flood waters of justice. Be swept along by that river of righteous living, and care for your neighbours. The Lord of heaven has not abandoned the earth, and neither will his kingdom people. You can rely on our covenant-keeping God.

"And this is my covenant with them' says the Lord. 'My Spirit will not leave them, and neither will these words I have given you. They will be on your lips and on the lips of your children and your children's children forever. I, the Lord, have spoken!'" (Isa 59:21)

~~~~~~~

MEDITATE & MEMORIZE:
Memorize these scriptures, and speak them out loud as often as you can, taking time to meditate on them and asking the Holy Spirit to open them up for you. Let faith come as you hear your own voice declaring the true word of God.

"He was amazed to see that no one intervened to help the oppressed. So he himself stepped in to save them with his strong arm, and his justice sustained him." (Isa 59:16)

"He (has) wrapped himself in a cloak of divine passion." (Isa 59:17)

PRAY & PROCLAIM:
See the world full of people in their need, and pray for God's mercy on all. Intercede for those nations that are suffering from the violence of greedy and hate-filled men, those living in troubled lands, and in failing communities. Let your compassion be stirred, with love triumphing over division. Now proclaim the good news of Jesus Christ over every situation, asking that Jesus leave no one behind in his mission to save and to heal. Proclaim that all God's daughters are your sisters and that all God's sons are your brothers. Pray that your own city be filled with a restored knowledge of the glory of the Lord.

GIVE THANKS & WORSHIP:
Worship the God who has clothed himself with a passion that the weak should be made strong; worship him by looking for situations and people in your life that you can have the same passion to serve and help. Thank the Holy Spirit for making you a breaker of chains, and a destroyer of prison doors.

TESTIMONY

Have you heard what God is doing in Ottawa?

"God, what is your plan for my life? Show me something, just a little sign, to help me know that you're there and you're with me." This was my prayer one winter's day. I was recently married, without a job or even a work permit, and I was starting to wonder if God really had a plan for me.

God definitely heard my prayer that day and he answered me. Twice. After praying, I prepared myself to go out and run a few errands. While waiting at the bus stop I got a text from a friend and mentor who had just moved out of town. It said "God is with you and He has a good plan for you. You are going to do great things in the Kingdom of God. And you've married a good woman who loves God and is going to support and encourage you." I looked up and around me, half expecting to see my friend standing there. Had he been in my house that morning? How did he know exactly what I had been praying about? I breathed a quiet thank you to God. "You're there. You heard. I got it."

But God wasn't done yet. He wanted to make sure that I really understood. I went to the mall and did my errands and as I was heading back to the bus stop, a total stranger stopped me. He said "You prayed this morning, asking for a little sign. Is that right?" Surprised, I said "yes." He then handed me a twenty dollar bill saying, "This is a sign from God. He wants you to know that he heard your prayer and that everything is going to be alright."

Since that day I don't doubt God's promises or his plan. I know that I don't have to worry about the future because he will always provide for me. "The Lord is my shepherd; I have all that I need" (Psa 23:1).

David Rukundo,
Ottawa

Part Six:

EZEKIEL'S RIVER

DAY 21

Ezekiel's River

"In my vision, the man brought me back to the entrance of the temple. There I saw a stream flowing…" (Ezek 47:1)

Jesus ascended into heaven after spending time with his disciples following his death and resurrection. He instructed them to wait for the coming of the promised Holy Spirit, who would be their constant guide. For those extraordinary weeks, Jesus focused on instructing his disciples on how God's government would actually work on earth. He provided the practical details of how his work of seeking out the lost, and the ongoing work of saving and healing, would continue until the whole earth was reached. Jesus did not birth a religious system or a way of holding church meetings; he didn't tell them that he had prepared a cave for them to hide in until their mansions were ready. He talked to them about the Kingdom of God.

Ezekiel didn't see a pool of stagnant water; he saw a stream that kept on flowing, kept on getting deeper the further away from the entrance that it travelled. The promise of God here is that as we reach out beyond our current boundaries to tell everyone the good news that Jesus has done enough to save us, his river of life will grow ever deeper in us every day. For some of us that will mean getting over our shyness and telling someone that we are a Christian, and that we know Jesus as a friend. For others it will mean reaching out to groups of people who are different from us, refusing to live out our entire lives with people who look and think exactly as we do, accepting and valuing many new neighbours.

For others it will mean new ministries bursting seemingly out of nowhere, ministries of Christ that he has kept hidden in the palm of his hand until now. For many it will mean raising our eyes to the horizon and seeing something more than our nation, or our continent, or our language or economic group; it will mean joining those disciples and listening to Jesus as he talks to us about the Kingdom that is filling the earth. The image that the prophet sees shows him the river of life that starts inside the temple throne room of God then flows outwards through the entrance that is Jesus, the gate of the sheepfold, growing deeper with the years and with distance until, in our day, it spreads out to cover the whole earth. This vision of the temple thus changes our perspective dramatically; it is no longer a place that we would long to go into, but cannot because of our great sin. It has become in Jesus a place where the healing, saving river of his life blood flows outward to cover the whole world. The life and holiness and glory of the Most Holy Place, once a place of death to us, now flows outwards to the ends of the earth. We rejoice that the veil of the temple was torn from top to bottom as the work of the cross was accomplished, as it gives us complete confidence to rush into the place where God lives. But we also see with Ezekiel that outwards through the torn veil rushes the very life of God, sufficient power to heal the nations, a great tsunami of mercy, hope and joy, as the blood of Christ shouts "forgiveness, forgiveness!" (Heb 12:24 NLT) to the four corners of the world that he loves so much. Expecting a deluge of judgement, we are instead inundated with a flood of forgiveness and love from heaven.

Jesus' work was one of rescuing individuals by his love and mercy, lifting suffering, sin, and sickness from their shoulders and carrying them off on his own. His work was one of restoring the nations of the earth. To achieve this end he sent to us as a constant companion: God the Holy Spirit.

"When the Spirit of truth comes, he will guide you into all truth. He will not speak on his own but will tell you what he has heard. He will tell you about the future." (John 16:13)

In just the same way that the Holy Spirit is given to us as a guide and teacher about the kingdom, Ezekiel is given a guide from heaven. He also is there to describe the future to his prophet, and it all centres on the entrance to the Temple. How do you feel about the future? It is a key question, and one that we need to ask ourselves frequently as a check on our faith towards God. Do you face the future with fear, with a sense of approaching tribulation and impending doom? Are you expecting that the children of faith will dwindle and diminish, as the blood-cleansed citizens of the Kingdom suffer defeat? Or are you just a little stirred up as you consider Christ's heroic love, as you contemplate his suffering, and try to comprehend the precious value of every drop of his blood, given for us? There are many of you who look at these things and find that there is fire in your bones, flames of fire on your head, and a love for Jesus that will not let you give up, that makes it impossible to stay silent. There are believers in the land who consider the works of God's hands, and who would give anything to exalt the sacrifice of Jesus on the cross. Just as the Holy Spirit moves over the nations determined that the blood of Jesus should have its full effect, so there are multitudes of Christians filled with that very Spirit who want to stand and shout that there is power in the blood of Jesus to cleanse, to forgive and to save all who call on his name! That's the truth that the Holy Spirit is guiding us into; let him be your guide and he will show you a future where Jesus Christ is Lord of all.

Ezekiel's vision shows a work of transformation that will touch every aspect of life and every corner of society. The land will be used differently, with each tribe receiving an equal share, with the way into the temple and the river of life that flows outwards from it at its heart. Old arrangements are swept away, and a new creation is revealed. We are lost if we retreat from our conviction that Jesus still has power in his name sufficient to transform and restore the fortunes of every people across the planet. You believe that everything you see in his creation came about as he spoke words of transformation from heaven; is it too hard a thing to believe that the greater power that is present in speaking his name can bring salvation and a new creation into the lives of multitudes? If you believe that God created all things by his word, then prove it in our generation by saying the name of Jesus and watching as the new creation is revealed. God said "let there be light"(Gen 1:3) and there was light! We say, 'in the name of Jesus Christ' and people are saved, bodies are healed, devils flee, and justice touches our communities! The glory of God is seen in the creation that is there because of his word; this generation of saints and godly ministers will show the greater glory of the new creation that is there because of the Word himself, Jesus Christ the King. All eyes are on the door into the place where God lives, and all life flows from that entrance.

"Jesus told (Thomas) 'I am the way, the truth and the life. No one can come to the Father except through me.'" (John 14:6)

On another occasion, Jesus specifically called himself the gate, the only entrance into the Temple where God lives.

"I tell you the truth, I am the gate for the sheep ... those who come in through me will be saved.

They will come and go freely and will find good pastures." (John 10: 7, 9)

So, whichever guide you listen to, the one sent from heaven for Ezekiel or the Holy Spirit sent from heaven for all of us, all eyes are directed to the entrance of God's dwelling place. Let your eyes be directed onto that gate, and consider Jesus, the origin and perfecter of our faith. If we are to be truly nation changers, then every believer's eye needs to be focused on that entrance into God's holy presence. Only Jesus can lead us on, only he can give us the gift of eternal, overflowing life. The entire work of the Holy Spirit is to keep us on track with the words and work of our leader, Jesus Christ.

"He will bring me glory by telling you whatever he receives from me. All that belongs to the Father is a mine; that is why I said 'The Spirit will tell you whatever he receives from me.'" (John 16: 14-15)

Ezekiel, in his vision, allowed himself to be led by his guide, humbly submitting to his teaching. As the church submits to the leading of the Holy Spirit, as we give ourselves over to all that he speaks to us about Jesus, we will stay in life. We should understand that following the guidance of the Holy Spirit in our Sunday morning meetings is mostly practice for when game-time arrives. Knowing what song or scripture should come next, or judging a word of prophecy, is just a way of warming up the servants of Christ who are destined to reach the nations. We never learn the names of athletes who work out but never compete. It's the runner who crosses the finish line at high speed who is memorable. We all know the name of Jesus because he completed his work, able to declare with conviction, "it is finished" (John 19:30). Similarly, Paul is happy to confirm:

"I have fought the good fight, I have finished the race, and I have remained faithful." (2 Tim 4:7)

Our lives before God are not a spectator sport, filled with observations of the efforts of others. We are all in it to win it, and the prize is the salvation of humanity and the glory of God. Let us live with purpose, live to help others find God's grace. And let's do that by allowing our guide to keep our attention focused on the gate of the sheepfold, the entrance to God's Temple.

"Since we are surrounded by such a huge crowd of witnesses to the life of faith, let us strip off every weight that slows us down, especially the sin that so easily trips us up. And let us run with endurance the race God has set before us. We do this by keeping our eyes on Jesus, the champion who initiates and perfects our faith." (Heb 12:1-2)

Our guide from heaven is keeping our eyes fixed on Jesus, the perfecter of our faith. It comes as no surprise to us that Jesus is the gateway into God's presence, begins and perfects our faith, is our champion in all things, and is the life that flows outward to us all.

"Then I saw a stream, flowing…" (Ezek 47:1)

We are left in no doubt that there is a river of healing, a river of life flowing out from beneath the entrance to the temple. There is life flowing out of heaven capable of transforming our troubled world into a well-watered garden. There is a river of water and precious blood flowing out of Jesus' tortured body that can wash us clean and deliver us back to our loving Father. There is life in heaven, flowing from heaven's door, and we can swim in it. The waters are freely given to anyone who will declare their thirst to Jesus, and we are to drink without measure.

"Don't be drunk with wine, because that will ruin your life. Instead, be filled with the Holy Spirit." (Eph 5:18)

In this busy, exciting, troubled world, there is a lot to look at, many things that fill and claim our time. So we need to make a deliberate, serious decision to orient our lives towards the entrance of the temple, out of which the river of life flows. We need to acknowledge and welcome the Holy Spirit as our advocate, counsellor and guide. He will keep our eyes fixed on Jesus because his eyes never stray from contemplating his face. The Spirit will keep us centred on the Son, and build up our faith in the power of his name. The Holy Spirit will keep us in the stream that flows from under the throne of God and of the Lamb, until it knocks us off our feet forever. Let the flowing of his river transform your life and make your service before the Lord effective. Without that river, nothing works, and our crops are dried out and ruined.

"And the people's joy has dried up with them." (Joel 1:12)

But when that river flows, the world changes. If your life has dried up and you can see no fruit, then fix your eyes on the gateway to the Temple, jump by faith into the river, and see what your God will do for you. The Lord will pour out his Spirit without measure on us all, and we will all be transformed by the fullness of the provision of our great God.

"In that day the mountains will drip with sweet wine, and the hills will flow with milk. Water will fill the streambeds of Judah, and a fountain will burst forth from the Lord's Temple." (Joel 3:18)

~~~~~~~

MEDITATE & MEMORIZE:

Memorize this scripture and speak it out loud as often as you can, taking time to meditate on it and asking the Holy Spirit to open it up for you. Let faith come as you hear your own voice declaring the true word of God.

"Since we are surrounded by such a huge crowd of witnesses to the life of faith, let us strip off every weight that slows us down, especially the sin that so easily trips us up. And let us run with endurance the race God has set before us. We do this by keeping our eyes on Jesus, the champion who initiates and perfects our faith." (Heb 12:1-2)

PRAY & PROCLAIM:

Proclaim this scripture as true in your own life: "I'm not going to slow down, I'm rejecting sin, I'm going to love everyone, and I'm running faster each day after Jesus!" Proclaim that Jesus is the champion, and that he is perfecting your faith not as you sit still but as you run! Pray that every time you say, "in Jesus' name" that new creation will be seen all around you to the glory of God. Salvation, healing, miracles and glory will fill your family, your friends, your community, until the whole earth can see it with you.

GIVE THANKS & WORSHIP:

Worship God, Father, Son and Holy Spirit today. Thank them for remembering you, and for washing you in the unstoppable river of life that flows out of the temple through

Jesus. Worship Jesus for giving his life for you, and tell him that you are going to live to the full for him. Surrender yourself into the control of this rushing river of his Spirit, and give thanks to Jesus for bequeathing you his precious peace.

TESTIMONY
Have you heard what God did in Peterborough?

During a bout of pneumonia, I experienced severe, sharp chest pains. An x-ray revealed my right lung was collapsed. My doctor said I would have to be on antibiotics forever and see a respirologist right away. On my way home I felt discouraged with this diagnosis and I remember telling the Lord that I could not be sick because I had a business to manage. My daughter dropped by to see how I was and she reminded me of James 5:14 which says if anyone is sick he should call the church leaders and ask them to pray over him and anoint him with oil in the name of Jesus.

Encouraged by this, I called right away. They asked if I could wait till the Sunday morning service when Steve Best would be back home from Norway. That suited me just fine. On Sunday morning we exalted the Lord and just before the time to pray, Steve said he wanted to tell about something that happened in Norway.

He said, "A man from the church in Norway came up to me and said a lady from my church was going to come to me and ask for healing. And when she comes and asks for healing that God will heal her. And he said, "God will restore everything just like that. She will come and ask particularly that you will pray for her.' I said, 'What is her name?" He pronounced her name as Joanie. He asked "Do you have a Joanie?" I said, "We don't have a Joanie."' He said, "I am never wrong in these things!" I asked "So how do you spell Joanie?" He said, "J-O-A-N-N-E." "This week Jo Anne Fallaise called and asked for prayer for a collapsed lung. The Lord moves in miraculous ways."

My hope for God to move was strong that morning and after hearing this story, I was totally amazed and jumping up and down on the inside. Then Steve prayed, anointed me with oil and people laid hands on me. I was so blessed by the prayers and the love I felt, but physically I did not feel any different yet. However, I knew God was working and I began thanking Him for healing me. As others were prayed for a lady from our church came to me and said that the Lord had told her to come and teach me how to breathe with my new lung. She showed me some exercises, which I continued to do each day, and also I kept on thanking the Lord for healing me even though I did not see the evidence.

It took about a week for the pain to gradually leave and I felt wonderful spiritually and physically. I still had to keep my appointment with the respirologist a week later, which involved x-rays. I was excited to tell him about my healing and my heart was soaring as he listened politely. But all he said was, "Let's just see what the x-rays show". I was sure they would show two healthy lungs....but they did not! I told the doctor that even though the lung looked collapsed, I still believed I was healed. He was always nice about it and smiled as he told me to come back in 6 weeks. This scenario continued for about a year with the x-rays never changing. I never stopped believing and I was enjoying good health with no pain. Finally, he told me to not come back as there was nothing more he could do to help me.

That was 15 years ago and my lungs continue to function well. Routine x-rays over the years now show no collapsed lung. At 81 years old, I am enjoying life with my good husband filled with the joy of grand and great grandchildren. I am forever grateful for God's Goodness.

Jo Anne Fallaise,
Peterborough

DAY 22

Seeing the Stream: Living with Your Eyes Open

"Then I saw a stream flowing…" (Ezek 47:1)

One need that is often expressed by God's people is their hunger to hear him more clearly and to be able to see into and participate in the workings of the Spirit. Jesus' declaration that the Father shows him everything can seem to make our situation even worse, as we feel unable to see what he saw every day.

"Jesus explained, 'I tell you the truth, the Son can do nothing by himself. He does only what he sees the Father doing. Whatever the Father does, the Son also does. For the Father loves the son and shows him everything he is doing. In fact, the Father will show him how to do even greater works than healing this man. Then you will truly be astonished.'" (John 5:19-20)

We, as his children, long to live our lives in just the same way. How can we grow to greater maturity in this ability to see? Firstly, we must at least try to swallow down this enormous and counter-intuitive truth, that Jesus could do nothing by himself. Jesus said so, and declared that he was telling the truth, so we believe it. Jesus Christ, fully man and fully God, could do nothing by himself, though he rules the universe by his word and power. Let's think about this reality together, and try to be sure that we are learning the correct lesson from Jesus, so that we can devote ourselves to living in the same way as he did. We give great attention, as we should, to the fruits of the Spirit, and to developing and modelling Christian character, as we long to be like Jesus. That's why so many ask themselves daily, "what would Jesus do?" But here is a whole new area, unrelated to our ongoing character development, in which we yearn to be like Jesus, this ability to see what God is doing in real time.

The first distinction is an obvious one, that there is a great difference between hearing Jesus ask, "What would the Father do?" and observing him looking into the supernatural to ask, "What is my Father doing?" Each day he was confronted with a sea of sick and oppressed people, and he loved them and was moved to do something for them by his great compassion for those sheep without a shepherd. He took away their sins and carried off their sicknesses; he exercised his governmental rule, knowing that as long as he was in a situation that he was the man in charge. He knew that his mission was to ease people's burdens and bring God's favour into every life. If he had asked only, "what would the Father do here?" then the answer would have been obvious, and no further looking into the supernatural world would have been needed. He healed them all, and offered forgiveness and fullness of life to everyone who received him.

The Father loves to destroy the works of the evil one as much as Jesus does and as much as the Holy Spirit does. Taking away the sins of the world, carrying off all our diseases, breaking the chains that bind us and breaking open the prison doors: that's simply who God is, his nature expressed in action. But if we hear Jesus, surrounded by multitudes, seeing daily the same crushing need, asking, 'what is my Father doing today?' then we understand that Jesus sees more than sin, sickness, and endless need surrounding him. He sees a stream, flowing. He sees Godly authority exerting kingdom rule. He reaches out to people, and they reach out to him, touching his clothes, and a river flows out of him, having its origin under the throne of his Father. We see the need, but Jesus sees the solution, understanding not just the inclination and will of a distant God but the constant, sacrificial flowing of life.

My wife and I recently spent a weekend with our closest friends during which we stood by a fast-flowing river that descended into a gushing waterfall into the valley below, surrounded by the awesome beauty of the fall colours of the many trees that surrounded us. Fish were rushing to leap up through the turbulent waters, to ascend through the rapids to lay their eggs and secure a future generation. It would not have made any sense for us to gaze at this scene and ask ourselves, "what would a river do?" The river was there, right in front of us, rushing by and bringing life to everything it touched in its journey. So instead we were able to joyfully admire the river that we could see, flowing down with all of its power and life.

Jesus can see a river of the Holy Spirit flowing out of the heart of each one of us, from our innermost selves, and it's the same stream that Ezekiel saw. It's a longer way downstream by now, of course, and so it is wider, deeper and irresistibly powerful, washing away sin, breaking prisoners free and healing every sickness. Seeing what is happening in the supernatural is not like looking for ghosts; it is not a game of hide and seek. It is the certain knowledge that someone extraordinary has come into the fight, that the highway of holiness has been used to usher in the arrival of a mighty Saviour, that the power of God is let loose in the world. Jesus can do nothing by himself, because he is never by himself, and he is joyfully aware of the power of the river flowing from the heart of his Father. The river of God is real, and it dominates the attention of Jesus. One key, then, to seeing into the spiritual is to be aware that we can do nothing by ourselves, but that we are surrounded always by the active ministry of someone else who is our constant companion and guide. The river of the Holy Spirit is bursting out of you. Can you see it?

So, make some appropriate decisions in your life. Stop trying too hard in your Christian journey; it always has been and always will be too difficult for you. Don't ever try to be someone else; you will be even less good at it than they are. You can have heroes and role models in faith and ministry, but don't try to be them. Stop talking and thinking about your failures, your less-than-stellar history, your embarrassments, your doubts and your many weaknesses. We understand that you are as human as we are, but all these supposed limitations seem trivial to us compared to the extraordinary stream of power that Jesus has caused to flow out of your newly created life by saving you and filling you with his Spirit. Jesus is the Son of God, all powerful, all knowing, and he modelled complete submission to the will, words, and actions of his Father. Rely completely on the fast-flowing, life-giving river of the Spirit that is rushing without ceasing out of you. That's just what Jesus did to you when you asked him into your life; so try to get over yourself a little and just watch the Spirit flow out of you.

Secondly, accept that you are never alone, but that God is always with you. The feeling that he is distant and that the heavens are closed to you is just that, a feeling; a stubborn, misleading, untrue feeling that contradicts the word of God. The only hope that your enemy has is that he can distract you from rejoicing over the life-giving river of the Holy Spirit that Jesus has given you. He often does that by this same old tired lie that God has deserted you; by this lie he hopes to force you to stop thinking about Jesus and the river of his Spirit and go all introspective again. When you think that you are the problem it's because you have taken your eyes off the life flowing out of you. So throw out the lie and rejoice in the truth. You can do nothing on your own, but you are never on your own. Speaking about learning the secret of living in all circumstances, Paul asserts:

"I can do everything through Christ, who gives me strength." (Php 4:13)

This truth, that we are never separated from Jesus, also leads us to make appropriate decisions in our lives. Stop trying so hard to make miracles happen by the power of your mighty intellect; stop screwing up your eyes in the empty hope that squinting will help you see the supernatural better. Peter, addressing the crowd who had just witnessed an extraordinary healing, asked why they thought that this miracle had been accomplished by their own power and godliness. Can't they see the river of the Holy Spirit that is flowing? No, they couldn't, but you can! Don't they know that speaking the name of Jesus Christ with faith has all the power of creation in it? No, they don't, but you do. They are condemned to try harder to increase their power levels, and they assume that their personal record of godliness is the key. Now, you wouldn't fall into the same trap, would you? No, you are convinced that you received power when the Holy Spirit came upon you and started flowing out of you with miraculous results. You pursue godliness in order to glorify Jesus and please your Father, not to earn a license to operate in the supernatural. Concentrate instead on loving Jesus. Put him first, read his word, talk to him often, pray consistently without strange words or unfamiliar tones and emphasis. Talk like you usually do, but to Jesus. Tell him what you actually feel, and confess that you need his help again today, and he will draw near to you.

So, to hear and see better, we have decided to give up trying stuff on our own, and to spend our time and energy in loving Jesus, and to watch with amazement the river of life he has given to us all. Lastly, we will ask the Father to show us how to do greater things, to help people and to give him glory. No matter what level of experience we feel we have reached, we can ask the Father to show us more, to tell us how to do greater things. If Jesus could do this (John 5:20), you and I certainly can! This brings us into a teacher-student relationship with God, one where we honour God by devoting ourselves to learning. When you have poured out your heart to the Lord, then begin to practice the helpful art of listening. I'm convinced that we would all hear and see much more of the supernatural if we could simply become good listeners once more in the house of God. Tear your gaze away from your smart phone; have a whole day without social media (go on, you can do it!); admit that the sports game will go on even if you're not watching it; settle down with your bible and give some quality listening time to Jesus. This same behaviour will work really well with your partner, your kids and friends too! The Spirit will help us to understand as we read our bibles. Not even he can help us much if we keep our bibles closed or never quite give the scriptures pride of place in our day. Time spent reading and studying our bibles, helped by the wise Holy Spirit, will cause our hearts and lives to become humbly teachable. Mark reveals the importance of this teacher-student relationship when Jesus wants to reveal a truth to his disciples about his approaching death and resurrection, though it is too much for them and they don't understand.

"Leaving that region they travelled through Galilee. Jesus didn't want anyone to know he was there, for he wanted to spend more time with his disciples and teach them." (Mark 9:30-31)

The disciples called Jesus 'teacher' and often bombarded him with questions. Jesus wanted to spend more time with them, to be with them and to teach them how to live. We recognize that Jesus would often walk away from the crowds to spend time with his Father in prayer, and become better able to minister to the crowds on his return as a result. But we must also make ourselves available to him, to turn away from the business and routine of our lives, to enjoy times with him when he can teach us greater things. He will teach us about ourselves, and instruct us in laying down our lives for others. He will teach us how to live a life of love, and he will teach us warfare. The Lord once left other nations in the land of promise to test the Israelites who were inexperienced in fighting.

"He did this to teach warfare to generations of Israelites who had no experience in battle." (Judg 3:2)

And again…

"He trains my hands for war, and gives my fingers skill for battle." (Psa 144:1)

Perhaps we ourselves have become inexperienced in the battle to destroy the devils works, unsure of ourselves in prayer against sin and sickness. Certainly we face a world occupied in many nations by forces of ungodliness, greed and violence, and the church needs to be up to the task of restoration. Ask him, and he will teach us how to go to war against the work and influence of the evil one.

So, to see the stream of God's Spirit better, we will stop trying too hard and depend on the Lord; we will take time to love Jesus and be with him, and we will be teachable, good listeners. Those of us who have been raised as Christian to be suspicious of 'Pentecostal' brothers and sisters, who feel that speaking in unlearned languages and prophesying the word of God is a little weird, need to get over that hesitation now. It has held you back, and you need to throw off those ashes and catch up with your Spirit-filled and empowered brethren. We need to rise up as one body in this, and embrace the Spirit baptized life.

"You should earnestly desire the most helpful gifts." (1 Cor 12:31)

"Let the Spirit renew your thought and attitudes." (Eph 4:23)

Don't you think it's time for Christians to leap ahead, to make progress towards maturity? Time also for you and me to be taught and trained for a broader form of real world effective service? If you are content as you are, then God bless you. But if you're not content at all, if you have fire in your bones that will not let you rest, then find others who feel the same way and shout to the Lord together as the young church once shouted.

"The Kings of the earth prepared for battle; the rulers gathered together against the Lord and against his Messiah…give us, your servants, great boldness in preaching your word. Stretch out your hand with healing power. May miraculous signs and wonders be done through the name of your holy servant Jesus." (Acts 4:26, 29-30)

Stop trying so hard and trust in God; concentrate not on achieving power but on loving Jesus; be humble, teachable, a student of your bible. Break out of the limitations of where you began your life as a Christian, and embrace your life as it will be, filled by the Holy Spirit. Call out to the Lord in fervent prayer for the salvation of the ends of the earth. Look around you and see the workings of God everywhere. See the mighty river from heaven flowing out to heal all the nations.

~~~~~~~

MEDITATE & MEMORIZE:

Memorize this scripture and speak it out loud as often as you can, taking time to meditate on it and asking the Holy Spirit to open it up for you. Let faith come as you hear your own voice declaring the true word of God.

"I can do everything through Christ, who gives me strength." (Php 4:13)

PRAY & PROCLAIM:
In seeing what the Holy Spirit is doing, I suggest you start with proclaiming this simple truth over and over until your heart, mind, and bones are filled with the fire of it. Imagine that you have a physical river flowing out of you, washing away every obstacle. Now, proclaim the scripture again and understand the true river of the Holy Spirit that is forever rushing out of you making all things possible. Pray that the blessing flowing out of your life will set the captives free!

GIVE THANKS & WORSHIP:
Worship the omnipresent God, available to bring justice and freedom everywhere in this wide world of diverse peoples and circumstances. Worship the omnipotent Lord, for whom nothing is impossible. Worship the omniscient God, who sees and knows everything, and who cannot be deceived or distracted from doing good. Thank your Father that the devil has none of these qualities, and that he was utterly defeated by the blood of Christ at the cross, and he has been walking in defeat ever since. Thank the Lord loudly for living in you by his Holy Spirit, so that you can do everything that Christ can do as he gives you himself, with all his strength flowing out of you like a river.

TESTIMONY
Have you heard what God is doing in Peterborough?

For years, we had been serving in a young and growing church. We had been asked to come and help our young adults transition out of the bubble of university and college into the world of careers, marriages, homes and children. We had seen much success, as many found partners, jobs and houses. We gave freely. But there came a point when we felt we had discharged all we were meant to bring; we were waiting for our next mission.

Each year we drove the three-hour journey from our home in Ottawa to visit our sister church in Peterborough for a week at a time. We would spend each evening spending time encouraging a different leader or member of the church, as we listened to them share their hearts. We loved it. We loved being an encouragement.

Then, one year Ali and I felt like we could move to be with the church in Peterborough. However, given our commitment to the church in Ottawa, we didn't tell anyone. We didn't even tell our kids.

Fast-forward three years. God had done something inside of us and we were gaining a fresh sense of our salvation and his call to us. But we never lost sight of Peterborough and our church friends there. Still, we never told anyone until one evening, a trusted friend and prophetic voice to us said, "Why is it that whenever I am praying for the church in Peterborough, I see you there?" We then shared our hearts and asked him to keep it to himself.

Two days later, we were in a meeting with the apostle who oversaw the churches in Canada. He preached from Mark 4, when Jesus and the disciples encountered the storm on the lake. He told the disciples they would go to the other side. So, when the storm came, they should not have been afraid. He promised they'd get to the other side – storm or not. Right then and there we knew the Lord was speaking to us – this storm of "what's our purpose?" would end and we would know again the deep calling of God to us as a family.

After the message, the apostle came to us and asked us if we would consider moving to Peterborough. Later we were assured he had not spoken to our friend the prophet. We knew that God was on the move with our family! We prayed, and felt that this had affirmed what we had felt three years earlier.

Moving to the church in Peterborough has been a "fit like a glove" move. Sure, there are challenges. But, when you are operating out of a revelation and a calling, challenges are not something that distract you; they are easily overcome. The word of God through these two different Holy Spirit servants of Christ made this move one of faith and certainty for us. We have loved this move in so many ways. Do we miss the people of Ottawa? Absolutely. But do we know coming here is a testimony of God's goodness – without a doubt. And for that reason I wouldn't trade this move for anything.

Pat and Ali McKinnon,
Peterborough, Ontario

DAY 23

Deep River: Deepening Your Experience of God

"Then he measured another 1,750 feet, and the river was too deep to walk across. It was deep enough to swim in, but too deep to walk through." (Ezek 47:5)

      I remember an old joke about teachers of bible doctrine that got a little lost in the presentation of their studies. A preacher was said to have 'gone down deeper, stayed down longer, and come up dryer' than any teacher before him. How could it be possible for a bible teacher to dive into the living word of God, and deliver such a dried-out message? Why has so much of our generation moved away from bible truth as being unrelated to their lives? Perhaps we need to call on God to give us preachers and teachers who are courageous enough to take us out of the shallows of the word, where they are pandering to our reluctance to change by giving us empty encouragement, by feeding us a self-improvement version of the good news. "Do this and you will be happier; do that and you will be wealthier; follow these seven secrets of a contented life." No, we will not give any more time to listening to preaching that leaves us trapped in immaturity, telling us that God is fine with us as we are, proclaiming peace where there is not and should not be peace. Neither do we want preachers to dive down deeper into the word in a dry, academic way without bringing up some food for us from those depths. Jesus knew that we needed good food, and commands his shepherds to guard the flocks of the Lord, leading them to green grass and pure water. If you are able to imagine it, I want you to conjure up an image in your minds of a flock of sheep with attitude, a demanding group of sheep crying out for better food, cleaner water and for an honest account of God's living word towards his people. We have no need to be nervous of a future judgment as long as we ask Holy Spirit teachers to hold us to the standards of scripture, submitting ourselves obediently to the present judgment of God's word.

Within a few weeks of becoming a Christian as a student, it was my attitude to the bible that got me into trouble. My younger life, wrapped as it was in a religion that was not exactly famous for being bible-based, may have raised suspicions in the mentors of the study group. Or maybe I was considered too young a believer to be asking questions. Whatever it was, I was taken aside and giving a rather chilling warning from one of the inter-varsity organization's leaders. What was my sin? I had noticed that some of my new Christian friends had lots of money, while others struggled; I had also noticed that the early church 'had no needy among them,' as the born again church experienced new-heart responses to strangers who were now made to be close family by the saving work of Jesus. I had just wondered out loud why we didn't try to live the word that we read to each other. A lot of Christian students around me devoted endless hours to studying and charting the end times, but otherwise seemed unaware of the needs around them. Later on, during my final year at university, a handful of believers around me actually did use their money to even out those differences by sharing money and resources, so that none would be poorer than his brother. No, we weren't discovering communism; we were discovering covenant love for our brothers and sisters, and it was one of the formative experiences of my young Christian journey. Our small community of care comprised four brothers and one sister, actually, and she was very lovely, and said 'yes' when I later asked her to marry me, so it was an absolutely great period in my life. Praise God, from whom all blessings flow!

The vision that the man explained to the prophet showed the need to go deeper into the life of God. Ezekiel was led downstream and then across the stream, which was ankle-deep. Refreshing, different, but not challenging to his ability to keep on walking. Many unbelievers have encountered church experiences in just this way, tried attending some meetings for a while, and then climbed out of the stream and kept on walking in their secular lives. I have met many Christians who have encountered the baptism and gifts of the Holy Spirit in much the same way. Attended some meetings, spoken a few words of a language unknown and unlearned, and then moved on. Many more, though, have a hungry desire to walk in deeper, until the waters of God's life are up to their knees, and then their waist. To feel the power of the Holy Spirit all around oneself, to understand how much bigger than us God really is can be truly amazing.

Times of revival always seem to involve powerful encounters with the real God, with many overwhelmed by the closeness of his presence. Joy inexpressible gets expressed in hilarious ways; knees wobble and strong men and women fall before their Lord. In one such time of refreshing our church in Swansea, South Wales was unable to meet in our usual venue one Sunday, so we decided to meet in one of that city's amazing parks. We sang, we prayed, God turned up, people fell to the ground at his closeness. A young woman, out for a Sunday morning walk, witnessed this unexpected scene, and came over to us to ask what was going on, as it certainly didn't look like church to her! I explained, and she asked if she could try it, too. I asked if she was a Christian, and she said, "no, I've never been interested." Not really being sure about what would happen, I agreed to her request, and we prayed a simple prayer of blessing over her. She fell just like the rest of us, having felt the power of a God who she had never believed in. If this walk of faith is all about our effort, then we are going to grow weary, quickly; but when the Holy Spirit turns up, then it is an exciting and joyful ride. My hope is that for myself and for this present generation, that nothing will hold us back from pressing ever deeper into the river of life. To turn an unbelieving world back to God, to truly get their attention, requires the witness of a Kingdom community that has gone all the way in to the river of life that flows from God's throne. We need to live radically changed lives, to be an amazing group of people, not argumentative with our neighbours, but able to demonstrate the Spirit's power and not just talk about it.

"For when we brought you the Good News, it was not only with words but also with power, for the Holy Spirit gave you full assurance that what we said was true." (1 Thes 1:5)

It's important to remember that the words Paul used were not weak or ineffective speeches, but were themselves power-filled.

"For the word of God is alive and powerful. It is sharper than the sharpest two-edged sword, cutting between soul and spirit, between joint and marrow. It exposes our innermost thoughts and desires." (Heb 4:12)

So Paul's words were not empty or religious, in need of help. That's not at all the point he is making to the community of believers. The bible is extraordinary; God's breathed-out life towards us. The words of preachers and teachers and evangelists are sharply effective, dangerous to sin and illuminating to our inner selves. Paul's assertion is that the astonishing interventions of the Holy Spirit's power are his way of saying amen and amen, these words are true! To speak about Jesus to people is a tremendous privilege; to speak about Jesus with signs and wonders following is nation-changing.

"So what makes us think that we can escape if we ignore this great salvation that was first announced by the Lord Jesus himself and then delivered to us by those who heard him speak? And God confirmed the message by giving signs and wonders and various miracles and gifts of the Holy Spirit whenever he chose." (Heb 2:3-4)

We must press in deeper, calling on God to give us greater boldness in preaching, and to confirm that his word is true by showing signs, wonders, and miracles. That is a river of life deep enough to knock people off their feet, deep enough to swim in. Only when the truth of Jesus' transforming power is revealed by a mighty encounter with God himself can we expect to see the tide turn in our world. To that end, leaders and ministers of every kind must press in together into God, striding out into deeper stretches of God's river. The river begins under the throne of God and of the Lamb, so we must more deeply express the government of God. It passes out of the temple into the whole world from east to west, so we must follow the Spirit out into the nations. It is a crystal clear river of life, so we must love the gospel, preaching Jesus boldly. And it is a powerful current that takes us off our feet, so we must go deeper into the supernatural gifts and abilities freely given to all who believe.

The river is a deep river, deep enough to win the day and bring multitudes to life in Christ. It is deep enough to fill the whole earth with a keen awareness of the glory of Jesus. Our desire to work in the depths of God must be our greatest desire, our preeminent ambition, so that we can come to God our King with the words of Esther:

"This is my request and deepest wish." (Est 5:7)

The depth of her cry came from the encouragement of Mordecai, who, believing this to be a crucial time in the history of his people, asked her:

"Who knows if perhaps you were made Queen for just such a time as this?" (Est 4:14)

Similarly, we have to ask ourselves why we are still here, why aren't we safe in heaven right now? Perhaps it is because the needs of the oppressed are so great, perhaps the cry of the hurting have ascended up to the throne. It may seem to us that the suffering peoples of so many nations need to see a serving, compassionate church community, filled with the name of Jesus and the power of the Spirit. When you watch the news, you probably wonder, "What kind of time are we living in? Rapture us out of it, O Lord!" How much better is it to ask ourselves, "Who knows if perhaps the saints are on earth for just such a time as this?" Our thoughts about the prophets have led us to understand that God is pleased with his people when they remember the poor, and help those who are in trouble. We don't want to be taken away from the world when so many are in harm's way, we want to preach life in Christ to them all, in the power of the Holy Spirit, surrounded by signs, wonders, and miracles. Let us look forward to being caught up in the clouds to meet the returning king on the last day. Let's make sure that everyone who should be there is in the sky with us! Not one of God's children will be left behind.

So many people of faith have laboured so hard, for so long, and though there has been great fruit from their labours, we all long for more. The mountain of the Lord will be raised up higher than all the mountains of the earth. The river is deep enough to cover everyone and everything on the planet. Let's go deeper!

"(Jesus) said to Simon, 'Now go out where it is deeper, and let down your nets to catch some fish … soon both boats were filled with fish and on the verge of sinking." (Luke 5:4, 7)

~~~~~~~

MEDITATE & MEMORIZE:

Memorize this scripture and speak it out loud as often as you can, taking time to meditate on it and asking the Holy Spirit to open it up for you. Let faith come as you hear your own voice declaring the true word of God.

"So what makes us think that we can escape if we ignore this great salvation that was first announced by the Lord Jesus himself and then delivered to us by those who heard him speak? And God confirmed the message by giving signs and wonders and various miracles and gifts of the Holy Spirit whenever he chose." (Heb 2:3-4)

PRAY & PROCLAIM:

Pray fervently that the word of God will be loved by his saints, and that the sharpness of the scriptures might cut us free from all doubt, unbelief and ordinariness. Call out to the Lord to raise up his people and bring us all into our full inheritance, with no part of it being unclaimed. Proclaim that the Holy Spirit has empowered his church and that signs and wonders and various miracles and gifts will always follow the true preaching of the message about Jesus.

GIVE THANKS & WORSHIP:

Give thanks to God for giving us his Son, his Word and his Spirit. Worship him in his majesty and holiness, and for his greatness in all that he does. Give thanks to the Holy Spirit for deciding to let his many gifts flow out of your inner being to water the world, to heal, deliver and save.

· TESTIMONY ·
Have you heard what God did in Toronto?

Back in 2002, my wife and I were living in Toronto with our young son. We had just moved to Toronto in 2001 from our prior home in Peterborough. I had been working for an IT company in downtown Toronto since 2000, but we only moved from Peterborough (which had a much, much lower cost of living) to Toronto (which has a very high cost of living) after my company dramatically increased my salary in late 2001. Our family joyfully welcomed our second child, a daughter, in 2002, and around this time, the company where I worked was purchased by a much larger firm. This was a period of great change, but I had kept my position through a couple of rounds of layoffs, we had two beautiful children and lacked nothing that we needed.

Then, just after our daughter was born, I developed a series of abdominal abscesses that left me in hospital for over six months. My wife was at home with our children, and I was the sole earner in the family. We had short term disability insurance and hospital room coverage through my employer, so we were not overly concerned about money and focused instead on my health.

A couple of months into my hospital stay, everything suddenly changed. First, we found out that my employer had only reported my starting salary to the insurance company. The large raise that had enabled our move to Toronto was never reported. Thus, the disability payments from the insurance company were insufficient to live on. To make matters worse, the insurance company took several months before they started making any payments at all. Our savings quickly dwindled, and we maxed out all of our available credit.

One day, in the midst of all this, my wife came into the room to visit and was clearly very upset. We had just received a bill from the hospital for $3028 for my semi-private room. My insurance company had not paid the hospital, and we were left with the bill and absolutely no means to pay it. We had no money and no credit. We talked for a bit, then I hugged her into me and we simply prayed that God would provide for us, and that He would make a way where we could see none.

The next morning, my wife came back to visit. She was clearly quite excited and was almost dancing with joyful energy. A cheque had just arrived in the mail for $3000 from some believers in Ottawa (over 400 km away) who knew I was ill, but who knew nothing of our financial needs. Naturally, we thanked God and paid the hospital bill. From that point, the money situation turned around. Within a couple of weeks, the insurance company started paying the hospital bills (backdated), and though they never did straighten out the discrepancy with my salary, the money that had been provided made up for this lack. We continue to praise God for his provision in that time. What really captured my attention is the fact that the answer to our prayer was already on its way and in the mail before we even asked God to provide the money that we lacked. Believers who were hundreds of kilometers away and who knew nothing of the specifics of our situation had simply obeyed the Spirit of God, and we were saved before we knew that we needed saving.

Cathy and Wesley Roebuck
Toronto

DAY 24

Life Giving River: From Death to Life

"There will be swarms of living things wherever the water of this river flows. Fish will abound in the Dead Sea, for its waters will become fresh. Life will flourish wherever this water flows." (Ezek 47:9)

The river that flows from the throne of God and of the Lamb brings the water of life to all who are thirsty to receive it. It flows from the throne down the centre of the main street of the city. It flows from the entrance of the temple, and out of the pierced side of our Saviour Jesus. He endured death on the cross in order that the power of death might be forever defeated, to deliver us from death and lead us into life forever. We look to the cross and see Jesus achieve victory over death and victory over separation from our Father, making us forever certain that neither death nor distance from our Father's protection will ever hurt us again. The river of the waters of life flow out of us as the Holy Spirit fills us and spills out of us. This river that flows turns despair into dancing as it turns death into indestructible life. Everywhere the waters flow, life bursts forth, even in you and me. Whatever you think about the life that flows from Jesus, you have seriously underestimated the enormity of its power to transform you. However powerful your present ministry is, you have just begun to dip your toes into the flood of blessing that is flowing down the valley in your direction. The good news that King Jesus has travelled the highway prepared for him and entered our world as our King is much, much better news than you've been thinking. There is a fresh revelation of the glory of the King that is about to burst in upon our grey, distracted world, and it is going to make all our possessions, all our toys, all our concerns seem trivial and dull compared to the light of his face and the joy of his life poured out for us.

Naaman was the commander of an invading army, who enjoyed the admiration of his king. The Lord had given him great victories, but he had leprosy. A young girl of Israel who had been captured became a maid to the commander's wife, and she courageously suggested that he seek out God's prophet in Samaria. Elisha called for Naaman to be sent to him so that Naaman might know that there was a true prophet of God in the land. He was quite upset at the idea that anyone should think that God had no servants that knew his greatness and who moved in his Spirit. That same indignation is starting to surface in the church of Christ, and it is driving new ministers of the Spirit to rise up and declare themselves to the world, a new generation of nation-changing women and men with transformative faith. They will speak as Elisha did, with bold declarations based on an unshakeable belief in God's word and the flowing river of the Holy Spirit.

"Go and wash yourself seven times in the Jordan River. Then your skin will be restored and you will be healed of your leprosy." (2 Kings 5:10)

Naaman got upset, muttered about better rivers back home, listened to reason from his officers, dipped himself in the Jordan and was healed, and declared:

"Now I know that there is no God in all the world except in Israel." (2 Kings 5:15)

He passed from death to life in his knowledge of the one, true God by allowing the waters of life to surround him. His skin, once leprous, was now clean and clear like a young child's. He was offended and put off by the prophet's words, though they were helpful and true. But he could not deny the miracle worked by the river of healing. The work of restoration took him beyond where he might have expected to be, with the skin of an adult man, and gave him the skin of a young child. Ask the Lord to restore you in body, mind and spirit, and the God who restores all things will take you beyond a simple answer into a greater blessing that you needed! Surrender yourself into the waters of baptism to bury the old life; come out of those waters into a brand new life and dive immediately and permanently into the deep waters of the Holy Spirit, as he baptizes you and fills you to the full.

When we see Ezekiel's river flowing into the valley of the Dead Sea, we would be impressed if we saw a little bit of life. But no, there are fish and fishermen everywhere. Nets are drying out from En-gedi on the west shore to En-eglaim on the far shore, life from east to west as far as the eye can see. The river of restoration doesn't improve things a little; it generates an overwhelming and passionate love of fruitfulness wherever it goes. Jesus didn't come to condemn us but to save us, and he brought rich, full lives for us to enjoy. He rips off our chains and lifts up the oppressed. He brings justice, not judgment, and sets the lame dancing. He searches out the lost and carries them out of sin and danger on his own shoulders, and takes them all the way home to his Father's house. When healing a man with a deformed hand on the Sabbath, he annoyed his religion-inclined enemies. But he was determined to conquer sickness, sin and death, and bring health, mercy and life to all who received him. He asked his critics:

"Is this a day to save life or to destroy it?" (Mark 3:4)

They wouldn't answer the question, but the river of mercy that flows out of Jesus gives life, and promotes it to the fullest measure. The river that flows from his side takes away death and leads us to himself as the source of our eternally settled lives.

"They have washed their robes in the blood of the Lamb and made them white. That is why they stand in front of God's throne and serve him day and night in his Temple. And he who sits on the throne will give them shelter. They will never again be hungry or thirsty; they will never be scorched by the heat of the sun. For the Lamb on the throne will be their shepherd. He will lead them to springs of life-giving water. And God will wipe every tear from their eyes." (Rev 7:14-17)

The power of the blood of Christ to wash us into righteousness is limitless to all who put their faith in Him. The passage from death to life delivers us forever from hunger and thirst; shields us from the oppressive heat of life' circumstances, and wipes away every tear from every eye. The love of the Lord is unquestionable, and his courage in facing suffering and death is extraordinary, too great for us to comprehend. Having taken us out of death's power, having washed away every stain, every memory of sin, he leads us to springs of life-giving water. Oh, what a saviour! Having delivered us from the very smell of death, he does not hesitate to give us everything we need in order to live our new lives to the full.

"By his divine power, God has given us everything we need for living a godly life." (2 Pet 1:3)

It is vitally important that we understand our need of this provision, to live this born again life with the river of the Spirit flowing freely. We couldn't live our old lives as we should have, weighed down as we were by the sinful nature. But neither can we ever hope to live this new creation life without constant connection to the waters of life that flow out of us because of the Holy Spirit. Jesus could live the Christian life, and did so in the fullness of the Spirit. Our hope is that Christ will be the one living that life in us, the fullness of the life of the Spirit of God.

"My old self has been crucified with Christ. It is no longer I who live, but Christ lives in me. So I live in this earthly body by trusting in the Son of God, who loved me and gave his life for me." (Gal 2:20)

Ezekiel, advised and guided by the man from heaven, observed the flowing of the life-giving stream, that becomes an all-encompassing deep river of blessing and life. He sees that the life-effects are not small, but universal, and that abundant life's victory over dried-out death is absolute. Lives that were as dead as could be made clean and fully alive by heaven's river. We have looked beyond this picture to consider the blood that washes us and the water that brings life flowing from Jesus' side, filled with purposeful love. The sight makes us want to live this life to the full, and to believe for the reversal of death, hatred, division and suffering in the lives of all our brothers and sisters. How can we not be filled with hope for the nations, as our faith responds to this word about the river of the water of life? If the lowest, driest, deadest place on the face of the earth can burst with life at the touch of God's river, then we can believe that all the earth will become aware of God's magnificent eternal glory.

~~~~~~~

MEDITATE & MEMORIZE:

Memorize this scripture and speak it out loud as often as you can, taking time to meditate on it and asking the Holy Spirit to open it up for you. Let faith come as you hear your own voice declaring the true word of God.

"They have washed their robes in the blood of the Lamb and made them white. That is why they stand in front of God's throne and serve him day and night in his Temple. And he who sits on the throne will give them shelter. They will never again be hungry or thirsty; they will

never be scorched by the heat of the sun. For the Lamb on the throne will be their shepherd. He will lead them to springs of life-giving water. And God will wipe every tear from their eyes."
(Rev 7:14-17)

PRAY & PROCLAIM:
Prayerfully and with reverence come before God's throne and see that you have washed your robes in the blood of the Lamb and made them white, robes of righteousness. Tell Jesus that you will serve him today, tomorrow and forever because of what he has done. Ask God to wipe away every tear from your eyes, and then pray for everyone that the Spirit brings into your mind, asking that he wipe away their tears also.

GIVE THANKS & WORSHIP:
Give thanks to God for sending Jesus to rescue us; express your deepest gratitude to Jesus for willingly laying down his life as a sacrifice. Acknowledge that you are clean and holy because of the spilling of his blood, and worship the God who loves us so much. Worship him by offering comfort, compassion, forgiveness, acceptance, mercy, faithful friendship, food and water to everyone you touch in life.

TESTIMONY
Have you heard what God did in Brooklyn?

When David Wilkerson, founder of Teen Challenge and author of The Cross and the Switch Blade, mentioned the street outreaches he was leading in Brooklyn, NY, I knew I had to go! My first day on the streets of Brooklyn, I was standing on a corner below a park. I heard a voice above me and looked up into a pair of very intense, hate-filled eyes.

"What are you doing here?" the man demanded.

"I'm inviting people to a free outdoor concert and to hear David Wilkerson speak about Jesus," I replied.

"Don't you know I could kill you right now?" he shot back.

I continued to look this young, troubled man directly in the eyes and said, "I suppose you could kill me, but you won't because right now God is speaking to you and telling how very much he loves you. He loves you so much, he sent his Son, Jesus to pay for your sins, so you could be free!" He listened quietly, warned me again that I was in a very dangerous place, took my invitation to the concert and walked away. Only God knows if he is one of the hundreds of people who came to the park and surrendered his life to Jesus.

Later that week at the outdoor concert, I was praying and asking the Holy Spirit to show me who I should sit near. He led me to a young, likely homeless woman I'll call Sherri. As David began to speak, the awesome, powerful presence of God descended on the park! There were several hundred people gathered, and they became very quiet and listened as the message of God's amazing love and kindness was preached. People were streaming into the park, many with tears flowing down their faces as they experienced the love of God and heard about freedom from sin. I turned my attention back to Sherri. She began to frantically dig through her bag for her hairbrush, then some makeup. She was so aware of the holy presence of God; she was trying to clean herself up. I moved closer and watched and waited. When David asked people to come to the stage if they wanted to meet Jesus, Sherri jumped to her feet! I introduced myself and asked Sherri if I could walk with her. She had tears in her eyes when she asked Jesus for his help and surrendered her life to him. We were able to connect Sherri with people who could also help her with her life situation.

Vicki Kreuzer,
Brooklyn, U.S.A.

DAY 25
Food and Healing

"Fruit trees of all kinds will grow along both sides of the river. The leaves of the trees will never turn brown and fall, and there will always be fruit on their branches. There will be a new crop every month, for they are watered by the river flowing from the Temple. The fruit will be for food and the leaves for healing." (Ezek 47:12)

Take a deep breath and accept that this prophetic image is describing you and me, picturing the children of the living God as gloriously fruitful, with eternity in their hearts. Because of the cross of Christ, and because of his blood sprinkled upon us, and because of the continuing work of the Holy Spirit poured down on us from heaven, we will never die, but live for eternity with God. It is not just today that is settled; we will fellowship with and worship our good, good Father forever. We will not wither away and fail, dropping like dried out leaves to the ground, no matter what our circumstances in life. Whatever people have said to you in the past and whatever they say about you in the future, your eternal destiny is certain as you trust in Jesus, drawing your life from him.

The children of God will grow up to fruitful maturity on both sides of the river; no walls between us, no denominational or historical divisions, nothing separating us from the love of Christ, just a river of life joining us together as we feed upon it as one people. Gone is any idea of living on 'the wrong side of the tracks,' excluded by poverty, powerlessness, language, colour, or culture; both sides of the river are doing great! Our sisters and brothers are everywhere we look, and they are fruitful, grown to adulthood, ready to share good food with the hungry, and they have healing in their hands. We have believed small things for too long, expected little excitement in our faith journey, and been invisible to the world when they needed us to stand up and be counted in their battle. Dare to believe that the river of God has brought vibrant life and overcoming godliness into our society; stand up and shout that the blood of the Lamb has triumphed over every evil! Today is the most important day of your entire Christian life, and I hear that tomorrow will be even better. The cross of Christ has not lost its power; the blood of Christ has not become diluted with time or changing circumstances or modern thought. Jesus Christ is Lord of all peoples and King over every nation, and his children are fruitful, healing trees planted by the river flowing from his throne.

The Lord loves trees: many, varied, and fruitful trees. Jesus loves us as family: many, varied, and fruitful children of God. He loves life, and living by the river that flows out of heaven keeps us in an abundant life that is joyful and satisfying. He knows that he can come to any one of us at any time and find food for the hungry. He is fully confident that he can come to us at any time of day and find a faithful community of people who have in their hands healing for the sick and justice for their communities. There will always be food and healing to be found when Jesus comes by to look for it. The same crowds that gathered around Jesus can now gather around his saints, and with the same, even greater, results because the river of the Spirit of Jesus is flowing out of us all. What a plan! Heaven's love for the world, our Father's great compassion, his unwillingness to allow sin to reign, his battle to set his children free - what an amazing plan it is that we see coming to its final victory in our world. It is important that the image of God that we carry in our hearts and minds should be that of a joyful God, a lover of life. He wants us to be real, and to love justice and mercy towards others as he does. He wants to bless us with life, and to save us from decay, making us fruitful in all that we do. He urges us to love the righteousness of his Kingly rule, and to seek after it with all our strength. He knows the effect that such a godly life will have on us.

"They are like trees planted along the riverbank, bearing fruit each season. Their leaves never wither, and they prosper in all they do." (Psa 1:3)

The prophet Jeremiah, like all prophets, knew that trusting in the Lord and living to please him brings guaranteed benefits to his people.

"Blessed are those that trust in the Lord and have made the Lord their hope and confidence. They are like trees planted by the riverbank, with roots that reach deep into the water. Such trees are not bothered by the heat or worried by long months of drought. Their leaves stay

green, and they never stop producing fruit." (Jer 17:7-8)

You will see from these and other statements that this image is a powerful one for the prophets and those who listen to God through them. A river flows out of heaven from the throne; it passes through the cross and out of Christ himself; it flows into and out of his holy people to make the earth a God-blessed well-watered garden. The lives of all those who put down their roots into this river of delights are fruitful, and useful to others. They are heat-resistant, and cannot be discouraged by the pressures of life. They are drought-resistant because they have a source of living water that flows from heaven and that only gets deeper with time. Our God never grows old, distracted or too busy to watch over every one of us, and so our leaves stay green throughout the most withering of seasons. When the Lord comes to inspect our progress he always finds plentiful food and leaves for healing, because his servants never stop producing fruit.

When I first gave leadership to a church in Wales, I followed on from the ministry of its previous leader, a much-loved modern day prophet. He used this idea of fruitfulness in God's children to give a scriptural direction to his own church family, to the saints in his care, declaring that they would:

"Take root downward, and bear fruit upward." (2 Kings 19:30, KJV)

The understanding that the expectation of discipleship in Jesus is to be deeply rooted in Christ, in his word and in the life of his Spirit, is foundational to making progress in our Christian journey. That understanding also encapsulates the concept of bearing fruit upwards to the Lord for his inspection and glory. His investment in us will produce a bountiful reward, a never-ending increase in his government and peace to the ends of the earth. Bearing fruit for God as we live on his words and flow in his Spirit is now the natural cycle of our supernatural living. Giving ourselves wholeheartedly to living by his word and his Spirit will lead us to success and help us pioneer forward effectively.

"In all that he did in the service of the Temple of God, and in his efforts to follow God's laws and commands, Hezekiah sought his God wholeheartedly. As a result, he was very successful." (2 Chron 31:21)

When we give ourselves with sincere passion to the work of the Lord, when we courageously speak out about putting God first always, then we can expect the pleasure of heaven and fruit in our lives. As we gather our courage and defend justice for all, as we use our strength to guard the weak, as we share our resources to aid the hungry, thirsty and naked, as we embrace our community in all its God-reflecting diversity, then the pace of the river's flow will quicken. The Lord rewards those who seek him earnestly, who are impressed by God more than anyone or anything else. Nehemiah pursued reforms in the lives and service of God's people, and knew that God would not forget him, or fail to recognise his works of faith.

"Remember this good deed, O my God, and do not forget all that I have faithfully done for the Temple of my God and its sacrifices." (Neh 13:14)

So, putting down our roots deeply into God by meditating on his word in our bibles every day is something we can do, and increase in. Putting down our roots into every word that comes out of the mouth of our Father is another. Earnestly seeking to live in complete dependence on the ever-present Holy Spirit is another way of being well-rooted, taking our very life from the river of God. Avoiding isolation by making fellowship a priority and by humbly opening ourselves up to the ministries around us is another way to have strong roots. Discover the present-day ministries of apostles and prophets, evangelists, pastors, and teachers, as they work to bring you, me, and all God's people into maturity. Their passion is to increase the measure of Christ's stature in all of us, so make their service joyful for them by receiving them with faith. All these things will strengthen our roots, and give us an expectation of bearing fruit upwards to our God.

Being fruitful and producing something useful is important to us and to the Lord. Ezekiel's river of the waters of life sustains many trees growing on its banks, which in turn produce fruit for food and leaves for healing. We have already noted that the final, glorious, fully realised picture of this river found in Revelation 22 similarly produced constantly available fruit, and leaves that were used as medicine to heal nations. For the one who came into our world to destroy the devil's work, Jesus' ministry often meant feeding the hungry with bread and with truth, quenching the thirst of those who needed to drink, and healing all who were sick. His ministry, and that of his disciples, provided sustenance, comfort and health to all who came to them for help. If we are to have a vision for the restoration of the Kingdom community and for the maturing of the saints, let it be this: that the entire world can come to the saints as they did to Jesus, finding food for their hunger, truth that will set them free, and healing for their disease.

When the crowd, impressed by the miracles of the loaves and the fish, came looking for more, Jesus attempted to get their roots down deeper into God:

"Jesus replied, I am the bread of life. Whoever comes to me will never be hungry again. Whoever believes in me will never be thirsty ... I tell you the truth, anyone who believes has eternal life." (John 6:35, 47)

And the sick and diseased from across the countryside found a fruitful Jesus willing and able to help them.

"They had come to hear him and to be healed of their diseases; and those troubled by evil spirits were healed. Everyone tried to touch him, because healing power went out from him, and he healed everyone." (Luke 6:18, 19)

When the hungry and thirsty came to Jesus, they found food for their bodies and food for their souls. They found a river of life and kindness flowing out of him, and they could drink freely. He would feed them and then sit them down to teach them, love and encourage them all. When they were ill, or harassed by evil spirits, he would touch them and speak over them, and he healed everyone. Whatever their burdens were, whatever the cause of their sadness or grief, he carried away their suffering by taking it on himself. Healing power flowed out of Jesus like a river, and he taught his disciples how to be just like him in this. We live in an age deluged by the Holy Spirit, who gives us power to live and gifts of healing, so that the river is still available. We will worship God with joyful praises, with hearts lifted up to him in adoration. We will fellowship together for prayer and for teaching. And we will allow the river of God's Spirit to flow out of us, so that the hungry will find food in us, and the sick find healing. The river of God will never run dry.

~~~~~~

MEDITATE & MEMORIZE:

Memorize these scriptures and speak them out loud as often as you can, taking time to meditate on them and asking the Holy Spirit to open them up for you. Let faith come as you hear your own voice declaring the true word of God.

"Fruit trees of all kinds will grow along both sides of the river. The leaves of the trees will never turn brown and fall, and there will always be fruit on their branches. There will be a new crop every month, for they are watered by the river flowing from the Temple. The fruit will be for food and the leaves for healing." (Ezek 47:12)

PRAY & PROCLAIM:

Pray sincerely and fervently for all the people who live on the 'other side of town.' Proclaim God's great love over them, asking for them to be as blessed as you are, because they are family to you. Pray for another nation, religious, ethnic or cultural group in the same way, proclaiming God's favour on them, because the whole earth belongs to the Lord of Lords.

GIVE THANKS & WORSHIP:

Worship God for sending Jesus to make peace between heaven and earth, to bring us back into his family, and to restore our relationship with all our sisters and brothers throughout our nation, and to the ends of the earth.

TESTIMONY
Have you heard what God is doing in Ottawa?

On a Saturday in the spring of 2014 I was opening our pool with my son-in-law. I had never opened a pool before and did a few things incorrectly in the process. We spent a couple of hours crouched down pulling on the large winter tarp while trying to pump the water off of it. Sunday evening – almost 30 hours later – I began to feel a pain in my lower back. It gradually got worse over the next couple of days. I have generally been quite healthy and fit and so I tried to ignore it with the idea that it would likely just go away. That plan went badly. By Thursday I was in terrible pain. It took me two hours to get out of bed in the morning even with assistance. Apparently I had a pulled muscle. Any movement that activated the muscle would cause it to go into excruciating spasms. That pain was the worst I have ever experienced in my life. My condition continued to deteriorate over the next few days. On Sunday evening I (foolishly) went out in the car on a short errand but, due to the pain, had to come home before completing it. When I arrived home I could not get out of the car. Any attempt to do so would send the muscle into spasms. Finally, with help from my wife and others, I did manage to get out and sit in a chair beside the car. But I simply could not stand up. So, reluctantly, at the urging of others, we called an ambulance. As you might have guessed, the doctor said I needed to rest it completely and that basically all that I had been doing for the last week had just made it worse. He gave me some medication and over the next week it improved a little. But I was still in pain and could really only get relief by lying down.

I am a Project Manager in commercial construction and we live in Ottawa. There was a very complicated lift with a crane that was taking place on the following Monday evening on one of my construction sites in Toronto. I felt I needed to be there. So during the day on Monday I drove to Toronto (this is now a little over two weeks since the problem started). It was painful but I managed to get to the site. The operation started at 8:00 pm and took about five hours. As I stood watching my back became more and more painful. I went and laid down in the car a couple of times but finally, at about midnight, I told the others I couldn't stay any longer and drove to my motel.

The next day I needed to visit three sites briefly and then start the four to five hour drive home. At the third site I was pointing out something as I walked and did not notice a change in elevation (a single step) in front of me. I stepped off and stumbled wrenching my back badly. I thought to myself that I have really done serious damage now. As I supported my weight on some equipment nearby and tried to let the pain subside, my co-worker, who was also a Christian, laid his hands on my back and prayed for God to heal it. I did not feel any improvement immediately but decided anyway to try to drive home. I did not want to be stuck in Toronto by myself in this condition. Driving now was considerably more difficult. I kept trying to take the weight off my back by pushing one hand down into the seat, for a short time, then switching to the other hand. I told myself to just focus on the road and take it one minute at a time. About an hour into the drive I suddenly felt that the pain was gone. I wiggled around in the seat – it felt OK. A few minutes later I pulled into a Service Centre along the highway. I stepped out of the car, bent over and touched my toes. I pulled one knee up towards my chest as if I was putting a sock on. Then I did the same with the other knee. I was completely healed! Thank you Lord Jesus! There has been absolutely no problem with my lower back muscles since!

Dale Bright
Ottawa

Part Seven:

AS THE WATERS COVER THE SEA

DAY 26

A Well-Watered Garden: He Came to Give Us Full Lives

"The Lord will guide you continually, giving you water when you are dry and restoring your strength. You will be like a well-watered garden, like an overflowing spring." (Isa 58:11)

In this chapter, Isaiah gives our own generation an opportunity to humbly examine our place in the world. What are we focused on and where does our energy go? What are our issues, our concerns? Are we happy enough as long as the worship goes well and the preaching doesn't challenge us too much? Are our thoughts on how the church and its meetings are doing, or on how the world is faring? As Christians we are sometimes vulnerable to majoring on minor issues, distracted by music, meetings, and the bewildering choice of local churches that many of us have. Isaiah's concerns are that God's people can be found to be filling their time with activities that neither interest God nor make the world a better, safer, happier place.

I hope that you have noticed in previous chapters how encouraged I am by this generation of believers. The grace and mercy of the Lord flows like a river as the Holy Spirit turns his people into a well-watered garden. Nevertheless, it is wise for us not to get too carried away with ourselves, and to humbly submit to the scrutiny of God's prophets. Our boast is in Jesus, not in ourselves; and we welcome and need Christ-sent ministries to help us to grow. Their responsibility is to equip God's people to do his work and build up the church, the body of Christ.

"Now these are the gifts Christ gave to the church: the apostles, the prophets, the evangelists, and the pastors and teachers…This will continue until we all come to such unity in our faith and knowledge of God's son that we will be mature in the Lord, measuring up to the full and complete standard of Christ." (Eph 4:11-13)

As a group of churches, we have recently been stirred by our apostolic and prophetic leadership to devote one Saturday a month for the next few years to dive into the word of God together. We have made use of technology that can bring everyone in to the feast of the word, however distant they are from Ottawa. Great teachers, women and men, are giving us a firm foundation of truth that will stir us into action. That's what ministries do, of course: they bring us to maturity, keep us out of the shallows of endless discussion of minor matters, and send us out equipped for service in the real world. One of the contributors to our bible school, a teaching prophet who has been a foundational inspiration to many, was asked a question at the end of his sessions: Why are there so few examples of healing and miracles to be seen in the church? He confessed that he really didn't know the answer; he then proceeded to tell us of the great miracles that he has witnessed, tremendous healings he has seen, and of the individuals that he has spoken to that have been raised from the dead! His observation was that the truly astounding miracles appear to be seen in regions of the world that are poorer than in the West, with fewer resources and greater needs seen in the population. This answer achieved what I imagine it was meant to achieve; a deep determination that nothing in our culture or material situation would be allowed any longer to keep us paddling in the shallows of God's mighty river. As we rise up in godly discontent, believing in Jesus and filled with the word, as we allow the fire in our bones to cause us to preach and act with boldness, then the heavens will open up the flow of life that is placed within each of us to give. The Ephesians 4 Christ-given ministries will be prominent factors in such a body of believers becoming relevant and effective in the real world outside of our cosy church walls. I was saddened to listen to a good Christian man being interviewed recently, who had concluded that his country had fallen so far into moral decay that "God must want to bring us to our knees, I guess." God does indeed want to bring us to our knees, but not driven there by his rebuke; rather he will listen to us as, on our knees, we make fervent, sincere petitions rise up to his waiting ears, asking that he might bless us. We will tell God that he is great, and that we know he is restoring all things. We will leave him in no doubt that we love the Son, and that, like the Holy Spirit, we will not allow one ounce of his suffering to be robbed of its effect, not one drop of the precious blood of the Lamb to fall to the ground without bringing healing to the sick and to the nations. We are far from despair, and not far at all from victory as we proclaim Christ crucified and gloriously risen from the dead!

There was a time when to express a belief in present day apostles and prophets was to face opposition and ridicule. Everyone loved evangelists, pastors, and teachers, of course. But apostles and prophets were all deemed to be safely dead, belonging to long-gone 'Bible times.' Not so today, of course. It's probably because too many of us noticed that the work assigned to these gift ministries from Jesus clearly still needed to be completed. I am a believer, a part of God's people, and I am in need of being better equipped for service to this great King. The thought of doing the work of Christ in our day and of making a difference in this troubled, needy world is a passionate ambition for so many of us. Oh God, build up the church! Unless you are more deeply impressed than I am with the level of maturity across the world church of Jesus, then the 'until' in Ephesians 4:13 surely still applies. We are certainly growing in our knowledge of Jesus, and will not rest until the whole earth is aware of his glory as the waters cover the sea.

Apostles, prophets, evangelists, pastors and teachers will help us to become mature, consistent and strong in Spirit, word, and life. What is our expected standard, our goal and finish line? It is the fullness and completeness of Christ's stature; a church impacting this age as Jesus impacted the crowds of his time on earth! Look around you, at your church and at the world (not just your part of it). If you feel that all is as it should be, that all is well, then God bless you. But if you see the need for restoration of missing ministries and spiritual gifts, if you understand that there are multitudes still crying out to heaven for help, if you grieve because the troubled and oppressed peoples of the world have been attacked and left bleeding in the gutter, then rise up in passionate prayer to our God. Let him hear the loud voice of the western church, joining with all our brothers in the east, in the north and the south, to see the glory of Jesus fill the earth. We will not accept that a suffering, forgotten church in other nations will see the miracles, while the western church turns away from our sisters and brothers, and becomes empty of Jesus' power. We will not turn off the news channels to watch comedy shows and play video games while the world needs help and the salvation found only in Jesus. This generation will not pass by on the other side. We will not build walls or proclaim that this is just the judgement of God on the wicked. This whole generation of Christians, one body in Christ, filled to overflowing with the mighty, supernatural Holy Spirit will give a world-wide witness to the love, power and mercy of King Jesus, the Lamb who was slain. We are finally realising that we don't need to wait for the fractured organized church to come to structural unity before the powerful river of God's blessing will flow. We are united already, have been made into one body by the headship of Christ, and have no need to wait for interdenominational conferences to say "Go," to tell us that we can get started on reaching the world. We love all the saints, have the heart and mind of Christ living in us, and we have been given our mission.

Ignore the walls, be blind to historical divisions, and find your faith-filled sisters and brothers. Go and preach the good news of Jesus, and signs and wonders will follow, flowing out of heaven in a mighty river of life. We are encouraged today because of the Lord's unfailing love and faithfulness. We are obedient to the scriptures as being God's breathed out word, and submit ourselves to that word.

"All scripture is inspired by God and is useful to teach us what is true, and to make us realize what is wrong in our lives. It corrects us when we are wrong and teaches us to do what is right. God uses it to prepare and equip his people to do every good work." (2 Tim 3:16, 17)

Generally, we read this scripture in the context of our own 'quiet times,' as we learn the wisdom of building a discipline of daily reading of our bibles with an attitude of faith. We are further inclined to admit that the scriptures are effective in helping us to realise what is still imperfect in our lives, and so we come to God's word humbly, expecting it to change us to be more like Jesus. It would be exciting, I think, to lift up our eyes a little, to better understand the apostle's intent in encouraging us to be devoted to our scriptures. Certainly, the word is good food for the individual, and we should read and apply it to our own lives, remembering also to encourage enthusiastically God's preachers and teachers by being responsive to their ministry. Paul is telling us, however, that God's use of his scriptures in our lives is also corporate ("his people") and has the work of God to the nations in mind ("every good work"). We must never lose our emphasis on the need for each individual to have his own personal relationship with God, and reading and meditating on our bibles is vital to healthy living. We must also never forget that God's love, and Jesus' sacrifice, are big enough to touch all the families of the earth. Perhaps we have had too little emphasis on this truth, this fruit of the Kingdom, which sees the church as an army trained for war, as an athlete trained for the race, every individual a child of their Father in heaven; the whole body as one, each part useful and equipped for every good work. These good works are to begin with those who are immediately around us: family, friends, and neighbours. But they are also good works on a national and global scale, so that the whole earth might know of his glory and love. The breathed out word of God that are our scriptures are also part of God's irrigation system, watering the seed that he puts within us to ensure maximum growth. If we want to see a mightier church, then we should devote ourselves to the public and private reading of the scriptures, so that individual saints might grow strongly, and that the church might come to its fullness in Christ, filled to overflowing with the river of his Spirit.

We are also thankful for the river of life that flows out of heaven down the main street of the city. We rejoice over the tree of life with its abundant fruit, and whose leaves provide medicine for the healing of all nations. We look to Jesus as Lord, as the cornerstone. We look to apostles and prophets to be our foundation:

"Together, we are his house, built on the foundation of the apostles and prophets. And the cornerstone is Christ Jesus himself." (Eph 2:20)

We receive these foundational helps, and, together with evangelists, pastors, and teachers we press on in obedient faith to maturity in Christ. We started out on this chapter by listening to one of the greatest of the prophets. Isaiah was fully aware of and acknowledged his role as a man of God and as a prophet towards God's people. In our lives we can soak in his prophetic word as it impacts our own time, learning lessons and principles so as to avoid the traps that ensnared the people. Isaiah can also strengthen our foundations, giving us a strong place to stand and a healthy attitude to the Lord. Listen to the prophets and become a well-watered garden of a life, with a fast-flowing river of the Spirit of life flowing out of your heart. Be humble enough to listen to God's servants and reap the rewards that are on offer.

"Humble yourselves under the mighty power of God, and at the right time he will lift you up in honour." (1 Pet 4:6)

When the people of God responded sincerely to the prophets, God blessed the nation. As we respond sincerely to the apostles and prophets of our own time, we can be assured that the Lord will bless our nation also. Humbling ourselves under the power of God while ignoring the words of the servant gifts of Christ is not an option. Our obedience to God is so often shown in our submission to each other, and to those who carry God-given authority.

Let the river of the Spirit flow out of you unhindered. Love the scriptures and feed on them as God's very own word. Love one another, and have the widest possible understanding of who is your neighbour. Seek out a living, faith-filled local church built on the foundation of apostles and prophets, with Christ Jesus as the undisputed cornerstone. Give your time, energy and focus to the important things that please God and help the poor, the needy and the oppressed in our world. Forget yourself, and live for Jesus. Where will he be?

"He will guide you continually…"

He is not far away from you, not easily offended. He is constant, faithful, and trustworthy. He is gentle, compassionate, and filled with love for you and for all of us.

"…giving you water when you are dry…"

You will no doubt have realised that being dry is a circumstance, not a sin, and it is easily resolved. When you are dry he will give you water to drink. When you feel lost he will come looking for you, pick you up, and carry you home. You will be a well-watered garden.

"…and restoring your strength." (Isa 58:11)

God is a great God, and he is restoring all things, including your strength. If you are tired, he will refresh you. If you are mourning, he will comfort you. If you are sick or in pain, he will heal your body. If it is your mind that is troubled, if your thoughts are anxious, he will set your mind at peace. He loves us, cares for us, and never ever forgets to watch over us. Trust in Jesus, and depend on his wisdom, grace, and strength.

"Come close to God, and he will come close to you." (James 4:8)

~~~~~~~

MEDITATE & MEMORIZE:

Memorize this scripture and speak it out loud as often as you can, taking time to meditate on it and asking the Holy Spirit to open it up for you. Let faith come as you hear your own voice declaring the true word of God.

"Together, we are his house, built on the foundation of the apostles and prophets. And the cornerstone is Christ Jesus himself." (Eph 2:20)

PRAY & PROCLAIM:

Pray for God's faithful servants, and ask the Lord to give them success. Pray for the apostles, prophets, evangelists, pastors and teachers, and proclaim your openness to their

Holy Spirit ministry. Declare that the church of Christ across time and throughout the whole world is one house, and pray that multitudes of people will receive Jesus as saviour and come to live there.

GIVE THANKS & WORSHIP:

Worship Christ as the cornerstone of God's house, as the beginning and the end, and thank him for all that he has done for us.

TESTIMONY
Have you heard what God is doing in Cape Breton?

He is raising up a new generation of song writers among other things. This is a song from Cape Bretoners Ethan and Chelsea Fenton (used with the permission of the writers).

Creation Cries Out
By Ethan & Chelsea Fenton

Verse 1
You moved the stars to their place, and You called them by name
They hung there in silence just to see what You'd say
The wind picked up pace as You said it was good
The sun rose that day just to bask in Your love
The clouds moved in closer to get a glimpse of Your face

Chorus
They sang Holy is The Lord, They sang Holy is The Lord

Verse 2
The sky paints a masterpiece to mark a day in Your reign
The leaves change their colour to watch the smile on Your face
And the waves stand up and bow down on repeat
And the trees dance together to the rhythm of Your beat
And all of creation cries out to sing of Your grace

Chorus
They sing Holy is The Lord, They sing Holy is The Lord

Bridge
If I do not praise then the rocks will cry out
If I do not glorify the heavens will shout
So I'll lift up Your name because You are good
You're so good to me

Chorus
So I'll sing Holy is The Lord, Yes, I'll sing Holy is The Lord

Ethan Fenton
Member & Booking Agent
RootsDeepDown | www.rootsdeepdown.ca
Cell: 902.322.5617

DAY 27

Strike the Water: Getting to Do God's Work

"Elisha picked up Elijah's cloak, which had fallen when he was taken up. Then Elisha returned to the bank of the Jordan River. He struck the water with Elijah's cloak and cried out, 'Where is the Lord, the God of Elijah?' Then the river divided, and Elisha went across."
(2 Kings 2:13-14)

Making sure that the anointing of the Lord is passed on to the next generation has always been a crucial factor in continuing the work of the Kingdom. One generation can experience great revival, or receive breath-taking new revelation of truth, but which of the children will pick up the cloak and strike the water with it? It is the will of God that the blessings of walking with him in love and obedience should touch many generations, that his Spirit might be on us and our children, and on our children's children. We often turn too late to succession planning for the house of God, but our Father always has his eye on those that are growing up, often unseen, around us. When governments change the legacy of the previous rulers can be lost in a day; the Kingdom of Jesus is not so fragile, as his government and rule will increase without end. It is still, however, the sacred duty of each generation of believers to pick up the sword of the Lord and continue the battle. A whole new team of athletes is about to come running on to the track, filled with his word and overflowing with the Holy Spirit. As they do so they will pick up the baton of their spiritual fathers and mothers, honour and protect the legacy of mighty women and men whose faith took them across the world to raise up the banner of Jesus in all of his house. I encourage you to increase your knowledge of previous generations of courageous pioneers now gone to their reward with God; read their stories and discover their source of inspiration, while rejoicing in their ministry. Then let us agree to rise up together and make this the generation that moves so powerfully in the Holy Spirit that justice and righteousness will fill the earth and bring back the King. The commandments given by God to all the nations of earth through Moses confirm this multi-generational focus to an extraordinary degree.

"I lavish unfailing love for a thousand generations on those who love me and obey my commands." (Exod 20:6)

I'm not exactly sure how long a thousand generations is, but I guess it includes many great, great, great, greats before the word "grandchildren"! The heart of the Lord is exposed here, in that even in the giving of these commandments to an often rebellious people, God's desire to shower us with his unlimited covenant love for eternity is made plain. The God of Abraham is also the God of Isaac and of Jacob, that all of Israel's descendants would be immersed in his mighty river. I never feel more holy than when I actually read all of those names in the genealogies found in scripture during my annual bible-reading plan. The temptation to skip the list and get to bed early is great indeed. The lists are there, of course, to convince us that the "thousand generations" promise of unfailing covenant love was seriously meant by a God who does not lie. The Lord wanted Elisha to pick up the cloak and test it out; he wanted a prophet in Israel who would continue the Holy Spirit era into the coming years. Elijah had ascended into heaven, and the final scene that he witnessed as he looked down from above was of a leader of a new generation of prophets striding towards the river. If you had been there, would you have picked up the cloak? Would you have struck the water and shouted, "Where is Elijah's God?"

Jesus willingly gave up his life on the cross, conquering sin and death, healing us all by his wounds. He rose again on the third day and spoke to many witnesses about the Kingdom rule of God. He warned them not to move on to the planning of how to reach the world until the promised Holy Spirit had fallen upon them from heaven. He would ascend into heaven, just as Elijah did, and he too would drop a cloak upon us all. Being baptized in the Spirit is not all about you and me getting over our nerves or being freed from our doctrinal bias so as to utter our first word of prophecy. Baptism in the Spirit is God's plan to ensure that the works of Jesus should continue on the earth, a dropping of his cloak of anointing on all flesh. The ability of this present generation of Christians to fully enter into our inheritance, and to take up our responsibilities as servants, rests on Jesus pouring out the Holy Spirit upon us. Elisha didn't use the cloak as a badge of rank (Elijah's heir!); he didn't use it to keep warm or safe. He immediately, and without hesitation, struck the water and called on Elijah's God to be with him also.

Crossing the River Jordan will do that to you. When Moses died, there was a similar need to see the journey of God's people continue under clear and courageous leadership. So the Lord spoke to Joshua, Moses' assistant.

"Moses my servant is dead. Therefore, the time has come for you to lead these people, the Israelites, across the Jordan River into the land I am giving them." (Josh 1:2)

Joshua and Elisha were charged with one command: to believe that the Lord was with them wherever they went, just as he had been with Moses and with Elijah. The church is charged with the same command today: to believe that we are to continue, even enlarge, the ministry of Jesus to the ends of the earth. The 'great commission' is not the beginning of evangelism but the continuation of it. Our absolute dependence on the guidance and equipping with power of the Holy Spirit mirrors Jesus' own humble reliance on his Father.

"Then Jesus, full of the Holy Spirit, returned from the Jordan River. He was led by the Spirit in the wilderness ... then Jesus returned to Galilee, filled with the Holy Spirit's power. Reports about him spread quickly through the whole region." (Luke 4:1, 14)

If you are taking the time to read this then I urge you, pick up the cloak and strike the water. Use your own life for God's glory; put all your trust in Jesus and surrender totally to the baptism in the Holy Spirit that he has sent to us all from heaven. Be filled with the Holy Spirit's power, and use it to enter into the mighty river pouring out from heaven's throne. Jesus wanted more than to get a few of us to go to church. After his resurrection, and in anticipation of the coming fires of Pentecost, he spoke to them about God's Kingdom. Our ambition is to see God's magnificent rule in all the nations; that his salvation will be available to all who call on his name. It is nowhere near enough for us to benefit from God's goodness in private – we need to go public with the joy of knowing Jesus' unfailing love. The name of Jesus is too great to be known and spoken by a few; the whole earth must be filled with the sound of that beautiful name.

The Jordan River appears again as Jesus is revealed in his greatness to the world. John the baptist, prophet of Jesus, is a voice shouting in the wilderness that all should come to the river.

"John announced: 'Someone is coming soon who is greater than I am – so much greater that

I'm not even worthy to stoop down like a slave and untie the straps of his sandals. I baptise you with water, but he will baptize you with the Holy Spirit!" One day Jesus came from Nazareth in Galilee, and John baptized him in the Jordan River. As Jesus came up out of the water, he saw the heavens splitting apart and the Holy Spirit descending on him like a dove." (Mark 1:7-10)

The will of God is that we not remain powerless, for he has sent Jesus as the baptizer in the Holy Spirit. He promised that we would receive power when the Holy Spirit came upon us, and he has, of course, kept that promise. The Spirit is poured out on all humanity, on women and men, on adults and children, on every nation, every people, every culture and language. Jesus has dropped his cloak from heaven, not so we can call ourselves Pentecostals, but to give us the power needed to continue his ministry until all his work on earth is done. All this is true, and yet there is a sense in which the cloak still lies on the ground, barely touched, little tested. We seem to have tip-toed into the shallows of the river, cloak in hand, and become somewhat intimidated by the enormity of the task. The world seems too big, so complex, and staying home in faithful attendance of local church meetings can seem warm and tempting. But the cries of those who need the Lord's help rise up to heaven. So very early in human history, a cry was heard that echoes still into our own time.

"Listen! Your brother's blood cries out to me from the ground." (Gen 4:10)

The cry of our brothers' blood, our sisters' blood, is heard in heaven, and the church must pick up the cloak and strike the water. The cry of many children's blood is heard loudly by our loving Father, and he is stirring us to action, to go out in love to help the lost and the oppressed. We cannot hide from the sadness of those who are hurting, and the Spirit of Christ within us won't allow us to close our eyes or cover our ears. Heaven is listening, and will answer with the blood of Christ and with the waters of the river of life, driven along by the unfailing love of our Father.

"In that day, I will answer,' says the Lord. 'I will answer the sky as it pleads for clouds. And the sky will answer the earth with rain. Then the earth will answer the thirsty cries of the grain, the grapevines, and the olive trees. And they in turn will answer, 'Jezreel' – 'God plants!' At that time I will plant a crop of Israelites and raise them for myself. I will show love to those I called 'Not loved.' And to those I called 'Not my people,' I will say, 'Now you

are my people.' And they will reply, 'You are our God!'" (Hos 2:21-23)

~~~~~~~

MEDITATE & MEMORIZE:
Memorize these scriptures and speak them out loud as often as you can, taking time to meditate on them and asking the Holy Spirit to open them up for you. Let faith come as you hear your own voice declaring the true word of God.

"Where is the Lord, the God of Elijah?" (2 Kings 2: 14)

PRAY & PROCLAIM:
Shout out these words of scripture, and also ask, "where is the God of Jesus our Saviour?" Proclaim that our Father is a good Father, that he has not grown old, distant, angry, or uncaring. Tell him that you love him and that you are asking him to renew his marvelous deeds in our own day. Pray for the mightiest outpouring of the river of the Holy Spirit that the world has ever seen, and proclaim that the earth will soon be filled with his glory!

GIVE THANKS & WORSHIP:
Worship God for who he is and because he is a God of covenant love and faithfulness. Thank him that he will never, never abandon us and that he is near to us whenever we call.

TESTIMONY
Have you heard what God is doing in Ottawa?

Healing
A few years ago my family and I were spending the day with a group of close friends. Our friend Wendy is a physiotherapist and at the time was a new mom. During our time together Wendy said that she needed to take some medication and go to sleep because she was dealing with recurring pain in her neck and back that was also causing headaches. I asked her if I could pray for her and told her that the Holy Spirit can heal any problem with our bodies. Wendy happily received prayer and after placing my hand on her shoulder and praying she looked at me in shock and said, "the pain and stiffness are gone, that's awesome, I've never seen God do anything like that before." Wendy was a believer, but until then hadn't experienced the healing power of the Holy Spirit that way before.

Meeting in the Market
A couple of friends and I were eating at a restaurant in downtown Ottawa. While we were talking, the Holy Spirit had highlighted a young man to me who was sitting across from us with two of his friends. I didn't know why the Holy Spirit was bringing this person to my attention; I just knew there was something significant about him. When he and his friends left the restaurant I walked over to him and got his attention. I told him, "I'm a Christian and I believe God was highlighting you to me for a reason. Do you know what that reason is or is there something I can pray for you?" Immediately the young man started crying, he told me that his dad was sick with cancer and he had asked God the night before to give him a sign that he is real and he felt me coming to speak with him was that sign. I prayed for healing for his dad and prayed for this man's relationship with God. He thanked me and said he was leaving the city to go back home the next morning.

Holy Smokes
I was at the grocery store one day and the Holy Spirit prompted me to pray for a lady who walked by. I introduced myself and asked her if there was anything she wanted prayer for. She was very receptive and told me that she was on her way to buy some cigarettes. She said that she had smoked since she was young, which had been decades, but had quit several months before. She didn't want to start smoking again, or to let her

husband and kids down who were so proud she had quit, but she had a strong urge that day that she couldn't resist. I shared with her about God being a father and about how much he loved her. She pointed to the name on the cigarette shop. The store was called Holy Smokes. She said, "I don't think it's a coincidence that the name of this shop is Holy Smokes," and she told me she felt God directed me to her to help her continue a non-smoking lifestyle. She said she was amazed that he cared that much about her. She asked me to pray that her desire to smoke would leave, which I did. Her daughter then came out of the grocery store and the lady left without a desire to smoke and a hope to continue that way.

Pat O'Halloran
Ottawa

DAY 28
To the Ends of the Earth

"May he reign from sea to sea, and from the Euphrates River to the ends of the earth."
(Psa 72:8)

The psalm that closes Book Two of the collection is one of the proclamations of the King and his Kingdom, a royal psalm. These psalms speak about the qualities of the King and the expectations of His rule over God's people. It is a kingly authority that reflects the very heart of God, and a reminder that we are, as Christians, the loyal subjects of a king. We are a royal Kingdom people, a holy nation, gathered around a throne. Because of this new status, we are equipped to show everyone the goodness of God. We no longer live in the darkness, for Jesus has called us out of the shadows to live in the full light of his glory. Understanding the Kingdom should prevent us from living as if the universe is centred on 'me and my needs.' It should serve to keep us focused on Jesus, seeing the full glory of who he is, an eternal King raised high above every other power. Without this knowledge of the rule of Jesus over his Kingdom we risk a return to living as individuals, subject only to our own desires.

"In those days Israel had no king; all the people did whatever seemed right in their own eyes."
(Judg 21:25)

By being reconciled into God's family by faith in his name, receiving Jesus as Lord and King, we are transformed. We are no longer like sheep, each turning to his own way. We are a brand new creation, the born-from-above people of God, and we have a responsibility to be servants of a righteous government that brings justice, that frees the wrongly imprisoned and oppressed, that releases our sisters and brothers from the fear of violent, greedy rulers. We proclaim a message of the great love of the Father, and of the coming of his Son Jesus to save us from our sins. We proclaim that we have received power when the Holy Spirit came upon us. All of these declarations are governmental in nature, speaking of the authority that has been given to the King in his rule.

The Father loves us, but that is the beginning of the story only; he is working to bring his righteous, compassionate rule into the lives of men, so that they might be brought back home to his house. Jesus has saved us from sin, requiring that we now move beyond being grateful for his aid and truly acknowledge him as Lord of our lives. We received power from the Holy Spirit, but not to impress each other; it is governmental power, authority to bring the will of heaven to the ends of the earth. A gift of healing is not meant to attract individuals into our meetings; taking away someone's pain is an act of government in the name of Jesus Christ. This is what the government of heaven looks like, and these are the works that reveal who he is to the world. I remember a few years ago seeing one of those funny t-shirts, meant to lighten our day with a little humour. This one read, "the meek will inherit the Earth (if that's all right with the rest of you?)." Of course, the real world isn't like that, as the men with the guns and the bombs are not inclined to listen to meek preachers putting forward humble teaching points. But that, of course, is not what faith in Jesus has made us into. If he had only saved us into church meetings, a kind of safe gated community, and told us to stay there for our own protection, then that would have been different. Then we would all have been free to sing comforting songs, as long as the worship band was to our liking, and to rate each week's preacher out of ten. We could bring an offering, or perhaps just occasionally throw in a few coins, because after all, this church is lucky to have me! And if someone offends me, then there are plenty more congregations that would love to sign me up, and I can just spend my life hopping from place to place, and then the end will come. Praise God, this is not at all what Jesus has done, nor is this form of dead religion in any way related to the work of the cross, or touched by his transforming blood. No, we have been made new, and we are called by the Holy Spirit to fill the earth with forgiveness and mercy, exercising authority over demons so that the people of the world might be freed from evil and that sinners might find salvation in the Son.

We are changed into God's flock, the army of God, brethren to Jesus. Now we can look to heaven and speak confidently to our Father, for that is who he is. We are transformed from believing in our own wisdom and opinions, into a people who love our bibles, and breathe in its truth. We are a well-taught people, as we willingly give ourselves to the apostle's teaching, to preachers and teachers who open the scriptures to us as the living word of a living God. We are no longer unteachable and impossible to correct, but disciples who joyfully follow godly leadership.

"Obey your spiritual leaders, and do what they say. Their work is to watch over your souls, and they are accountable to God. Give them reason to do this with joy and not with sorrow. That would certainly not be for your benefit." (Heb 13:17)

Psalm 72, then, is a royal psalm about a godly ruler, and we are an obedient kingdom people. We have faith to have influence at the national and international level because of the power of the cross, and because we are ourselves obedient to the government of God expressed in our church leadership. In this also we are like Jesus, under authority and therefore able to exercise that same authority to bring light and life into the nations. The first cry to the Lord from the psalmist is that God might give the king the Lord's own love of justice. We have already seen in many scriptures, and in the declarations of so many of the Lord's faithful prophets, a solemn reminder that God loves justice, and expects to see the same in his church. The goal of God is not for us to achieve the perfect Sunday gathering, and sustain it week after week; the goal of God is that the nations might be filled with songs of praise to a King who has restored justice, freeing the innocent from the violence of brutal, greedy rulers, bringing in a different kind of Kingdom. The river of the Holy Spirit is not there to keep the church behind a moat; it is bringing healing to the nations as the loving protection of a new King is extended over the planet. Don't give up all of your time and attention to the minor issues of church life, as it will not prove to be sufficient to bring the light of Christ to the ends of the earth. Raise your expectations, and proclaim that what Jesus has done is mighty, bringing not cozy religion but godly government. Let us encourage one another to great faith, to live our lives for a worthwhile cause, that the whole earth might soon be aware of the glory of God.

Even such important factors as vibrant, spiritual praise and worship, passionate preaching and fervent prayers lose their power if God's people forget their love of justice for all. He accepts our worship, stirs our preachers with boldness, and hears our prayers when the church reaches out to those who are in trouble. The psalmist cries out that God might cause the king to rule in righteousness, and to raise his sons as righteous children, flowing in the kindness of God. He calls neither for flawed judgement nor for an absence of judgment, but for godly, righteous judgement. Isaiah, after rebuking the people for their sin and rejecting their sacrifices to the Lord because of their insincerity, calls for righteous judges to be given to us by God so that they might lead us on a path back to fullness.

"Then I will give you good judges again and wise counsellors like you used to have. Then Jerusalem will again be called the Home of Justice and the Faithful City." (Isa 1:26)

Cry out, people of God, for godly leaders who will judge rightly and without the fear of men, and then follow them faithfully. Put no value on preachers who tell you how great you are when Jesus wants to teach you a better way. Don't judge your church by whether it agrees with you and leaves you comfortable; look for wise counsellors and brave preachers who will keep you from straying and build you as a true kingdom community. Welcome leaders who shepherd God's people into radical Kingdom communities that act as a letter to the watching world, as a model of heaven come down to the earth. Thank God for giving us men and women who can sharpen us and are unafraid to challenge us onwards in character and into maturity. Seek out and find in your community apostles, prophets, evangelists, pastors, and teachers, who are working with elders, deacons and other local leaders, to bring us all to maturity.

"Their responsibility is to equip God's people to do his work and build up the church, the body of Christ. This will continue until we all come to such unity in our faith and knowledge of God's Son that we will be mature in the Lord, measuring up to the full and complete standard of Christ." (Eph 4:12-13)

If this is what you want, what you hunger and thirst for, then accept that God has made us into a Kingdom people, with King Jesus in the driver's seat. He has Lordship over us individually as Christians, something that we have long understood. But he is King over all his kingdom and rules over nations, with plans for everyone and renewed hope for the poor. The oppressed and voiceless across the planet can rejoice that a righteous, loving King is on the throne, as he will champion their cause and act against their enemies. He is a king of restoration, interested in all the nations. He has promised his people that he will restore and rebuild until his glory is seen in every nation.

"In that day I will restore the fallen kingdom (or house or tent) of David, I will repair its damaged walls. From the ruins I will rebuild it and restore its former glory. And Israel will

possess what is left of Edom, and all the nations I have called to be mine. The Lord has spoken, and he will do these things." (Amos 9:11-12)

If you are reading this as you live in a ruined nation, or a fear-filled city, then put your trust in the King and his Kingdom. Call on Jesus to extend his rule over your community and to send his mighty Holy Spirit to bring in the rule of the King. Call on the Lord of heaven and earth to extend his government, his covering and protection over you, not just in the life to come, but here and now in our present world. Call on Jesus to lay a foundation of righteousness in your nation, to raise the flag of justice over you and your neighbours. If you are living a ruined life from whatever cause, an individual experience that is unsatisfying or without hope, call on Jesus to save you and to extend his rule over your life, and he will do that for you. The King loves you and has come looking for you so that he might help you in your life and cover you with his protection. Ask the Lord to extend his mercy over you so that you might be saved. Looking at Jerusalem, and looking right now at your community, Jesus cries:

"How often I have wanted to gather your children together as a hen protects her chicks beneath her wings." (Mat 23:37)

Be like Ruth who asked Boaz to "spread the corner of your covering over me, for you are my family redeemer" (Ruth 3:9). In the same way, call out to the Lord and he will answer you, and spread out his wings, his covering, over you. Join a living church with faithful, godly leaders, and they will spread their wings over you also, protecting, teaching and guiding you with Kingdom authority. Be devoted to the teaching of apostles and respond with faith to the Lord's prophets, and find yourself built on their firm foundation, with Christ Jesus himself as the cornerstone. And if it is your very nation that is devastated, and it seems as though no one can deliver you, put your trust in a King who is mightier than all the violent destroyers that have ruined your homes. The Lord says to hateful, violent people:

"I will cut you down to size among the nations; you will be greatly despised. You have been deceived by your own pride because you live in a rock fortress and make your home high in the mountains. 'Who can ever reach us way up here?' you ask boastfully. But even if you soar as high as eagles and build your nest among the stars, I will bring you crashing down, says the Lord." (Obad 1:2-4)

Jesus is King of Kings, Lord of Lords, and his Kingdom rule is eternal and irresistible. He cannot be denied his rule by any terrorist, any hate-filled servant of violence. He is big enough to bring peaceful restoration even to our present troubled world, and he will do it. The church is waking up from its sleep, looking beyond its meeting places into the ends of the earth. We are a missionary people, unwilling to pass by on the other side, ignoring the plight of those who are suffering in our world. Jesus Christ the King is Lord of all, and will act, not in a small way, but in a great way. In rejoicing over the marvelous truth that God would fully restore the people of Israel, the Messiah is proclaimed to do even more than that. He will restore you and rebuild the nations by his mighty rule. There will be justice and righteousness for all the earth. Ezra understood that with God's help, and only with his help, the nation that had fallen so far could be restored only by the grace extended to it by the King of heaven. Almost overwhelmed by the reality of their condition, he says:

"But now we have been given a brief moment of grace … he has given us security in this holy place. He has brightened our eyes and granted us some relief … he revived us so we could rebuild the Temple of our God and repair its ruins." (Ezra 9:8-9)

The King of Kings is an agent of restoration for individuals and for nations in ruins. He will give us grace to bring relief, revival, rebuilding, and repair, so that ruins are transformed into temples to his grace and kindness. The whole earth is in his heart; Jesus is the rescuer, the Messiah for all who cry out to him. Of him it is said:

"You will do more than restore the people the people of Israel to me. I will make you a light to the Gentiles, and you will bring my salvation to the ends of the earth." (Isa 49:6)

~~~~~~~

MEDITATE & MEMORIZE:

Memorize these scriptures and speak them out loud as often as you can, taking time to meditate on them and asking the Holy Spirit to open them up for you. Let faith come as you hear your own voice declaring the true word of God.

'Who can ever reach us way up here?' you ask boastfully. But even if you soar as high as eagles and build your nest among the stars, I will bring you crashing down, says the Lord." (Obad 1:2-4)

PRAY & PROCLAIM:

Shout out these words of scripture, aiming them at the agents of hate and terror, firing these words in the spirit at everyone who would divide us from any of our sisters and brothers around the world. Proclaim loudly that it is not God's will that any human being should perish, and that salvation is preached to all peoples, and that his will is going to be accomplished on earth just as it is in heaven. When you are finished say, "Amen and Amen!"

GIVE THANKS & WORSHIP:

Worship God for sending Jesus to oppose wickedness and to destroy the devil's work. Thank him that he has taught you how to know the difference between his purpose and the purpose of the cruel thief at work in our world. Worship the God who is love, thanking him that love will always overcome division, suspicion and hate. Let his love for the world fill your own heart and mind right now.

TESTIMONY
Have you heard what God is doing in Malaysia?

Of all the prophecies spoken over my life since being born again, one stood out and kept resurfacing. I was sixteen, a high school student living in Southeast Asia. It was a church youth camp and a pastor spoke over my life and prophesied that I would one day speak to (a room full of) leaders, government leaders, and individuals with power and that they would listen. Over the course of my late adolescence and adult life, the same prophecy would come up, at different times, locations and through different people.

However, growing up in a lower middle class neighbourhood located in a 'third world' country, I had a hard time reconciling between what was spoken over my life and the reality of my surroundings and upbringing - at the time. My dad was a factory worker who toiled his whole life making ends meet while my mom stayed home to raise four children. I remembered the financial troubles we had growing up and the stress associated with it. Over time, this led to a sense of inadequacy, lack and to an extent - hopelessness.

Unable to see beyond my worldly constraints, I found myself being more of an observer than a participant/actor of the prophecy. Occasionally, I'd put the prophecy to test by intentionally refraining from taking on any activities I thought could aid the fulfillment of the prophecy or cause it to be "self fulfilled". I wanted to know for certain that the prophecy was indeed from God. Later I learned that the bible does ask us to test all things (that are been said) and hold on to what is good (1 Thessalonians 5:21).

Despite my doubts, God continued to remind me of His steadfast love and plan for my life. One day shortly after my 22nd birthday, my dad came into my room and broke the news that he would no longer be able to support me through college and that I would have to halt my tertiary studies for lack of financial resources. Unlike in North America, it was economically unfeasible and culturally incompatible to work and go to school at the same time. It didn't help that there were preferential and discriminatory education policies that made the pursuit of a university degree for families from a lower socio-economic background, who belong to a certain ethnic group, that much more difficult, at times impossible. At the time, I was already considered a late student compared to other peers my age.

However, just as I couldn't understand how a person born in a "poor family" with no prospect of getting a proper education could possibly speak to/advise government leaders and individuals in power, I realized something; God, our loving Father chooses to use the lowly things of this world, and showed me that it is irrelevant what my circumstance is/was and that He can put into motion things beyond our earthly understanding.

In less than two months after my dad broke the news, I was on a plane to Canada to complete my university degree! Now that's hard to fathom considering just 'a moment' ago I was going to have to drop out of college and now I'm paying international fees in a Canadian university?? It just didn't make sense. However, I'm reminded that God's ways are not our ways (Isaiah 55:8) and that He can defy our earthly logic and rationale and transform our lives completely in a single moment, if only we allow Him to work in us.

To cut the long story short, it's been over 11 years since I came to Canada. God remains faithful and steadfast and the prophecy spoken over my life is more alive today than ever before! I'm now a public servant working for the Canadian federal government. This year alone (2016), I've had the opportunity to provide advice to the Minister's office, written policy briefs, Cabinet documents and help develop national policies and recommendations that the Prime Minister of Canada himself will have to sign-off! All Glory to God.

"For [HE] knows the plans [HE has] for you," declares the LORD, "plans to prosper you and not to harm you, plans to give you hope and a future" (Jeremiah 29:11).

Nicholas Yee,
Ottawa (and Malaysia!)

DAY 29

God So Loved the World

"May all the godly flourish during his reign. May there be abundant prosperity until the moon is no more. May he reign from sea to sea, and from the ... river to the ends of the earth." (Psa 72:7-8)

This Kingdom psalm is filled with the love of God for the peoples of his world, confidently proclaiming his blessing upon those who look to King Jesus, enthroned over heaven and earth. The river that is set in motion from God's place of government flows out to water every family, making everyone under his rule become a well-watered garden, to the ends of the earth. The Lord loves justice and will not rest until the last captive is freed, all of the oppressed lifted up. He insists that the poor and powerless in this world should be treated with fairness, looking to the saints to initiate compassionate action in the sharing of resources, and that righteous judgement should prevail. Following King Jesus as faithful disciples leads to prosperity, not for a few super-rich, but for all. Praise God for leaders, politicians, NGOs, philanthropic foundations and policymakers who see the need for change and give their life's work to achieve progress. And praise God once again for his church joyfully joining in the task of ensuring that all the families of the earth will be blessed, just as God promised to the father of our faith.

Prosperity for all is made possible by the river of love flowing from heaven, and from the cross of Christ. He blesses the hills to make them fruitful. We have heard of rural communities where this river of blessing has miraculously improved the quality of the land and the size of the harvest in response to the faith and needs of the people. Carrots twice as big as normal may not sound as exciting as national revival, but when your family is hungry it can sound like the best kind of news! Being down to our last jar of oil isn't as worrying as it used to be now that we know that the Lord can multiply the jar's contents. We honour the scientists who are dedicated to increasing the harvest to meet the tremendous need for food across the planet, and welcome the Lord who can do quite a lot with a few fish and a bag of bread rolls! My wife and I, together with millions of others around the planet, looked up at the sky last night to see a super moon, a full moon that had approached to its closest distance to earth since 1948. The will of God and the prayer of Christ's kingdom is that everyone will prosper as part of a unified family of believers until the moon is gone from our skies. We should all try to match our ambitions and dreams to the fullness of the stature of God's own vision of kingdom life! Think big; leave no one behind; try to out-give and out-love your Father in heaven. The mighty power of the King is there to defend the poor, and to rescue the children of all who need support, a rescue driven by the torrent of God's unfailing, unwavering kindness. If violent people rise up to fill the nations with fear, he will crush them as the champion of the oppressed (verse 4).

John understood the heart of the Father, and knew that the love of heaven would crush the sin of man, at the unthinkable cost of the crushing of the Son of God, who was beaten so that we could be whole, whipped so that we could be healed. And so he encourages us to live in love.

"Dear friends, let us continue to love one another, for love comes from God. Anyone who loves is a child of God and knows God. But anyone who does not love does not know God, for God is love." (1 John 4:7-8)

"Everyone who believes that Jesus is the Christ has become a child of God. And everyone who loves the Father loves his children, too." (1 John 5:1)

"I am writing to remind you, dear friends, that we should love one another. This is not a new commandment, but one we have had from the beginning." (2 John 1:5)

It is important that we fully realize the unstoppable power of the Father's love; that it is impossible to halt the flood of his kindness towards those who look to him. His love is so great, his kindness and mercy so ingrained in his nature, his determination is so absolute to find us and save us from the dangers of sin and the powers loose in this world, that no ungodly power can hold his blessing back. God loved the world so completely that he gave his own beloved Son, so that all who received him and believed in his name might be saved. The power of Christ's sacrifice, his courage in facing the cross, the power of his precious blood can never be prevented from achieving all he has set himself to achieve. So, blessed we will be, no matter what our circumstance, even if men have destroyed our city, wounded our family. His river of love is overwhelming, and it cannot be resisted by lovers of hate and violence. It is admirable that we honour and thank those who give their lives as military personnel, who by their great skill, courage and selflessness defend all that we cherish, putting themselves in harm's way to defend our freedom. How much more, then, shall we honour, respect and praise the Lamb of God who gave his life as a willing sacrifice to take away our sin and sickness?

"I am about to shake the heavens and the earth. I will overthrow royal thrones and destroy the power of foreign kingdoms. I will overturn their chariots and riders." (Hag 2:21-22)

The love of God will never give way to the hatred and greed of man, and his love for his world means that he will never forget the children of the earth. He will act to "overturn the chariots" of all those who seek to use their power to crush the innocent. He will shake all things, not only to reveal his will, but also to rescue the families of the earth from oppressive governments. Scripture shows us God's righteous judgment in action. Looking at a great city that has fallen into wickedness, he decides that the time has come to rise up in his rule and judge the affairs of men. As God judges Nineveh, he provokes genuine repentance expressed in specific actions, and as a result he changes his mind. God withdrew the judgement on their sin in response to a sincere change of heart in the people. The prophet, Jonah, more impressed with himself than with the mercy of a loving God, is upset at the Lord. So the Lord explains himself.

"Nineveh has more than 120,000 people living in spiritual darkness, not to mention all the animals. Shouldn't I feel sorry for such a great city?" (Jonah 4:11)

Even for the cities of our day that are filled with spiritual darkness, God's light shines for the people, and his loving kindness extends towards them. Christians are sometimes a little more impressed with the power of evil than they should be, and can be heard declaring that their own city, or parts of it, are deeply dark places, hard to reach with the gospel. A young man, young enough that he had to stand on a chair to be seen by the adults present, declared in our Sunday meeting yesterday that no matter how dark it is, just turning on the light will change everything. The light of Christ overcomes all the darkness, bringing hope into our troubled world. Part of our progress in promoting justice is that we must have a right view of our own burdens, compared to the suffering of our sisters and brothers across all nations, and that we spare some thought and prayer time for others. As we look around our hurting world, at failed states and terrorized communities, our faith in the power of Christ's love must be absolute. No shrinking back then, from the task that faces the church, and no descent into fearfulness in the hearts of the saints. God loves the world, and so do his children. We are to be like Jesus as we allow our hearts and lives to overflow with his love. Paul commends Philemon for just these qualities.

"I always thank my God when I pray for you, Philemon, because I keep hearing about your faith in the Lord Jesus and your love for all God's people … your kindness has often refreshed the hearts of God's people." (Philm 1:4, 5, 7)

Let it be our aim to act in such a way that we too can be spoken of like this by the apostles and prophets. Paul encourages Philemon to show love and kindness, to hold on to his rights lightly, and to forgive any wrongs. Too much time is given over in our churches to dealing with small hurts and offences that could be quickly immersed in a rising tide of mercy, forgiveness and godly memory loss. We have larger issues to deal with if we are to reach the lost and see God's restoration in the nations. Let's be quick on our feet when dealing with small offenses and lack of perfection in our brothers and sisters. Being immediate in our forgiveness of others simply builds up a store for us in heaven that we will be grateful we invested in on our own judgment day. The love of God for his people is captured beautifully in the image of the saints of God as the bride of Christ. We must never see ourselves as God's project, hard work filled with disappointment for him as we fail to match up to his expectations of holiness. No, we are God's beloved children, being made ready as a bride readies herself for her wedding. "You have captured my heart, my treasure, my bride" (SS 4:9) says the Lord – so come to a place of restful confidence that God fully knows and loves you. Paul uses the image of the saints as Jesus' bride to encourage the Corinthians to keep to his revelation of the gospel of Christ.

"For I am jealous for you with the jealousy of God himself. I promised you as a pure bride to one husband – Christ." (2 Cor 11:2)

The love of God for us is personal, and there is a celebration coming which none of us will want to miss.

"'Blessed are those who are invited to the wedding feast of the Lamb.' And he added, 'these are the true words that come from God.'" (Rev 19:9)

Are you worried that you have nothing suitable to wear for such an occasion?

"'She has been given the finest of pure white linen to wear.' For the fine linen represents the good deeds of God's holy people." (Rev 19:8)

The love of God flows to us from his throne like a mighty river, passes through the cross and person of Christ and out of the entrance to the temple. Let that same love fill you full and flow out of you to refresh the lives of others. Be hard to offend, quick to forgive, and full of kindness towards others. Don't use up all your love on your favourite people, or focus too much on any one nation. Let your own concerns be widened beyond your present horizons to include all God's holy people. Fill your day with good deeds by remembering the fearful and oppressed, by lifting multitudes up to the Father in prayer. We are a big people, made for eternity, with no need to think small or feel limited. The Holy Spirit will help us to cry out to God with impactful prayers that will have the force of heaven behind them. Our prayers are effective because our loving God is mighty.

"Jesus gave his life for our sins, just as God our Father planned, in order to rescue us from this evil world in which we live." (Gal 1:4)

In our weakened state Jesus' salvation was powerful and sufficient to save us from this evil world, this corrupt generation. And in our still weakened state of humble prayer, he helps us again.

"And the Holy Spirit helps us in our weakness. For example, we don't know what God wants us to pray for. But the Holy Spirit prays for us with groanings that cannot be expressed in words. And the Father who knows all hearts knows what the Spirit is saying, for the Spirit pleads for us believers in harmony with God's own will." (Rom 8:26-27)

MEDITATE & MEMORIZE:

Memorize these scriptures and speak them out loud as often as you can, taking time to meditate on them and asking the Holy Spirit to open them up for you. Let faith come as you hear your own voice declaring the true word of God.

"Dear friends, let us continue to love one another, for love comes from God. Anyone who loves is a child of God and knows God. But anyone who does not love does not know God, for God is love." (1 John 4:7-8)

PRAY & PROCLAIM:

Tell the Father that you love all of his created people, those that know him now, and those who are yet to receive him. Tell the Father that you love all of your sisters and brothers, even those that you have thought of as your enemies. Proclaim that you will dedicate the rest of your life to loving others, to respecting and valuing everyone that you meet, and that you will allow kindness and compassion to flow out of your heart and mind like a river.

GIVE THANKS & WORSHIP:

Give thanks for the love that has flowed out of heaven towards you, and for the extraordinary grace that comes to you from the cross of Christ. Worship God for his mercy towards you, and thank him for his never-ending grace in your life.

DAY 30

Glory!

"Praise his glorious name forever! Let the whole earth be filled with his glory. Amen and amen!" (Psa 72:19)

At the time that I became a Christian by responding to the preacher at a student meeting, I discovered that most of my fellow believers held a rather pessimistic view of the future. The most commonly held view about how the world would end involved a tiny group of faithful but beleaguered survivors huddled together on a remote Scottish island being rescued by a last minute miracle as they flew off into the stormy sky. The church, decimated by the evils of the earth, found itself caught in a 'now would be a good time to beam us up' kind of moment. I was fascinated by this view, and didn't really worry for several years that I couldn't find such a picture in my bible. You can imagine my surprise when I first began to encounter Christians with a very different expectation of how things would end. They believed that the prayer of the psalmist would be answered, and that everyone on earth would become aware of the glory of the Lord, displayed in every nation. So how will it be to see the entire planet filled with the Father's glory?

Our churches in Canada took another whole Saturday together recently, joined across several cities and provinces by technological means beyond my comprehension, to study the scriptures together. This Saturday morning's session was taught from Wales by an old friend of mine, who, with his usual skill and passion, encouraged us to value our bibles as the breathed out word of God. He was great, but something happened to our video screen as the morning passed by. Minute by minute the light levels on the image ahead of us increased, until the teacher was surrounded by a holy glow. The last half hour of his final session left him surrounded by brilliant white light of a heavenly intensity, with his glasses being the last feature to fade into the general glory. Is this how the earth will look as it becomes saturated with an awareness of God's true glory?

Some of the descriptions in scripture of our final destination as his people certainly have glorious qualities to expound.

"I heard a loud shout from the throne, saying, 'Look, God's home is now among his people! He will live with them, and they will be his people. God himself will be with them. He will wipe every tear from their eyes, and there will be no more death or sorrow or crying or pain. All these things are gone forever.' And the one sitting on the throne said, 'Look, I am making everything new!' And then he said to me, 'Write this down, for what I tell you is trustworthy and true.' And he also said, 'It is finished! I am the Alpha and the Omega—the Beginning and the End. To all who are thirsty I will give freely from the springs of the water of life. All who are victorious will inherit all these blessings, and I will be their God, and they will be my children.'" (Rev 21: 3-7)

The final result of the King's rule in our lives is that we find ourselves in a place where God lives openly with his people, wiping away every last tear from our eyes, in a place without pain, exhaustion, despair, suffering, regret, or sorrow. The curses of life are no more, and only the blessing and life that flows like a river from his throne remain. It will be a bright city without the terrors of night, because the Lord himself will be its light. God, whose first recorded words in Genesis produced great lights in the heavens, is in himself full of light. As his glory fills the earth, deeds of darkness will be forced to retreat at the advance of God's faithful servants.

"After this, the man brought me back around to the east gateway. Suddenly, the glory of the God of Israel appeared from the east. The sound of his coming was like the roar of rushing waters, and the whole landscape shone with his glory. This vision was just like the others I had seen, first by the Kebar River and then when he came to destroy Jerusalem. I fell face down on the ground" (Ezek 43:1-3)

The cry of the prophets, the expectation of scripture and the hope of the church is that the whole earth will be filled with God's glory. Our expectation is that every eye should see Jesus and every life be touched by his love. His love of justice will be the glory of God to the oppressed. Those who have been held down by the greed and ambition of self-centred rulers will shout out a welcome to the righteous judge who has delivered them. It will seem a thing of glory that the poor are treated as fairly as the rich. The lions will lie down with the lambs as the rich and powerful find community with their voiceless brothers and sisters, sitting at the table with them. The mountains and the hills will have a harvest available to all, so that all will prosper, caring for each others' comfort.

"All the believers were united in heart and mind. And they felt that what they owned was not their own, so they shared everything they had. The apostles testified powerfully to the resurrection of the Lord Jesus and God's great blessing was upon them all.

There were no needy people among them because those who owned the houses would sell them and bring the money to the apostles to give those in need." (Acts 4:32-35)

The glory of the Lord seems to be multi-faceted like a great jewel. The good deeds of the saints, dynamic faith in the risen Jesus, the caring community of believers, our renewed love of justice and single-minded pursuit of righteousness, signs and wonders and miracles, all reflecting the light of God's glory into the earth. The weight of his presence will increase as God's joy in the holiness of his people is demonstrated to us all.

"Moses could no longer enter the Tabernacle because the cloud had settled down over it, and the glory of the Lord filled the Tabernacle." (Exod 40:35)

"The priests could not continue their service because of the cloud, for the glorious presence of the Lord filled the Temple of the Lord." (1 Kings 8:11)

Our generation has not been left without a witness of God's glorious presence, and many Christians know exactly what it is to be unable to stand up in his glory. The Lord has not abandoned us, indeed he lives closely with his people, and it is often impossible to continue our service as we are overcome by the weight of his nearness. To feel small as we get a taste of his greatness is to feel happy and free. To surrender like defenceless lambs as the Lion of the tribe of Judah prowls the room is the very heart of worship. The effect of Immanuel, God with us, is and should be a profound experience for his people. But God's glory is more than a sight, more than a feeling. His glory has meaning, significance beyond its physical effects on his servants.

When the glory of the Lord fills the tabernacle, his people remember justice for all peoples. When the heavy glory of Jesus fills the temple, we remember the poor and share our resources. The immediate effect of Pentecostal glory was that the people saw each other as being united under the fire of God, and they connected with other languages, other nations. The glory of the Lord filled the upper room, and the saints were quite unable to maintain their separation from the concerns of their neighbours. The body of Christ was baptized in the Holy Spirit and there were no needy people among them. The glory of God baptises us, inside and out, with his power and fire, with his greatness and his loving Father's heart. You just don't get the option to love God and forget your sister living in oppression. The glory of the Lord won't allow it. You aren't given the choice of speaking in unknown languages while abandoning your brother to unjust imprisonment. The glory of God overwhelms our emotions and our physical bodies for sure; the greater effect, though, is on our attitudes and actions.

The transformation of our lives achieved by the courageous sacrifice of Christ is to the glory of our Father, who sent Jesus to rescue us. We no longer live for our own little world experience, but have hearts and minds that have opened wide to value others. The world has lost its grip on us, as we no longer care much for our own ambitions, and have a hunger only for God's plan for the nations.

"As for me, may I never boast about anything except the cross of our Lord Jesus Christ. Because of that cross, my interest in this world has been crucified, and the world's interest in me has also died. It doesn't matter whether we have been circumcised or not. What counts is whether we have been transformed into a new creation. May God's peace and mercy be upon all who live by this principle; they are the new people of God." (Gal 6:14-16)

Paul always encourages us to understand this transformation of our very lives, and points us forward into a radical new way of living for God's glory.

"So we keep on praying for you, asking our God to enable you to live a life worthy of his call. May he give you the power to accomplish all the good things your faith prompts you to do. Then the name of the Lord Jesus will be honoured by the way you live, and you will be honoured along with him. This is all made possible because of the grace of our God and Lord, Jesus Christ." (2 Thes 1:11-12)

Our transformed lives, made possible by the cross, and by our Lord's grace towards us, cause us to live in a radical kingdom way. The glory of God's presence produces more than a sense of closeness to God; it fills us with the significance of his work in restoring our lives in unity with all of mankind. We are captured by it. We are always aware of Jesus' love for 'me,' but consumed with spreading the awareness of that love to all others. We therefore gladly honour those ministries of Christ that give their lives to announcing God's grace, and glory in the cross of Christ.

"Some of the traveling teachers recently returned to me and made me very happy by telling me about your faithfulness and that you are living according to the truth. I could have no greater joy than to hear that my children are following the truth. Dear friend, you are being faithful to God when you care for the traveling teachers who pass through ... please continue ... for they are traveling for the Lord ... support them so that we can be their partners as they teach the truth." (3 John 1:3-8)

Heaven has equipped the church with ministers of Christ, apostles and prophets, evangelists, pastors, and teachers, who travel throughout the whole world to spread the good news about Jesus. We do well to honour them, to show them support and hospitality, to see that their needs are met. In doing this, we become their partners in making the whole world aware of the glory of God. We have, each one of us, received power into our newly created lives, as the Holy Spirit has been and is being poured out upon all of us. We are partners with the 'traveling teachers,' and also empowered to build Kingdom communities driven by radical lifestyles. Make sure that you are regularly exposed to all the ministries and fellowship that God has provided so that your life might be extraordinary, filled as it should be with the glory of the Lord. Be teachable!

"The teacher sought to find just the right words to express truths clearly. The words of the wise are like cattle prods – painful but helpful. Their collected sayings are like a nail-studded stick with which a shepherd drives the sheep. But, my child, let me give you some further advice: Be careful, for writing books is endless, and much study wears you out. That's the whole story. Here now is my final conclusion: fear God and obey his commands, for this is everyone's duty. God will judge us for everything we do, including every secret thing, whether good or bad." (Eccls 12:10-14)

A church that is serious about seeing our world filled with God's glory will accept the words of the ministries of Christ, acknowledging that those words can be 'painful but helpful'! Christians that wish to work together, refusing to acknowledge denominations, divisions, and barriers that seem to separate the saints, will grow to become an exceptional, extraordinary generation of faith. As we join together to seek the fullest favour of God we will understand the need to commit ourselves to the work of his hands, which is to seek salvation, healing, freedom, restored sight, and the end of oppression for all. We will forget ourselves and remember others, living for the fullest blessing of the forgotten, the suffering and the lost, devoting ourselves to lifting burdens from their lives. We will live in the light of God's glory without becoming dazzled by it, and we will devote our lives and strength to see all the families of the earth emerging into the light of Jesus. My wife and I have been blessed by six wonderful grandchildren; one of them, an 18-month-old beautiful boy, is presently obsessed with lights. He likes nothing better than to be carried to a bank of light switches so that he can turn them on and off for hours. He is impossibly cute, and we love him to bits, but we still hope that he will have grown out of this activity before he gets to high school! There is a danger that some of us may become so dazzled by the conferences and 'Holy Spirit' meetings that we enjoy so much that we will just keep enjoying the experience of basking in the light of his presence, forgetting that when the meeting is over there is work to be done. Jesus enjoyed intimate fellowship with his Father every day; and every day he took the love and power of his glorious Father into the town squares, so that the helpless might see that their Messiah had come.

The best place for us to finish is at the feet of Jesus, gazing up into his face. When the whole earth is filled with an awareness of the glory of God, it will be an overwhelming experience that will feel a lot like being under water, baptized by full immersion into the powerful river of God. The poor will rejoice at the good news about Jesus, while the once oppressed and captive peoples of the nations will enjoy their freedom will all the saints. Rich people will acknowledge their brethren and share all that they have so that there might be no needy person in our community. The lion will lie with the lamb, and the ends of the earth will worship their King. The glory of God will indeed be seen in the astonishing light that fills the heavens and the earth, not from Sun, moon or city lights, but from the face of the Lamb of God, who came and took away the sins of the world. King Jesus, the Messiah.

"For God, who said, "Let there be light in the darkness," has made this light shine in our hearts so we could know the glory of God that is seen in the face of Jesus Christ." (2 Cor 4:4)

AFTERWORD

I hope that you enjoyed, and were encouraged by, the stories of God's help and grace that end each chapter of this book. God is a good God who loves you greatly, and if you call on Him he will help you and save you just as he has helped these writers. My thanks go out to these contributors and much-loved friends:

Aboubacar; Sandie Morency; Murray and Vicki Kreuzer; Jon and Janie Tenthory; Fidele Bolton; Dale and Jen Bright; Robyn and Noah Bright; Pat and Ali McKinnon; Maryann Roebuck; Pat O'Halloran; Lesley Ford; Maurice "Mo" Caron; Wes Roebuck; Todd Pulsifer; David Rukundo; Ethan and Chelsea Fenton; Nicholas Yee; Jo Anne Fallaise; one writer who is anonymous but provided an inspiring true account, and others who tried hard but missed the deadline and will appear in another book! Thanks to all who gave their stories, and to the many more who encouraged me throughout this process.

ABOUT THE AUTHOR

Originally from the United Kingdom, Mike Nicholson has served as a pastor and teacher in churches in the Canada and the UK for 35 years. He and his wife Hazel have four amazing daughters and six wonderful grandchildren. Mike currently serves as an elder at All Nations Church in Ottawa, Ontario and has a sincere passion to teach God's people to live in the fullness of the Holy Spirit.

global giving initiative

As we pursue our mission to help people get their voices and ideas out into the world, we at Unprecedented Press realize that others are concerned with more pressing needs. Finding creativity in every person is important work, but getting food, shelter, and dignity to individuals must come first. That's why Unprecedented Press donates a portion of all book revenue to the Everyone Gobal Giving Initative whose goal is to meet the practical needs of individuals around the world and to share the love of Jesus. To learn more, visit everyoneglobal.com

Other titles from
Unprecedented Press

40 Shocking Facts for 40 Weeks of Pregnancy - Volume 1:
Disturbing Details about Childbearing & Birth

By Joshua Best

40 Shocking Facts for 40 Weeks of Pregnancy - Volume 2:
Terrifying Truths about Babies & Breastfeeding

By Joshua Best

She Can Laugh
A Guide to Living Spiritually, Emotionally & Physically Healthy

By Melissa Lea Hughes

Once Upon A Year
Experience a year in the life of Finn

By Joanna Lenau

All titles available from Amazon or from unprecedentedpress.com/shop

Y - Christian Millennial Manifesto
Addressing Our Strengths and Weaknesses to Advance the Kingdom of God

Y, The Workbook
A Companion

By Joshua Best

Crumbs
100 Everyday Stories about 100 People

By Rose White

www.ingramcontent.com/pod-product-compliance
Lightning Source LLC
Chambersburg PA
CBHW050528300426
44113CB00012B/2002